THE ORIGINAL & GENUINE

GREENBOOK®

GUIDE TO THE

WALT DISNEY CLASSICS COLLECTION

THIRD EDITION

GREENBOOK ®

**The Most Respected Guides To Popular Collectibles
& Their After Market Values**

P.O. Box 645
Pacific Grove, CA   93950
831.656.9000
FAX 831.656.9004
www.greenbooks.com

Printed in Canada

ISBN 0-923628-73-8

The GREENBOOK would like to thank –

The Walt Disney Company for assisting in the compilation of the factual information contained in this Guide.

Becky Hoff & the staff at **The Sunday Funnies** in Tukwila, WA.

The **collectors, retailers, secondary market dealers** and **newsletter publishers** across the country who take their valuable time to supply us with information including secondary market status and price.

GREENBOOK TRUMARKET™ VALUES are obtained from trades and information provided by retailers, dealers and collectors. Manufacturers verify factual information only and are not consulted or involved in any way in determining our GREENBOOK TRUMARKET VALUES.

Disney artwork & materials ©The Walt Disney Company.

©1999 GREENBOOK. ALL RIGHTS RESERVED.
All names and illustrations contained herein are copyrighted.
Their reproduction or use elsewhere, in any form whatsoever,
without the written permission of the copyright owners is strictly forbidden
NO PART OF THIS BOOK MAY BE REPRODUCED OR UTILIZED IN
ANY WAY including, but not limited to, electronic, mechanical,
photocopying, or by information storage and retrieval methods
WITHOUT WRITTEN PERMISSION OF THE GREENBOOK.

Louise Patterson Langenfeld is unique in collectible annals, for she grew up immersed in collectibles. Her father developed the BRADEX, the first comprehensive listing of collector plates and their secondary market values, for the world renowned BRADFORD EXCHANGE. A graduate of Michigan State University, during summers and school breaks, Louise helped her Dad with his successful limited edition plate publishing business. Louise attended many South Bend Conventions, greeting and getting to know collectors in the exhibit.

After graduation, Louise gained a thorough education in retailing, working for New York Department Stores Abraham & Strauss. In the early eighties, she joined her father full time.

In 1985, they realized that there was no comprehensive, complete guide to one of the most popular new products, Enesco's Precious Moments Collection. Encouraged by her Dad, Louise proudly published the first GREENBOOK Guide to the Enesco Precious Moments Collection in 1986.

Louise can muddle through the most confusing complexity of information, reducing it to comprehensible components. Collectors appreciate her clear thinking and ability to discern the important facets of a collection. GREENBOOK Guides, deceptively simple in appearance, are chock-full of every fact any collector seeks. Every new Guide enjoys ever growing audiences, and imitators. Like the words Kleenex or Xerox have come to represent facial tissues and photocopies, GREENBOOK has come to mean secondary market price guide to many. GREENBOOK Guides are vastly different, collectors learn, for no detail is overlooked, and pricing is based on research, not fiction.

GREENBOOK is Louise. Her vision and concern for the collector is legend. As collectors' tastes and interests change, Louise is at the forefront, documenting and reflecting current enthusiasms. Her innovation and understanding of the collectible marketplace led GREENBOOK to be the first to document the Enesco Cherished Teddies Collection, and, more recently, Ty Beanie Babies. When a new product becomes hot, collectors, retailers, secondary market dealers and even makers turn to GREENBOOK, urging publication of the definitive GREENBOOK Guide.

1997 saw the launch of the very first GREENBOOK Guide on CD-Rom. Computer-savy collectors are delighted, for this innovative product makes everything much easier, from insurance documentation to shopping wishlists.

Louise's husband, Nick, joined GREENBOOK in 1998 to bear the administrative load leaving Louise free to develop even more Guides. And to enjoy some leisure time watching their 10-year-old daughter, Ally, compete on her horse, Bubble Bath.

Editor and Publisher, Louise Langenfeld

TABLE OF CONTENTS

GREENBOOK
- What We Do & How We Do It 6
- The WALT DISNEY CLASSICS COLLECTION 7
- BACKSTAMPS – The Mark Of Authenticity 9
- Annual Production Marks 10
- The Special Anniversary Mark 13

THE FILMS & CARTOON CLASSICS
- Aladdin 17
- Alice In Wonderland 19
- Bambi 25
- Beauty And The Beast 31
- Canine Caddy 37
- Cinderella 41
- Delivery Boy, The 54
- Don Donald 58
- Donald's Better Self 60
- Double Dribble 64
- Dumbo 66
- Fantasia 69
- Hercules 81
- How To Play Baseball 85
- Hunchback Of Notre Dame, The 87
- Jungle Book, The 89
- Lady And The Tramp 95
- Lion King, The 99
- Little Mermaid, The 105
- Little Whirlwind, The 114
- Make Mine Music 116
- Mickey Cuts Up 119
- Mickey's Birthday Party 122
- Mickey's Christmas Carol 124
- Mr. Duck Steps Out 128
- Mulan 133
- On Ice 135
- One Hundred And One Dalmatians 139
- Peter Pan 146
- Pinocchio 154
- Pluto's Christmas Tree (Holiday Series) 161
- Pocahontas 170
- Puppy Love 172
- Reluctant Dragon, The 176
- Scrooge McDuck And Money 178
- Simple Things, The 180
- Sleeping Beauty 182

Snow White And The Seven Dwarfs	191
Song Of The South	206
Steamboat Willie	210
Symphony Hour	213
Tarzan	219
Three Caballeros, The	223
Three Little Pigs	227
Touchdown Mickey	235
Toy Story	237
Who Framed Roger Rabbit?	242
Winnie The Pooh And The Honey Tree	244
Wise Little Hen, The	249

SPECIAL SERIES AND COLLECTIONS

Mickey Through The Years	251
Theme Park Attractions	255

WALT DISNEY COLLECTORS SOCIETY 260

Charter Membership Gift Sculpture	264
Membership Gift Sculptures	265
Animators' Choice	268
American Folk Heroes	272
Display Bases for Membership Sculptures	274
Members-Only Ornaments	275
Members-Only Sericels	278
Disney Villains	280
Five-Year Anniversary	282
Members-Only Numbered Limited Edition	283
Scene Completer	284

ANNOUNCEMENTS AS WE WERE GOING TO PRESS 285

Winnie The Pooh And The Honey Tree	285
First Aiders	286

QUIKREFERENCE

Disneyana Exclusives	288
Gold Circle Dealer Exclusives	288
The Tribute Series	288

INDEXES

By Subject	289
By Title	292
By Item Number	295

Table Of Contents 5

GREENBOOK
WHAT WE DO & HOW WE DO IT

ARTCHARTS & LISTINGS

The GREENBOOK ARTCHARTS developed for the Walt Disney Classics Collection feature color photographs, factual information and TRUMARKET PRICES for each piece.

Factual information consists of:
- Title
- Description
- Item Number
- Series or Collection
- Size
- Date of Issue
- Plussing
- Production Changes
- Item Particulars
- Status

GREENBOOK TRUMARKET PRICE Listings include:
- Year of Production
- Annual Production Mark
- Suggested Retail Price (issue or current price)
- GREENBOOK TRUMARKET Secondary Market Value

A COMPLETE GUIDE

As a collectible grows, it becomes too difficult for the producer to create material that traces the history of the collection, detailing every nuance about every item. This is where the GREENBOOK becomes an invaluable tool for the collector. Each edition adds the new and the newly known. Everything is right at the collector's fingertips, in handy, easy to read formats.

GREENBOOK TRUMARKET PRICES

Secondary market prices are reported to us by retailers and collectors. The data is compiled, checked for accuracy, and a price established as a benchmark as a result of this research. There are many factors which determine the price a collector will pay for a piece; most acquisitions are a matter of personal judgement. The price will fluctuate with the time of year, section of the country and type of sale. GREENBOOK takes all of these factors into consideration when determining TRUMARKET Values, and so **GREENBOOK TRUMARKET Values are never an absolute number**. Use them as a basis for comparison, as a point of information when considering an acquisition, and as a guide when insuring for replacement value.

The GREENBOOK does not trade on the Secondary Market. The GREENBOOK monitors and reports prices, in the same way as the Wall Street Journal reports trades on the stock markets in the United States and abroad.

WALT DISNEY CLASSICS COLLECTION AN INNOVATIVE VENTURE

The Walt Disney Company has a long history of inadvertently creating hotly sought after collectibles. Mickey Mouse and his compatriots are beloved everywhere, by all age groups, in every medium imaginable.

Each new property spawns a wealth of products that find willing acceptance 'round the globe. Companies are lined up for years in advance of a new release for the right to reproduce, in some fashion, the latest characters.

At the same time, characters that were created sixty and more years ago are still popular.

Americans grew up with Mickey. Everyone loves reliving and sharing good times. Mom and Dad, Grandma and Grandpa, Aunts and Uncles and friends can't wait to introduce Baby to their first Mickey or Donald or Pooh or Snow White.

Mickey has been a popular contemporary collectible subject for the past twenty years, as a result of limited edition collector plates and Christmas ornaments, just to name a few. And ceramic and plastic decorative accessories featuring Disney characters have found acceptance from the nursery to the living room and den.

It was indeed a great concept then to conceive a collection that would call upon the skills of the world's best artisans to craft sculptures that would do justice to the heritage of Walt Disney and his gifted team of artists and animators.

In the always innovative Disney fashion, developers took the concept of a range of figurines one step further than usual. A complete scene or vignette from the favored film is developed, not just individual characters. Furthermore, for the first few years, the scenes originated in a film crafted under the personal direction of Walt Disney. The scene sculptures appear in the context of the story, and not as isolated personalities relating to nothing. It was a brilliant idea, for Mickey as the Sorcerer's Apprentice is wonderful, but Mickey with the Broom is outstanding: full of life and movement. Thus the concept became the Walt Disney Classics Collection. This is the *very first time* a collection of fine animation sculptures has been created directly by Disney artists and animators.

The Collection debuted with teaser ads for retailers in the Fall, 1991 issues of their trade magazines. These ads featured a glimpse of the Field Mouse from *Bambi*. The prototypes were unveiled over the Fall and the Collection premiered in the early Spring, in California. Excitement mounted, until after months of painstaking work, the sculptures were shipped to dealers in October of 1992.

The rest is history. The **Walt Disney Collectors Society** debuted in 1993, and more than 50,000 people signed up. Innovation follows innovation and Disney product development teams search the world for unique accents to embellish and enhance the sculptures. Each year holds excitement as collectors await not only the announcement of the subjects to be honored, but the unique touches, termed **"plussing"** that the Disney innovators will devise.

The Collection can be divided into three groups, based on the film inspiration for each character and setting.

Timeless Treasures are those early feature films personally touched by Walt Disney.

Modern Masterpieces, beginning in 1970, show that the legacy endures, touching the hearts–both young and old–of today's audiences.

Cartoon Classics include all the early animated short films, through which Walt created the cast of characters who would introduce Disney magic to the world.

BACKSTAMPS

– The Mark of Authenticity

The Backstamp is an integral part of a ceramic product. For centuries manufacturers have marked the back or underside of their products in some fashion. From time to time, the marks are altered and a record kept of these changes. The word stamp is employed because a stamp of the company's current mark was made, dipped into a colored glaze and then stamped on the underside of the piece. Prior to the ability to make stamps, hand marks were used. It is these marks that enable antique dealers, museum curators and auctioneers to determine where and when a piece was crafted.

Today many companies own no manufacturing facilities themselves, but have their products made under contract by experts. In this case, the backstamp is also used as a quality assurance symbol. Only products that meet the standards established by the importer/producer bear the mark. As a result, the mark is rarely a stamp, but a beautifully crafted "decal" that is fired onto the piece during manufacture. (Because "decals" are made separately, occasionally a mix-up can occur and the wrong backstamp is applied to a sculpture.)

Backstamps can also indicate where a product was crafted, as American regulations require that country of origin appear on a product. Disney uses a vinyl sticker to denote the country.

Disney has employed three marks or backstamps to date:

Open Backstamp *or* "Floating Logo":
"CLASSICS" & "COLLECTION" in Teal Green; *Signature* in Gold; or all one color (Example–Scroll)
Period of use: 1992 to mid–1994.

Teal Green Background:
"CLASSICS" & "COLLECTION" in reverse-out White; *Signature* in Gold. PROBLEMS: The White filled in and the Gold could not be seen.
Period of use: Mid to end of 1994. (All Admiral Duck; some Uncle Donald; Mr. Smee; Medium and Large Mushrooms.)

Boxed–in Backstamp:
Teal Green ruled Box, enclosing "CLASSICS" & "COLLECTION" in Teal Green and *Signature* in Gold.
Period of use: Mid–1994 onward.

ANNUAL PRODUCTION MARKS

Chinese potters were the first to employ marks that indicated when an object was made. The marks detailed the dynasty of the Emperor ruling at the time. Some marks were imitated so that counterfeit items could be sold in place of the genuine article. The study of marks is fascinating, and follows history and events of importance.

With the onset of the popularity of contemporary collectibles, annual production marks took on a life and value of their own. Originally intended to allow future generations to easily identify the time of manufacture, some are sought after for their rarity.

"First Marks" often bring higher prices on the Secondary Market, and some collectors specialize, or limit their collections to these pieces. In particular, if a piece is introduced and shipped to retailers at the beginning of the year, it had to be manufactured in the final months of the previous year. So the avid collector often seeks those pieces.

The Annual Production Mark is usually incised into the base of the sculpture, from the mold. It is employed for the twelve calendar months of the year. Every January a new mark is inaugurated.

The Walt Disney Classics Collection uses the Annual Production Mark to honor a specific milestone of Disney history. Disney makes the announcement of the mark a special event, revealing one mark at a time, to date. The production marks and their milestone are:

Steamboat Willie   1992
To honor Mickey Mouse's debut in the cartoon short, *Steamboat Willie*, 1928.

Treble Clef 1993
To honor Disney's Academy Award–winning Silly Symphonies cartoons.

Dancing Flower 1994
To honor 1932's *Flowers And Trees*, the first full–color cartoon ever created and the first Disney Academy Award–winner.

Trowel 1995
Represents the Academy Award-winning, 1933 cartoon, *Three Little Pigs*. This short was also the first to introduce an original song, "Who's Afraid Of The Big Bad Wolf?" The tune was the first of many Disney hit songs.

Donald Duck's Hat 1996
Represents Donald's debut in *The Wise Little Hen*, 1934. Cast as a minor character, the film made Donald a star.

Music Stand 1997
Honors *The Band Concert,* Mickey Mouse's first color cartoon. It is the combination of the superb Mickey character as bandleader and Donald Duck as the mischievous peanut vendor that brought the film alive with comedy and music. This is the Maestro's Music Stand.

Pickax 1998
This symbol, from *Snow White And The Seven Dwarfs*, honors the Diamond Anniversary milestone of the Walt Disney Company. This was the first feature-length animated film.

Sorcerer's Hat 1999
This symbol from the *Fantasia* segment, The Sorcerer's Apprentice adds to the ongoing celebration of the Mouse that began it all. Fantasia was a marriage of two art forms–music and story visualization.

Annual Production Marks

SUNDAY FUNNIES™

(Established 1988)

16833 Southcenter Parkway
Tukwila, WA 98188
206-575-3565 or 1-800-664-4891
Fax 206-575-7572

Website: http://www.sundayfunnies.com

*Charter Gold Circle Dealer for the Walt Disney Classics Collection
And OFFICIAL HISTORIAN for the
GREENBOOK Guide to the Walt Disney Classics Collection*

PRESENTS

Classic Madness™

*Our Monthly Newsletter
Showcasing the latest news and images of
these special collections since 1994*

$22 for one year (free with annual purchase of $300+)
Visa, MC, AMEX, Discover & Checks Accepted
CALL 1-800-644-4891
(Also available on our website)

THE SPECIAL ANNIVERSARY MARK

Most of the Walt Disney films were innovative, ground-breaking works. Many won Academy Awards – Oscars – the highest accolade of the Hollywood film community. A number were responsible for technical inventions involving new machinery, like cameras, as well as techniques. Each had something special that set them apart.

There are many anniversaries to celebrate, from the introduction of a character, to the actual production itself. The Walt Disney Classics Collection devised a unique way to honor these milestones. A special message is incorporated into the backstamp of the sculptures concerned with the anniversary. Often in script, it clearly denotes the occasion being highlighted. The special backstamps appear on the designated sculpture for the anniversary year, and then appear no more. There have been a dozen anniversaries celebrated thus far.

- The **1992** Fiftieth Anniversary of *Bambi*.
- The **1992** Fiftieth Anniversary of *Symphony Hour*.
- The **1993** Fortieth Anniversary of *Peter Pan*.
- The **1993** Sixtieth Anniversary of *Three Little Pigs*.
- Donald Duck's Sixtieth Birthday was marked with a special message on all *Mr. Duck Steps Out* sculptures produced in **1994**.
- The **1995** Fiftieth Anniversary of *The Three Caballeros*.
- The **1996** Fiftieth Anniversary of *Song Of The South*.
- The **1997** Thirtieth Anniversary of *The Jungle Book*.
- The **1997** Thirtieth Anniversary of *Scrooge McDuck And Money*.
- Mickey Mouse's Seventieth Birthday was marked with a special message on all Mickey sculptures produced in **1998**.
- The **1998** Sixtieth Anniversary of *Donald's Better Self*.
- The **1998** Tenth Anniversary of *Who Framed Roger Rabbit?*
- The **1999** Fortieth Anniversary of *Sleeping Beauty*.
- The **1999** Fifth Anniversary of *The Lion King*.

OTHER GUIDES FROM GREENBOOK

GREENBOOK Guide to
>Precious Moments® by Enesco

GREENBOOK Guide to
>The Cherished Teddies® Collection

GREENBOOK Guide to
>Department 56® Villages including The Original Snow Village®, The Heritage Village Collection® and Seasons Bay™

GREENBOOK Guide to
>Department 56® Snowbabies™

GREENBOOK Guide to
>Hallmark Keepsake Ornaments

GREENBOOK Guide to
>Hallmark Kiddie Car Classics

GREENBOOK Guide to
>Harbour Lights™

Coming in 1999:

GREENBOOK Guide to
>The Boyds Collection Ltd. Plush

GREENBOOK Guide to
>The Boyds Collection Ltd. Resin

GREENBOOK Guide to
>Charming Tails

GREENBOOK Guide to
>Harmony Kingdom

GREENBOOK Guide to
>Shelia's Collectibles ... AND MORE!

GREENBOOK Introduces
GREENWARE™

The Collectors' Personal Inventory Software For

Perfect For Your Insurance Needs!

CLASSICS *Walt Disney* **COLLECTION**

This complete, easy-to-use software program is designed to help collectors and dealers track their **Walt Disney Classics Collection** inventory. Our unique CD-ROM is created from the collector's stand-point, utilizing all the information found in the all new 1999 Edition bestselling GREENBOOK Guide to **The Walt Disney Classics Collection**.

Our program incorporates:
- Pre-entered factual information & data on every single piece
- Current Secondary Market Values
- Beautiful full color photographs

Only $39.95 USA!

With this software you'll track your personal collection in a spreadsheet format that lays it all out for you. You can enter every detail of your collection, including quantity, condition, purchase price & date, dealer & collector contacts. You can customize & then print a dozen high quality reports tailored to your specific needs, including Insurance, Inventory, Financial, Swapping & Selling… Upgrades will be available annually for $19.95. Make tracking your collection a pleasure instead of a pain. This GREENBOOK CD-ROM is just what you've been looking for!

For more information please call (831) 656-9000
or visit our website at www.greenbooks.com

Minimum System Requirements: • PC Compatible Computer w/Microsoft Windows 3.x, '95. '98 or NT • 486DX processor • 8 MB RAM • 12 MB hard drive space • CD-ROM drive • SVGA display (256 colors)

On the following pages the films and cartoon classics appear in Alphabetical order.

Within each, the pieces appear in Availability order.

Use the QUIKREFERENCE at the beginning of each film or classic as your map through each section.

November 22, 1992

Aladdin

The desert, a land of mystery with scorching heat by day and often bitter cold by night, is home to street-smart Aladdin. One of the classic Disney heroes, born and brought up among a den of villains, yet brave, intelligent and clean, he is a diamond in the rough. Based on the ancient tale from *The Thousand And One Nights*, this is a musical fantasy in which Aladdin dreams of winning the hand of the Sultan's beautiful daughter, Princess Jasmine, in spite of the scheming vizier, Jafar. He is aided in his quest by his pet monkey Abu, a Genie he has freed from a magic lamp, and by a flying carpet. *Aladdin* continues with the recurring theme also seen in *The Little Mermaid* and *Beauty And The Beast* of a father's idea of what is best for his daughter being radically different from her own. It also continues the trend of concentrating a considerable amount of animation effort on objects that in the real world would be regarded as inanimate.

While researching *Aladdin*, animators went to the Middle East to study mosques, dwellings, architecture, marketplaces and elaborately-patterned carpets. They also borrowed from highly stylized Persian miniatures and Arabian calligraphy.

Aladdin set a new record for a Disney film: $217.4 million in ticket sales in the US and Canada alone.

ALADDIN QUIKREFERENCE

	TITLE	ITEM#	AVAILABLE
LIMITED EDITION:			
Genie	"I'm Losing To A Rug"	41269	4/98

COMPLEMENTARY PIECES:

WALT DISNEY COLLECTORS SOCIETY
DISNEY VILLAIN SERIES: (see page 280)
| Jafar | "Oh Mighty Evil One" | 41280 | 1998 |

"I'm Losing To A Rug"

TITLE: "I'm Losing To A Rug"
FIGURINE: Genie
ITEM NUMBER: 41269
SIZE: 7.5"
DATE OF ISSUE: 4/98

PLUSSING: Chess Board, Carpet Tassels and Earring: Bronze. **Chess Pieces:** Brass.
PRODUCTION CHANGES: The piece the rug holds is black on some, white on others.
PARTICULARS: Certificate of Authenticity. Incised Annual Production Mark.
STATUS: LIMITED EDITION: 12,500 Hand Numbered Pieces.

YEAR	MARK	SRP	GBTru
☐ 1997		$450	**$450**
☐ 1998		450	**450**

Aladdin

ALICE in WONDERLAND
July 28, 1951

Adapted from the literary masterpiece written by Lewis Carroll, Disney combined characters and events to tie the episodes he chose to animate together into one tale. A major decision for the studio was a way to make story-sense of an illogical string of episodes and fit it into the 75 minute time frame. Some story characters were left out and others were interwoven because, according to Disney's own count, the book contains over 80 characters. As it is, *Alice In Wonderland* contains more characters than any other Disney animated feature. Using Alice's curiosity, Disney evolved a story line to create the reactions of little girl to a fantasy world.

Walt Disney, fascinated by the Lewis Carroll stories, worked on the idea of an "Alice" film from 1933. When it was finally completed he remarked that it "had the pace of a three-ring circus."

ALICE IN WONDERLAND QUIKREFERENCE

	TITLE	ITEM #	AVAILABLE
SCROLL:			
Scroll	*Alice In Wonderland* Opening Title	41378	3/99
OPEN EDITIONS:			
Alice	"Yes, Your Majesty."	41375	3/99
Card Painter	Playing Card	41414	3/99
King of Hearts	"...And The King"	41419	3/99
ANNUAL:			
Queen of Hearts	"Let The Game Begin!"	41413	3/99

COMPLEMENTARY PIECES:

ENCHANTED PLACES

LIMITED EDITION:			
Sculpture	A Tea Party In Wonderland	41295	6/98 - 3/99
RETIRED EDITIONS:			
Sculpture	White Rabbit's House	41202	7/95 - 3/99
Miniature	White Rabbit	41213	4/96 - 3/99

WALT DISNEY COLLECTORS SOCIETY

MEMBERSHIP GIFT SCULPTURE: (see page 265)

Cheshire Cat	"'Twas Brillig"	41057	1994

MEMBERS-ONLY ORNAMENT: (see page 277)

White Rabbit	"No Time To Say Hello - Goodbye"	41373	1999

MEMBERS-ONLY SERICEL: (see page 279)

White Rabbit	"I'm Late"	1035092	3/15 - 5/30/99

Alice In Wonderland Opening Title

TITLE: *Alice In Wonderland* Opening Title
SCROLL: Opening Title
ITEM NUMBER: 41378
SIZE: 1.6"
DATE OF ISSUE: 3/99

PLUSSING: None.
PRODUCTION CHANGES: None.
PARTICULARS: Certificate of Authenticity. Decal backstamp with WDCC logo and Annual Production Mark.
STATUS: OPEN EDITION.

YEAR	MARK	SRP	GBTru
❏ 1999	🎩	$29	**$29**

"Yes, Your Majesty."

TITLE: "Yes, Your Majesty."
FIGURINE: Alice
ITEM NUMBER: 41375
SIZE: 7"
DATE OF ISSUE: 3/99

PLUSSING: Special Commemorative Backstamp: Approximately 125 pieces with the Special Backstamp message *"Celebrating The Classics March 1999"* were sold at the First Walt Disney Art Classics Convention, 3/19 to 3/21/99, in Orlando, Florida. (In addition, Gold Circle Dealers each received 2 pieces.) Item Number for Special Backstamp is 41441.
PRODUCTION CHANGES: None.
PARTICULARS: Certificate of Authenticity. Incised Annual Production Mark.
STATUS: OPEN EDITION.

YEAR	MARK	SRP	GBTru
❏ 1998	⚱	$145	**$145**
❏ 1999	🎩	145	**145**

Playing Card

TITLE: Playing Card
FIGURINE: Card Painter
ITEM NUMBER: 41414
SIZE: 5"
DATE OF ISSUE: 3/99

PLUSSING: Special Commemorative Backstamp: Approximately 125 pieces with the Special Backstamp message *"Celebrating The Classics March 1999"* were sold at the First Walt Disney Art Classics Convention, 3/19 to 3/21/99, in Orlando, Florida. (In addition, Gold Circle Dealers each received 2 pieces.) Item Number for Special Backstamp is 41454.
PRODUCTION CHANGES: None.
PARTICULARS: Certificate of Authenticity. Incised Annual Production Mark.
STATUS: OPEN EDITION.

YEAR	MARK	SRP	GBTru
☐ 1998	⊤	$120	**$120**
☐ 1999	♟	120	**120**

"...And The King"

TITLE: " ...And The King"
FIGURINE: King of Hearts
ITEM NUMBER: 41419
SIZE: 4.5"
DATE OF ISSUE: 3/99

PLUSSING: Crown: Oversized with shiny gold paint. **Special Commemorative Backstamp:** Approximately 125 pieces with the Special Backstamp message *"Celebrating The Classics March 1999"* were sold at the First Walt Disney Art Classics Convention, 3/19 to 3/21/99, in Orlando, Florida. (In addition, Gold Circle Dealers each received 2 pieces.) Item Number for Special Backstamp is 41442.
PRODUCTION CHANGES: None.
PARTICULARS: Certificate of Authenticity. Incised Annual Production Mark.
STATUS: OPEN EDITION.

YEAR	MARK	SRP	GBTru
☐ 1998	⊤	$90	**$90**
☐ 1999	♟	90	**90**

Alice In Wonderland

"Let The Game Begin!"

TITLE: "Let The Game Begin!"
FIGURINE: Queen of Hearts
ITEM NUMBER: 41413
SIZE: 7"
DATE OF ISSUE: 3/99

PLUSSING: Flamingo croquet mallet: Metal neck. **Crown:** Shiny gold finish. **Special Commemorative Backstamp:** Approximately 125 pieces with the Special Backstamp message *"Celebrating The Classics March 1999"* were sold at the First Walt Disney Art Classics Convention, 3/19 to 3/21/99, in Orlando, Florida. (In addition, Gold Circle Dealers each received 2 pieces.) Item Number for Special Backstamp is 41443.
PRODUCTION CHANGES: None.
PARTICULARS: Certificate of Authenticity. Incised Annual Production Mark.
STATUS: 1999 ANNUAL.

YEAR	MARK	SRP	GBTru
❒ 1998		$175	**$175**
❒ 1999		175	**175**

A Tea Party In Wonderland

TITLE: A Tea Party In Wonderland
SCULPTURE: Alice, Mad Hatter, March Hare, Dormouse
ITEM NUMBER: 41295
SIZE: 5.5"
DATE OF ISSUE: 6/98

PLUSSING: Characters: Cast in pewter. **Detailing:** Place settings and some chairs have pewter parts. **Lanterns:** Hang from real ropes. **Gate:** Real hinges allow it to open and close.
PRODUCTION CHANGES: None.
PARTICULARS: Enchanted Places. Certificate of Authenticity. Incised Annual Production Mark. Hand Engraved Serial Number. Sculpture comes with a wood display base with engraved brass nameplate.
STATUS: LIMITED EDITION: 4,500 Hand Numbered Pieces. EDITION CLOSED.

YEAR	MARK	SRP	GBTru
❒ 1998		$395	**$395**

White Rabbit's House

TITLE: White Rabbit's House
SCULPTURE: White Rabbit's House
ITEM NUMBER: 41202
SIZE: 4.5"
DATE OF ISSUE: 7/95

PLUSSING: Props: Water bucket, boot scraper, barrel, hoe, wheelbarrow, pots, blue bin and flowers are cast in pewter.
PRODUCTION CHANGES: New logo and **backstamp** mid-1996. **Annual Production Mark** added mid-1996.
PARTICULARS: Enchanted Places. Certificate of Authenticity. Incised Annual Production Mark. Hand Engraved Serial Number. Registration Card redeemable for a deed "signed" by the setting's original "owner," transferring ownership.

Sculpture comes with a wood display base with engraved brass nameplate.
STATUS: RETIRED 3/99.

YEAR	MARK	SRP	GBTru
☐ 1995		$175	**$175**
☐ 1996		175	**175**
☐ 1997		175	**175**
☐ 1998		175	**175**
☐ 1999		175	**175**

White Rabbit

TITLE: White Rabbit
MINIATURE: White Rabbit
ITEM NUMBER: 41213
SIZE: 1"
DATE OF ISSUE: 4/96

PLUSSING: Miniature: Bronze, hand painted.
PRODUCTION CHANGES: None.
PARTICULARS: Enchanted Places. Burgundy box, no picture on box, no Annual Production Mark.
STATUS: RETIRED 3/99.

YEAR	MARK	SRP	GBTru
☐ 1996	No Mark	$50	**$50**

Alice In Wonderland

Bambi
August 13, 1942

Bambi is famous for its painstaking, realistic detail. The superb natural effects resulted from the animators studying a small family of wildlife creatures brought to live at the studio. No expense was spared to ensure that every detail was believable and exact. When too much pampering tamed the animals, Disney sent a camera crew to the wilds of Maine to capture the creatures and their habitats on film. Combining human emotions with animal realism gave the film its unique touch.

It took seven years to bring *Bambi* to the screen. Work began in 1935 with character development assigned part-time to four of the "Nine Old Men:" Ollie Johnston, Eric Larson, Milt Kahl and Frank Thomas. At the same time they worked on major projects like *Pinocchio*, *Dumbo* and *Snow White* and yet were able to nearly finish this moving epic by 1941. Everyone applied their talents and the film debuted in the summer.

So successful were Disney's artists that the New York Times criticized the work and Disney for trespassing "beyond the bounds of cartoon fantasy into tight naturalism ... the cartoon caricatures have made way for a closer resemblance to life...". What a left-handed compliment! Today *Bambi* is regarded as a true masterpiece. It more than meets Walt's goal of restoring "our sense of kinship with the earth and all its inhabitants."

BAMBI QUIKREFERENCE

	TITLE	ITEM #	AVAILABLE
SCROLL:			
Scroll	*Bambi* Opening Title	41015	10/92
LIMITED EDITIONS:			
Bambi and Flower	"He Can Call Me A Flower If He Wants To"	41010	10/92 - 4/93
Field Mouse	Little April Shower	41012	10/92 - 1/93
RETIRED EDITIONS:			
Friend Owl	"What's Going On Around Here?"	41011	10-92 - 4/98
Thumper	"Hee! Hee! Hee!"	41013	10/92 - 4/98
Thumper's Sisters	"Hello, Hello There!"	41014	10/92 - 4/98
Bambi	"Purty Flower"	41033	4/93 - 4/98
Flower	"Oh...Gosh!"	41034	4/93 - 4/98

"Bambi Opening Title"

TITLE: *Bambi* Opening Title
SCROLL: Opening Title
ITEM NUMBER: 41015
SIZE: 1.6"
DATE OF ISSUE: 10/92

PLUSSING: None.
PRODUCTION CHANGES: None.
PARTICULARS: Certificate of Authenticity. Decal backstamp with WDCC logo and Annual Production Mark.
STATUS: OPEN EDITION.

YEAR	MARK	SRP	GBTru
☐ 1992		$29	**$35**
☐ 1993		29	**29**
☐ 1994		29	**29**
☐ 1995		29	**29**
☐ 1996		29	**29**
☐ 1997		29	**29**
☐ 1998		29	**29**
☐ 1999		29	**29**

Bambi

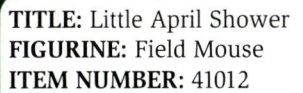

"He Can Call Me A Flower If He Wants To"

TITLE: "He Can Call Me A Flower If He Wants To"
FIGURINE: Bambi and Flower
ITEM NUMBER: 41010
SIZE: 6"
DATE OF ISSUE: 10/92

PLUSSING: Handmade Flowers: Nine colorful blossoms are handmade, petal by petal. **Limited Edition Backstamp:** Each is crafted with a gold backstamp. **Anniversary Backstamp:** A special gold script message *'50th Anniversary'* was added to the backstamp of all sculptures.
PRODUCTION CHANGES: Some pieces were made with an incorrect backstamp reading "He Can Call Me Flower If He Wants To."
PARTICULARS: Hand Numbered Certificate of Authenticity. Incised Annual Production Mark.
STATUS: LIMITED EDITION: 10,000 Hand Numbered Pieces. EDITION CLOSED 4/93.

YEAR	MARK	SRP	GBTru
❏ 1992	✸ Anniv. Mark	$298	**$500**

Little April Shower

TITLE: Little April Shower
FIGURINE: Field Mouse
ITEM NUMBER: 41012
SIZE: 5.75"
DATE OF ISSUE: 10/92

PLUSSING: Crystal Dewdrop: A shiny Austrian Crystal dewdrop slides off leaf, suspended above the mouse's outstretched paws. **Limited Edition Backstamp:** Each is crafted with a gold backstamp. **Anniversary Backstamp:** A special gold message *'50th Anniversary'* was added to the backstamp of all sculptures.
PRODUCTION CHANGES: Three versions: 1) **Not Touching/Above Paws:** The dewdrop hangs suspended above the field mouse's paws, 2) **Not Touching/Next to Paws:** Allowed for supporting foam to be added for shipping, and, 3) **Touching:** To prevent breakage, the dewdrop was lengthened to touch at least one paw.
PARTICULARS: Hand Numbered Certificate of Authenticity. Incised Annual Production Mark. 1993 NALED Figurine of the Year.
STATUS: LIMITED EDITION: 7,500 Hand Numbered Pieces. EDITION CLOSED 1/93.

YEAR	MARK	SRP	GBTru
❏ 1992	✸	$195	**$1400**
Anniv. Mark, *Not* Touching/*Above Paws*			
❏ 1992	✸	195	**1350**
Anniv. Mark, *Not* Touching/*Next to Paws*			
❏ 1992	✸	195	**1200**
Anniv. Mark, *Touching*			

Bambi 27

"What's Going On Around Here?"

TITLE: "What's Going On Around Here?"
FIGURINE: Friend Owl
ITEM NUMBER: 41011
SIZE: 8.75"
DATE OF ISSUE: 10/92

PLUSSING: Anniversary Backstamp: A special gold script message *'50th Anniversary'* was added to the backstamp of sculptures crafted in 1992.
PRODUCTION CHANGES: None.
PARTICULARS: Certificate of Authenticity. Incised Annual Production Mark.
STATUS: RETIRED 4/98.

YEAR	MARK	SRP	GBTru
☐ 1992	Anniv. Mark	$195	$195
☐ 1993		195	195
☐ 1994		195	195
☐ 1995		195	195
☐ 1996		195	195
☐ 1997		195	195
☐ 1998		195	195

"Hee! Hee! Hee!"

TITLE: "Hee! Hee! Hee!"
FIGURINE: Thumper
ITEM NUMBER: 41013
SIZE: 3"
DATE OF ISSUE: 10/92

PLUSSING: Anniversary Backstamp: A special gold script message *'50th Anniversary'* was added to the backstamp of sculptures crafted in 1992.
PRODUCTION CHANGES: SRP Change: $55 to $65 in 1998.
PARTICULARS: Certificate of Authenticity. Incised Annual Production Mark.
STATUS: RETIRED 4/98.

YEAR	MARK	SRP	GBTru
☐ 1992	Anniv. Mark	$55	$75
☐ 1993		55	65
☐ 1994		55	65
☐ 1995		55	65
☐ 1996		55	65
☐ 1997		55	65
☐ 1998		65	65

Bambi

"Hello, Hello There!"

TITLE: "Hello, Hello There!"
FIGURINE: Thumper's Sisters
ITEM NUMBER: 41014
SIZE: 3.6"
DATE OF ISSUE: 10/92

PLUSSING: Anniversary
Backstamp: A special gold script message '*50th Anniversary*' was added to the backstamp of sculptures crafted in 1992.
PRODUCTION CHANGES: SRP Change: $69 to $75 in 1998.
PARTICULARS: Certificate of Authenticity. Incised Annual Production Mark.
STATUS: RETIRED 4/98.

YEAR	MARK	SRP	GBTru
❒ 1992	Anniv. Mark	$69	**$75**
❒ 1993		69	**75**
❒ 1994		69	**75**
❒ 1995		69	**75**
❒ 1996		69	**75**
❒ 1997		69	**75**
❒ 1998		75	**75**

"Purty Flower"

TITLE: "Purty Flower"
FIGURINE: Bambi
ITEM NUMBER: 41033
SIZE: 6"
DATE OF ISSUE: 4/93

PLUSSING: None.
PRODUCTION CHANGES: None.
PARTICULARS: Certificate of Authenticity. Incised Annual Production Mark.
STATUS: RETIRED 4/98.

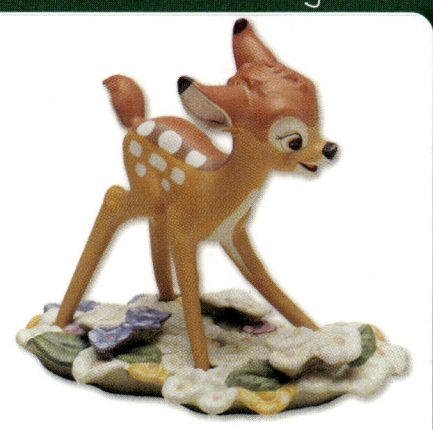

YEAR	MARK	SRP	GBTru
❒ 1992		$195	**$240**
❒ 1993		195	**195**
❒ 1994		195	**195**
❒ 1995		195	**195**
❒ 1996		195	**195**
❒ 1997		195	**195**
❒ 1998		195	**195**

"Oh...Gosh!"

TITLE: "Oh…Gosh!"
FIGURINE: Flower
ITEM NUMBER: 41034
SIZE: 3"
DATE OF ISSUE: 4/93

PLUSSING: None.
PRODUCTION CHANGES: SRP Change: $78 to $85 in 1998.
PARTICULARS: Certificate of Authenticity. Incised Annual Production Mark.
STATUS: RETIRED 4/98.

YEAR	MARK	SRP	GBTru
☐ 1992		$78	**$185**
☐ 1993		78	**85**
☐ 1994		78	**85**
☐ 1995		78	**85**
☐ 1996		78	**85**
☐ 1997		78	**85**
☐ 1998		85	**85**

Notes: _____

_____
_____
_____
_____
_____
_____
_____
_____
_____
_____
_____
_____

Bambi

Disney's Beauty and the Beast

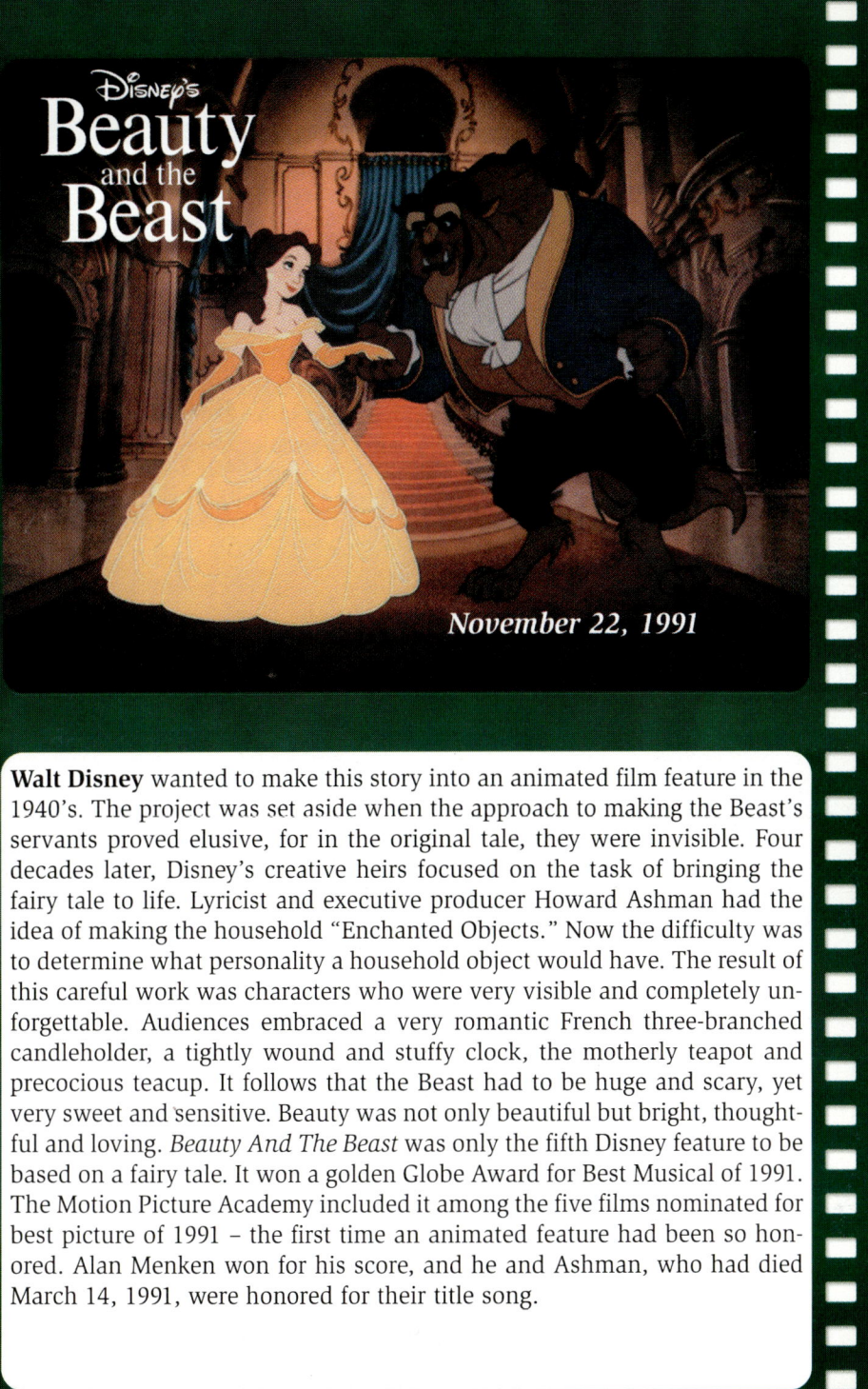

November 22, 1991

Walt Disney wanted to make this story into an animated film feature in the 1940's. The project was set aside when the approach to making the Beast's servants proved elusive, for in the original tale, they were invisible. Four decades later, Disney's creative heirs focused on the task of bringing the fairy tale to life. Lyricist and executive producer Howard Ashman had the idea of making the household "Enchanted Objects." Now the difficulty was to determine what personality a household object would have. The result of this careful work was characters who were very visible and completely unforgettable. Audiences embraced a very romantic French three-branched candleholder, a tightly wound and stuffy clock, the motherly teapot and precocious teacup. It follows that the Beast had to be huge and scary, yet very sweet and sensitive. Beauty was not only beautiful but bright, thoughtful and loving. *Beauty And The Beast* was only the fifth Disney feature to be based on a fairy tale. It won a golden Globe Award for Best Musical of 1991. The Motion Picture Academy included it among the five films nominated for best picture of 1991 – the first time an animated feature had been so honored. Alan Menken won for his score, and he and Ashman, who had died March 14, 1991, were honored for their title song.

BEAUTY AND THE BEAST QUIKREFERENCE

	TITLE	ITEM#	AVAILABLE
SCROLL:			
Scroll	*Beauty And The Beast* Opening Title	41189	3/97
OPEN EDITIONS:			
Belle and Beast	"Tale As Old As Time"	41156	3/97
Lumiere	Vive L'Amour!	41181	3/97
Cogsworth	Just In Time	41182	3/97
Mrs. Potts & Chip	"Good Night, Luv"	41183	3/97

COMPLEMENTARY PIECES:

ENCHANTED PLACES

OPEN EDITIONS:			
Sculpture	The Beast's Castle	41225	7/96
Ornament	The Beast's Castle	41294	7/98
Sculpture	The Enchanted Rose	41343	1/99

Beauty And The Beast Opening Title

TITLE: *Beauty And The Beast* Opening Title
SCROLL: Opening Title
ITEM NUMBER: 41189
SIZE: 1.6"
DATE OF ISSUE: 3/97

PLUSSING: None.
PRODUCTION CHANGES: None.
PARTICULARS: Certificate of Authenticity. Decal backstamp with WDCC logo and Annual Production Mark.
STATUS: OPEN EDITION.

YEAR	MARK	SRP	GBTru
❏ 1997		$29	**$29**
❏ 1998		29	**29**
❏ 1999		29	**29**

"Tale As Old As Time"

TITLE: "Tale As Old As Time"
FIGURINE: Belle and Beast
ITEM NUMBER: 41156
SIZE: 10"
DATE OF ISSUE: 3/97

PLUSSING: Belle's Dress: Opalescent paint to add shimmery highlights. **Belle's Earrings:** Opalescent paint. **Buttons:** Beast's jacket buttons painted gold. **Beast's Cravat Pin:** Painted gold.
PRODUCTION CHANGES: None.
PARTICULARS: Certificate of Authenticity. Incised Annual Production Mark.
STATUS: OPEN EDITION.

YEAR	MARK	SRP	GBTru
❏ 1996		$295	**$295**
❏ 1997		295	**295**
❏ 1998		295	**295**
❏ 1999		295	**295**

Vive L'Amour!

TITLE: Vive L'Amour!
FIGURINE: Lumiere
ITEM NUMBER: 41181
SIZE: 5.5"
DATE OF ISSUE: 3/97

PLUSSING: Candelabra Arms: Bronze with metal candlewicks. **Candelabra Stem:** In shiny gold paint.
PRODUCTION CHANGES: None.
PARTICULARS: Certificate of Authenticity. Incised Annual Production Mark.
STATUS: OPEN EDITION.

YEAR	MARK	SRP	GBTru
☐ 1997		$115	**$115**
☐ 1998		115	**115**
☐ 1999		115	**115**

"Just In Time"

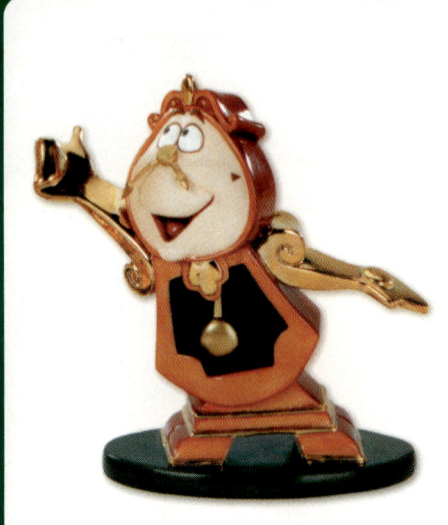

TITLE: "Just In Time"
FIGURINE: Cogsworth
ITEM NUMBER: 41182
SIZE: 4.2"
DATE OF ISSUE: 3/97

PLUSSING: Clock Hands: Bronze. **Pendulum:** Bronze, movable. **Arm Side Pieces:** Shiny gold paint.
PRODUCTION CHANGES: None.
PARTICULARS: Certificate of Authenticity. Incised Annual Production Mark.
STATUS: OPEN EDITION.

YEAR	MARK	SRP	GBTru
☐ 1997		$120	**$120**
☐ 1998		120	**120**
☐ 1999		120	**120**

Beauty And The Beast

"Good Night, Luv"

TITLE: "Good Night, Luv"
FIGURINE: Mrs. Potts and Chip
ITEM NUMBER: 41183
SIZE: 4.5"
DATE OF ISSUE: 3/97

PLUSSING: Chip's Cup Rim: Created with a chip missing.
PRODUCTION CHANGES: None.
PARTICULARS: Certificate of Authenticity. Incised Annual Production Mark.
STATUS: OPEN EDITION.

YEAR	MARK	SRP	GBTru
❑ 1997		$125	**$125**
❑ 1998		125	**125**
❑ 1999		125	**125**

The Beast's Castle

TITLE: The Beast's Castle
SCULPTURE: The Beast's Castle
ITEM NUMBER: 41225
SIZE: 10"
DATE OF ISSUE: 7/96

PLUSSING: Painting: 200 separate paint applications.
PRODUCTION CHANGES: None.
PARTICULARS: Enchanted Places. Certificate of Authenticity. Incised Annual Production Mark. Hand Engraved Serial Number. Registration Card redeemable for a deed "signed" by the setting's original "owner," transferring ownership. Sculpture comes with a wood display base with engraved brass nameplate.
STATUS: OPEN EDITION.

YEAR	MARK	SRP	GBTru
❑ 1996		$245	**$245**
❑ 1997		245	**245**
❑ 1998		245	**245**
❑ 1999		245	**245**

Beauty And The Beast

The Beast's Castle

TITLE: The Beast's Castle
ORNAMENT: The Beast's Castle
ITEM NUMBER: 41294
SERIES: Enchanted Castles Ornament Series – 2nd of 6
SIZE: 3.5"
DATE OF ISSUE: 7/98

PLUSSING: None.
PRODUCTION CHANGES: None.
PARTICULARS: Enchanted Places. Certificate of Authenticity. Sticker Annual Production Mark.
STATUS: OPEN EDITION.

YEAR	MARK	SRP	GBTru
☐ 1998	T	$45	**$45**
☐ 1999	⛵	45	**45**

The Enchanted Rose

TITLE: The Enchanted Rose
SCULPTURE: Table and Rose
ITEM NUMBER: 41343
SIZE: 7"
DATE OF ISSUE: 1/99

PLUSSING: Rose: In clear resin. **Table:** Top is painted to resemble marble with edge painted in gold. Base is painted to resemble heavy carved mahogany.
PRODUCTION CHANGES: None.
PARTICULARS: Enchanted Places. Certificate of Authenticity. Annual Production Mark.
STATUS: OPEN EDITION.

YEAR	MARK	SRP	GBTru
☐ 1998	T	$100	**$100**
☐ 1999	⛵	100	**100**

Beauty And The Beast

CANINE CADDY
1941

Trusty pal Pluto takes the role of caddy when he hits the golf course with Mickey. But Pluto can't stop the antics of a pesky gopher and tears up the course chasing him. Plowing tunnels through the hills and sandtraps, Pluto finally triumphs in time to see Mickey sink his shot.

CANINE CADDY QUIKREFERENCE

	TITLE	ITEM #	AVAILABLE
SCROLL:			
Scroll	*Canine Caddy* Opening Title	41417	5/99
OPEN EDITIONS:			
Mickey Mouse	"What A Swell Day For A Game Of Golf!"	41149	5/97
Pluto	A Golfer's Best Friend	41314	5/99
Display Base	*Canine Caddy* Display Base	41423	5/99

Canine Caddy Opening Title

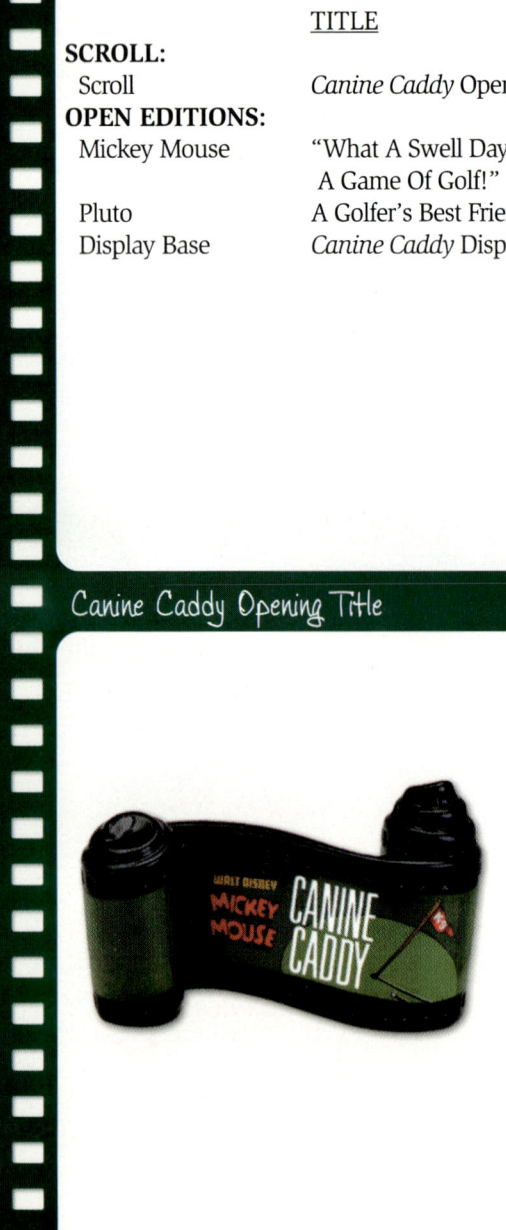

TITLE: *Canine Caddy* Opening Title
SCROLL: Opening Title
ITEM NUMBER: 41417
SIZE: 1.6"
DATE OF ISSUE: 5/99

PLUSSING: None.
PRODUCTION CHANGES: None.
PARTICULARS: Certificate of Authenticity. Decal backstamp with WDCC logo and Annual Production Mark.
STATUS: OPEN EDITION.

YEAR	MARK	SRP	GBTru
❏ 1999	🎩	$29	**$29**

Canine Caddy

"What A Swell Day For A Game Of Golf!"

TITLE: "What A Swell Day For A Game Of Golf!"
FIGURINE: Mickey Mouse
ITEM NUMBER: 41149
SIZE: 5.25"
DATE OF ISSUE: 5/97

PLUSSING: Golf Club: Metal shaft.
Mickey's Ears: Shaded paint to provide a two-dimensional look.
PRODUCTION CHANGES: None.
PARTICULARS: Certificate of Authenticity. Incised Annual Production Mark.
STATUS: OPEN EDITION.

YEAR	MARK	SRP	GBTru
❏ 1997		$150	**$150**
❏ 1998		150	**150**
❏ 1999		150	**150**

A Golfer's Best Friend

TITLE: A Golfer's Best Friend
FIGURINE: Pluto
ITEM NUMBER: 41314
SIZE: 4.75"
DATE OF ISSUE: 5/99

PLUSSING: Golf Bag: Leather strap. **Ears & Tail:** Pluto's ears are pewter, tail is metal.
PRODUCTION CHANGES: None.
PARTICULARS: Certificate of Authenticity. Incised Annual Production Mark.
STATUS: OPEN EDITION.

YEAR	MARK	SRP	GBTru
❏ 1999		$125	**$125**

Canine Caddy   39

Canine Caddy Display Base

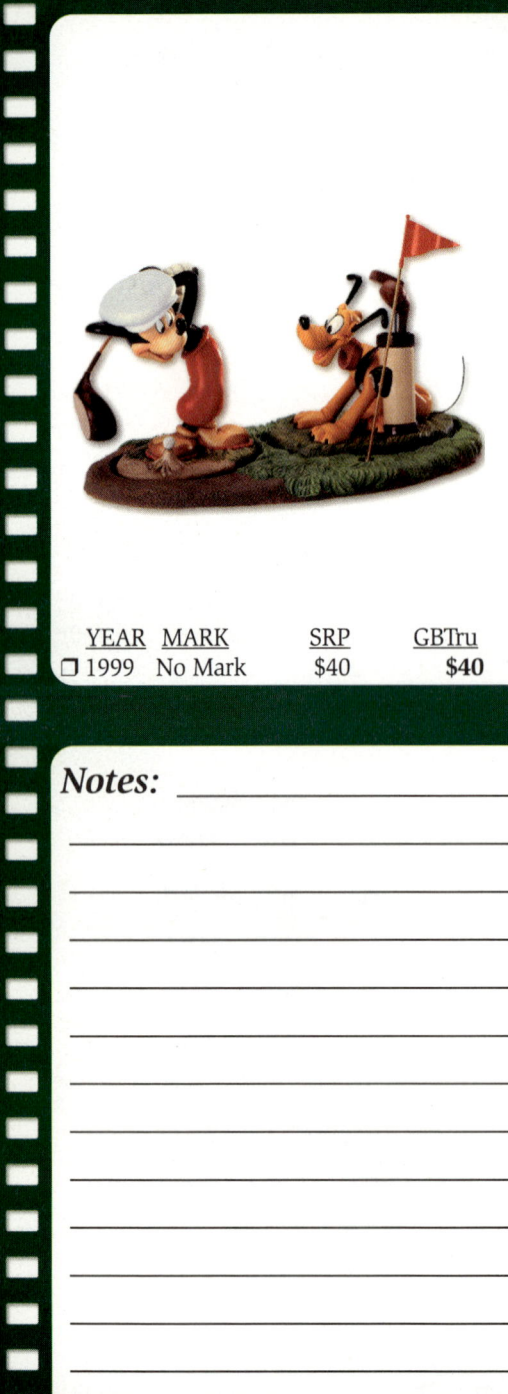

TITLE: *Canine Caddy* Display Base
ACCESSORY BASE: Display Base
ITEM NUMBER: 41423
SIZE: 7.5"
DATE OF ISSUE: 5/99

PLUSSING: Base: Plussed with a metal flag.
PRODUCTION CHANGES: None.
PARTICULARS: Base is made of resin with inserts for both Pluto and Mickey. No Annual Production Mark.
STATUS: OPEN EDITION.

YEAR	MARK	SRP	GBTru
☐ 1999	No Mark	$40	**$40**

Notes: _____
_____
_____
_____
_____
_____
_____
_____
_____
_____
_____
_____
_____
_____

Cinderella
From the Original Classic
February 15, 1950

Walt Disney took one of the world's best known, best loved fairy tales and made magic. *Cinderella*, often called one of Disney's all time greats, was a smash hit. The first full-length animated feature since 1942's *Bambi*, the film was brought to the public in the Winter of 1950.

Walt Disney knew that everyone loves cheering for good versus evil, for the triumph of the underdog. And dreams of wealth, success and most importantly, true love, are the motivating factors in most peoples' lives. That's why Disney films appeal to such vast audiences.

The movie creatively filled the screen with music, comedy, imagination and charm. Animator Marc Davis said that Cinderella had to be believable. Each movie goer had to sense her strength, feel sympathy as she battled villains, smile in wonderment as some of the screen's cutest creatures came to her rescue, and feel the magic as Cinderella and Prince Charming fell in love.

The tale tells of a young woman living with her stepmother and two stepsisters. Cinderella is treated poorly, accepts the injustice that is her fate, yet hopes and wishes for changes and opportunities that may never come her way. It is her goodness that is rewarded by her Fairy Godmother. Wishes come true, and "happily ever after" becomes a fact.

CINDERELLA QUIKREFERENCE

	TITLE	ITEM #	AVAILABLE
SCROLL:			
Scroll	*Cinderella* Opening Title	41009	10/92
OPEN EDITIONS:			
Cinderella & Prince Charming	"So This Is Love"	41079	10/95
Cinderella & Prince	Fairy Tale Wedding Cake Topper	41267	5/98
EVENT PIECES:			
Fairy Godmother	"Bibbidi, Bobbidi, Boo"	41108	7/96 - 12/96
Jaq & Gus	Tea For Two	41410	11/13 & 14/99
LIMITED EDITION:			
Cinderella's Dress	"A Lovely Dress For Cinderelly"	41030	12/92 - 7/93
RETIRED EDITIONS:			
Cinderella	"They Can't Stop Me From Dreaming"	41000	10/92 - 7/93
Lucifer (Cat)	"Meany, Sneaky, Roos-A-Fee"	41001	10/92 - 7/93
Bruno (Dog)	"Just Learn To Like Cats"	41002	10/92 - 7/93
Open Sewing Book	Cinderella's Sewing Book	41003	10/92 - 8/94
Needle Mouse (Suzy)	"Hey, We Can Do It!"	41004	10/92 - 8/94
Birds with Sash	"We'll Tie A Sash Around It"	41005	10/92 - 8/94
Chalk Mouse (Perla)	"No Time For Dilly-Dally!"	41006	10/92 - 8/94
Gus (Mouse)	"You Go Get Some Trimmin'"	41007	10/92 - 8/94
Jaq (Mouse)	"You Go Get Some Trimmin'"	41008	10/92 - 8/94

COMPLEMENTARY PIECES:

ENCHANTED PLACES

OPEN EDITIONS:			
Sculpture	Cinderella's Coach	41208	9/96
Miniature	Gus (Mouse)	41218	9/96
Miniature	Jaq (Mouse)	41242	4/97
Ornament	Cinderella's Coach	41244	7/97
Ornament	Cinderella's Castle	41293	7/98
RETIRED EDITION:			
Sculpture	Cinderella's Castle	41210	1/97 - 1/98

Cinderella Opening Title

TITLE: *Cinderella* Opening Title
SCROLL: Opening Title
ITEM NUMBER: 41009
SIZE: 1.6"
DATE OF ISSUE: 10/92

PLUSSING: None.
PRODUCTION CHANGES: The word 'Technicolor' was removed for trademark protection issues.
PARTICULARS: Certificate of Authenticity. Decal backstamp with WDCC logo and Annual Production Mark.
STATUS: OPEN EDITION.

YEAR	MARK	SRP	GBTru
☐ 1992	⚓ *w/Technicolor*	$29	**$45**
☐ 1993		29	**35**
☐ 1994		29	**29**
☐ 1995		29	**29**
☐ 1996		29	**29**
☐ 1997		29	**29**
☐ 1998		29	**29**
☐ 1999		29	**29**

"So This Is Love"

TITLE: "So This Is Love"
FIGURINE: Cinderella and Prince Charming
ITEM NUMBER: 41079
SIZE: 9.5"
DATE OF ISSUE: 10/95

PLUSSING: Gown: Cinderella's satin gown has 23 different paints and 6 kiln firings to create opalescent shimmer and shaded fabric folds. **Prince's Uniform:** Epaulettes on the Prince's jacket, collar, buckle, and pant-stripes are gilded with 11 karat gold.
PRODUCTION CHANGES: None.
PARTICULARS: Certificate of Authenticity. Incised Annual Production Mark.
STATUS: OPEN EDITION.

YEAR	MARK	SRP	GBTru
☐ 1995		$295	**$315**
☐ 1996		295	**295**
☐ 1997		295	**295**
☐ 1998		295	**295**
☐ 1999		295	**295**

Fairy Tale Wedding

TITLE: Fairy Tale Wedding
FIGURINE – CAKE TOPPER: Cinderella and Prince
ITEM NUMBER: 41267
SIZE: 9.5"
DATE OF ISSUE: 5/98

PLUSSING: Prince's Uniform: Epaulettes have gold accents.
PRODUCTION CHANGES: None.
PARTICULARS: Certificate of Authenticity. Incised Annual Production Mark.
STATUS: OPEN EDITION.

YEAR	MARK	SRP	GBTru
☐ 1998		$195	**$195**
☐ 1999		195	**195**

"Bibbidi, Bobbidi, Boo"

TITLE: "Bibbidi, Bobbidi, Boo"
FIGURINE: Fairy Godmother
ITEM NUMBER: 41108
SIZE: 9"
DATE OF ISSUE: 7/96

PLUSSING: Wand: Frosted glass wand.
PRODUCTION CHANGES: None.
PARTICULARS: A Cinderella with Fairy Godmother Lithograph was a gift with purchase. In addition, every retailer holding a Fairy Godmother Event received 10 Glass Slippers with an option for an additional 10 as part of the Event package. These have the WDCC logo on them, the GBTru$ is $65. Glass Slippers were also available at Disneyland. These have the Disneyland logo on them; the GBTru$ is $100. Certificate of Authenticity. Incised Annual Production Mark.
STATUS: EDITION CLOSED. Event piece was available 7/96 to 12/96.

YEAR	MARK	SRP	GBTru
☐ 1996		$125	**$175**

Cinderella

Tea For Two

TITLE: Tea For Two
FIGURINE: Jaq & Gus
ITEM NUMBER: 41410
SIZE: 4.5"
DATE OF ISSUE: 11/13 & 14, 1999

PLUSSING: Exclusive Porcelain Saucer: Available for guests to purchase has 1999 Open House backstamp and WDCC and Royal Doulton logos on bottom. **Teacup:** Contains two full-figure mice with metal tails and gold paint detailing.
PRODUCTION CHANGES: None.
PARTICULARS: Saucer, Item Number 1204894, sold separately as "purchase with purchase," in other words, it is available to purchase with the purchase of the event sculpture. Prototype shown.
STATUS: Event piece available 11/13 & 14, 1999.

YEAR	MARK	SRP	GBTru
☐ 1999	🎩	$87	**$87**

"A Lovely Dress For Cinderelly"

TITLE: "A Lovely Dress For Cinderelly"
FIGURINE: Cinderella's Dress
ITEM NUMBER: 41030
SIZE: Dress: 9", Miniature: 1"
DATE OF ISSUE: 12/92

PLUSSING: Bronze Miniatures: Hand-painted bronze miniature bluebirds and mice, made in the USA, placed on the piece. **Mouse Tails:** Solid brass wire is hand shaped, fitted, soldered to the bronze body before painting. **Jaq:** Separate Jaq miniature is numbered to match the Dress. **Scissors & Thread:** Tiny metal scissors dangle from a spool of real pink thread draped over dressmaker form.
PRODUCTION CHANGES: None.
PARTICULARS: Dome and stained wood base came with each dress for display purposes. Hand Numbered Certificate of Authenticity. Incised Annual Production Mark.
STATUS: LIMITED EDITION: 5,000 Hand Numbered Pieces. EDITION CLOSED 7/93.

YEAR	MARK	SRP	GBTru
☐ 1992	⚓	$800	**$2300**
☐ 1993	§	800	**2000**

Cinderella

"They Can't Stop Me From Dreaming"

TITLE: "They Can't Stop Me From Dreaming"
FIGURINE: Cinderella
ITEM NUMBER: 41000
SIZE: 6"
DATE OF ISSUE: 10/92

PLUSSING: Blown Glass Soap Bubbles: Cinderella balances a bubble on hand; more are found in bucket. **Water:** Clear glass-like resin is used to simulate water puddles around the bucket and scrub brush. **Bucket Handle:** Metal.
PRODUCTION CHANGES: Bubble: Original photographs showed the glass bubble at the tip of Cinderella's fingers. For production, the ball was moved onto her palm to prevent breakage. **Bubbles In Bucket:** Larger bubbles in ✵, fill the bucket; smaller ones in §, take up less space.
PARTICULARS: Certificate of Authenticity. Incised Annual Production Mark.
STATUS: RETIRED 7/93.

YEAR	MARK	SRP	GBTru
☐ 1992	✵	$195	**$450**
☐ 1993	§	195	**425**

"Meany, Sneaky, Roos-A-Fee"

TITLE: "Meany, Sneaky, Roos-A-Fee"
FIGURINE: Lucifer
ITEM NUMBER: 41001
SIZE: 2.6"
DATE OF ISSUE: 10/92

PLUSSING: Sooty Paw: The underside of Lucifer's paw is painted as if it's covered with soot. He plans to mess up Cinderella's freshly cleaned floor.
PRODUCTION CHANGES: None.
PARTICULARS: Certificate of Authenticity. Incised Annual Production Mark.
STATUS: RETIRED 7/93.

YEAR	MARK	SRP	GBTru
☐ 1992	✵	$69	**$135**
☐ 1993	§	69	**125**

Cinderella

"Just Learn To Like Cats"

TITLE: "Just Learn To Like Cats"
FIGURINE: Bruno
ITEM NUMBER: 41002
SIZE: 4.4"
DATE OF ISSUE: 10/92

PLUSSING: None.
PRODUCTION CHANGES: None.
PARTICULARS: Certificate of Authenticity. Incised Annual Production Mark.
STATUS: RETIRED 7/93.

YEAR	MARK	SRP	GBTru
❏ 1992	✱	$69	**$135**
❏ 1993	♪	69	**125**

Cinderella's Sewing Book

TITLE: Cinderella's Sewing Book
FIGURINE: Open Sewing Book
ITEM NUMBER: 41003
SIZE: 11.75" x 7.75"
DATE OF ISSUE: 10/92

PLUSSING: Book: A real book was used to craft this unique version of Cinderella's Sewing Book. **Display Stand:** Wooden display stand included.
PRODUCTION CHANGES: An Annual Production Mark was added in 1993. *(Appears on lower corner page of book.)* **Display Stand:** (No Mark) was 3-piece stand; ♪ and ⚹ were 2-piece stand.
PARTICULARS: Certificate of Authenticity. There was a dealer **porcelain display book**, Item Number 11K-11003-0. Five are known to exist; GBTru$ is $1,600.

STATUS: RETIRED 8/94.

YEAR	MARK	SRP	GBTru
❏ 1992	No Mark	$69	**$80**
❏ 1993	♪	69	**70**
❏ 1994	⚹	69	**69**

Cinderella 47

"Hey, We Can Do It!"

TITLE: "Hey, We Can Do It!"
FIGURINE: Suzy
ITEM NUMBER: 41004
SIZE: 5.8"
DATE OF ISSUE: 10/92

PLUSSING: Sewing Needle: Suzy holds a real chrome and gold-plated needle atop her spool-of-thread perch. **Mouse Tail:** A solid brass wire is hand shaped, fitted and then attached to the mouse. **Tail Bow:** A tiny ceramic bow is attached to her tail.
PRODUCTION CHANGES: Needle: Changed to a blunt point.
PARTICULARS: Certificate of Authenticity. Incised Annual Production Mark.
STATUS: RETIRED 8/94.

YEAR	MARK	SRP	GBTru
☐ 1992	✲	$69	**$120**
☐ 1993	⸞	69	**120**
☐ 1994	⸞	69	**100**

"We'll Tie A Sash Around It"

TITLE: "We'll Tie A Sash Around It"
FIGURINE: Birds with Sash
ITEM NUMBER: 41005
SIZE: 6.4"
DATE OF ISSUE: 10/92

PLUSSING: None.
PRODUCTION CHANGES: None.
PARTICULARS: Certificate of Authenticity. Incised Annual Production Mark.
STATUS: RETIRED 8/94.

YEAR	MARK	SRP	GBTru
☐ 1992	✲	$149	**$150**
☐ 1993	⸞	149	**150**
☐ 1994	⸞	149	**149**

Cinderella

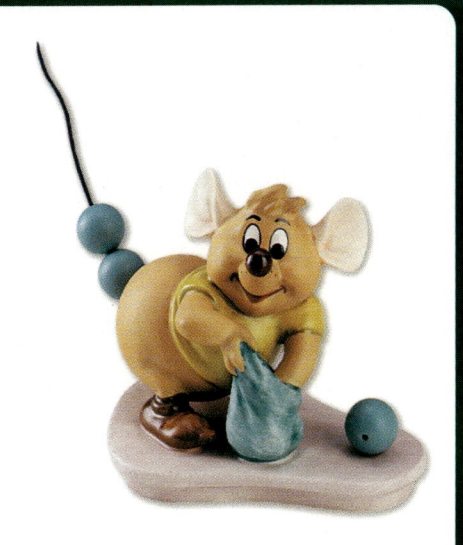

"No Time For Dilly-Dally!"

TITLE: "No Time For Dilly-Dally!"
FIGURINE: Perla
ITEM NUMBER: 41006
SIZE: 3.4"
DATE OF ISSUE: 10/92

PLUSSING: Mouse Tail: A solid brass wire is hand shaped, fitted and then attached. **Tail Bow:** A tiny ceramic bow is attached to her tail.
PRODUCTION CHANGES: None.
PARTICULARS: Certificate of Authenticity. Incised Annual Production Mark.
STATUS: RETIRED 8/94.

YEAR	MARK	SRP	GBTru
☐ 1992	✦	$65	**$120**
☐ 1993	♧	65	**100**
☐ 1994	♁	65	**100**

"You Go Get Some Trimmin'"

TITLE: "You Go Get Some Trimmin'"
FIGURINE: Gus
ITEM NUMBER: 41007
SIZE: 3.4"
DATE OF ISSUE: 10/92

PLUSSING: Mouse Tail: A solid brass wire is hand shaped, fitted and then attached. **Real Beads:** Gus' tail sports real wooden beads, strung there by Jaq. His tail fits into Jaq's hand. The mice display as a pair.
PRODUCTION CHANGES: None.
PARTICULARS: Certificate of Authenticity. Incised Annual Production Mark.
STATUS: RETIRED 8/94.

YEAR	MARK	SRP	GBTru
☐ 1992	✦	$65	**$135**
☐ 1993	♧	65	**130**
☐ 1994	♁	65	**120**

Cinderella

"You Go Get Some Trimmin'"

TITLE: "You Go Get Some Trimmin'"
FIGURINE: Jaq
ITEM NUMBER: 41008
SIZE: 4.2"
DATE OF ISSUE: 10/92

PLUSSING: Mouse Tail: A solid brass wire is hand shaped, fitted and attached to the mouse. **Real Beads:** Designed to work with Gus, Jaq has a real wooden bead on his base. It is to be strung on Gus' tail, which fits into Jaq's hand. The mice display as a pair.
PRODUCTION CHANGES: None.
PARTICULARS: Certificate of Authenticity. Incised Annual Production Mark.
STATUS: RETIRED 8/94.

YEAR	MARK	SRP	GBTru
☐ 1992		$65	**$125**
☐ 1993		65	**120**
☐ 1994		65	**110**

An Elegant Coach For Cinderella

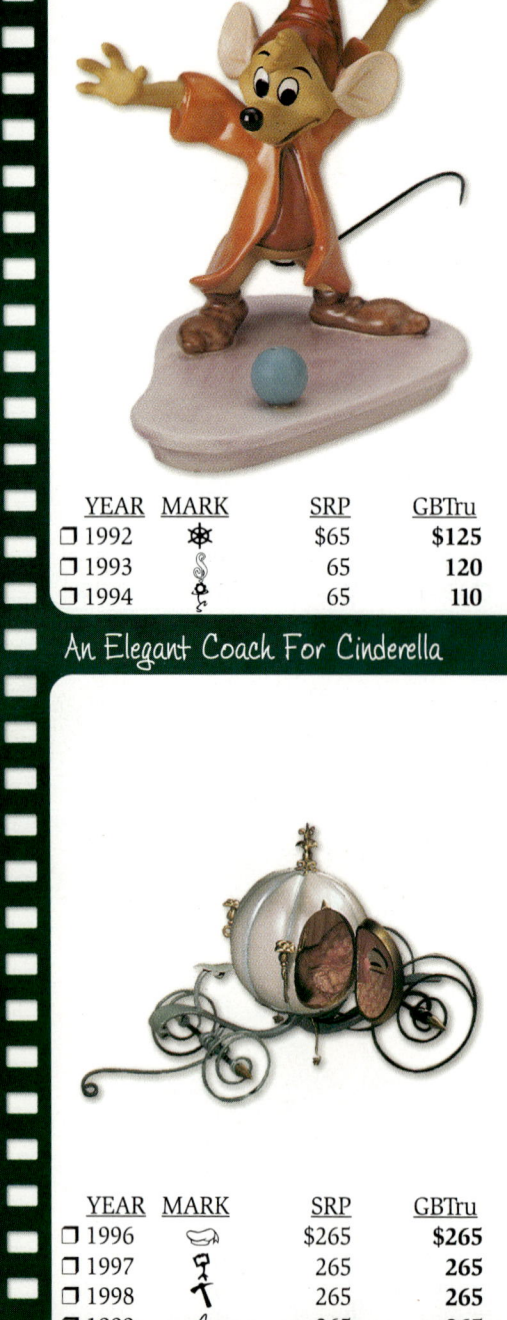

TITLE: An Elegant Coach For Cinderella
SCULPTURE: Cinderella's Coach
ITEM NUMBER: 41208
SIZE: 5.5"
DATE OF ISSUE: 9/96

PLUSSING: Coach: Metal chassis. **Door:** Brass hinges allow door to open and close. **Wheels:** Turn. **Miniature Lamp:** Inside Coach.
PRODUCTION CHANGES: None.
PARTICULARS: Enchanted Places. Certificate of Authenticity. Incised Annual Production Mark.
STATUS: OPEN EDITION.

YEAR	MARK	SRP	GBTru
☐ 1996		$265	**$265**
☐ 1997		265	**265**
☐ 1998		265	**265**
☐ 1999		265	**265**

Cinderella

Gus

TITLE: Gus
MINIATURE: Gus
ITEM NUMBER: 41218
SIZE: .75"
DATE OF ISSUE: 9/96

PLUSSING: Miniature: Bronze, hand painted.
PRODUCTION CHANGES: None.
PARTICULARS: Enchanted Places. Green box, no picture on box, no Annual Production Mark.
STATUS: OPEN EDITION.

YEAR	MARK	SRP	GBTru
❏ 1996	No Mark	$50	**$50**

Jaq

TITLE: Jaq
MINIATURE: Jaq
ITEM NUMBER: 41242
SIZE: .75"
DATE OF ISSUE: 4/97

PLUSSING: Miniature: Bronze, hand painted.
PRODUCTION CHANGES: None.
PARTICULARS: Enchanted Places. Green box, picture on box, sticker Annual Production Mark on box and on base of miniature.
STATUS: OPEN EDITION.

YEAR	MARK	SRP	GBTru
❏ 1997		$50	**$50**
❏ 1998		50	**50**
❏ 1999		50	**50**

Cinderella

An Elegant Coach For Cinderella

TITLE: An Elegant Coach For Cinderella
ORNAMENT: Cinderella's Coach
ITEM NUMBER: 41244
SIZE: 3.25"
DATE OF ISSUE: 7/97

PLUSSING: None.
PRODUCTION CHANGES: None.
PARTICULARS: Enchanted Places. Certificate of Authenticity. Annual Production Mark.
STATUS: OPEN EDITION.

YEAR	MARK	SRP	GBTru
☐ 1997		$45	**$45**
☐ 1998		45	**45**
☐ 1999		45	**45**

A Castle For Cinderella

TITLE: A Castle For Cinderella
ORNAMENT: Cinderella's Castle
ITEM NUMBER: 41293
SERIES: Enchanted Castles Ornament Series – 1st of 6
SIZE: 3.25"
DATE OF ISSUE: 7/98

PLUSSING: None.
PRODUCTION CHANGES: None.
PARTICULARS: Enchanted Places. Certificate of Authenticity. Sticker Annual Production Mark.
STATUS: OPEN EDITION.

YEAR	MARK	SRP	GBTru
☐ 1998		$45	**$45**
☐ 1999		45	**45**

Cinderella

A Castle For Cinderella

TITLE: A Castle For Cinderella
SCULPTURE: Cinderella's Castle
ITEM NUMBER: 41210
SIZE: 10"
DATE OF ISSUE: 1/97

PLUSSING: None.
PRODUCTION CHANGES: None.
PARTICULARS: Enchanted Places. Certificate of Authenticity. Incised Annual Production Mark. Hand Engraved Serial Number. Registration Card redeemable for a deed "signed" by the setting's original "owner," transferring ownership. Sculpture comes with a wood display base with engraved brass nameplate.
STATUS: RETIRED 1/98.

YEAR	MARK	SRP	GBTru
☐ 1997		$225	**$225**
☐ 1998		225	**225**

Notes:

Cinderella

THE DELIVERY BOY
1931

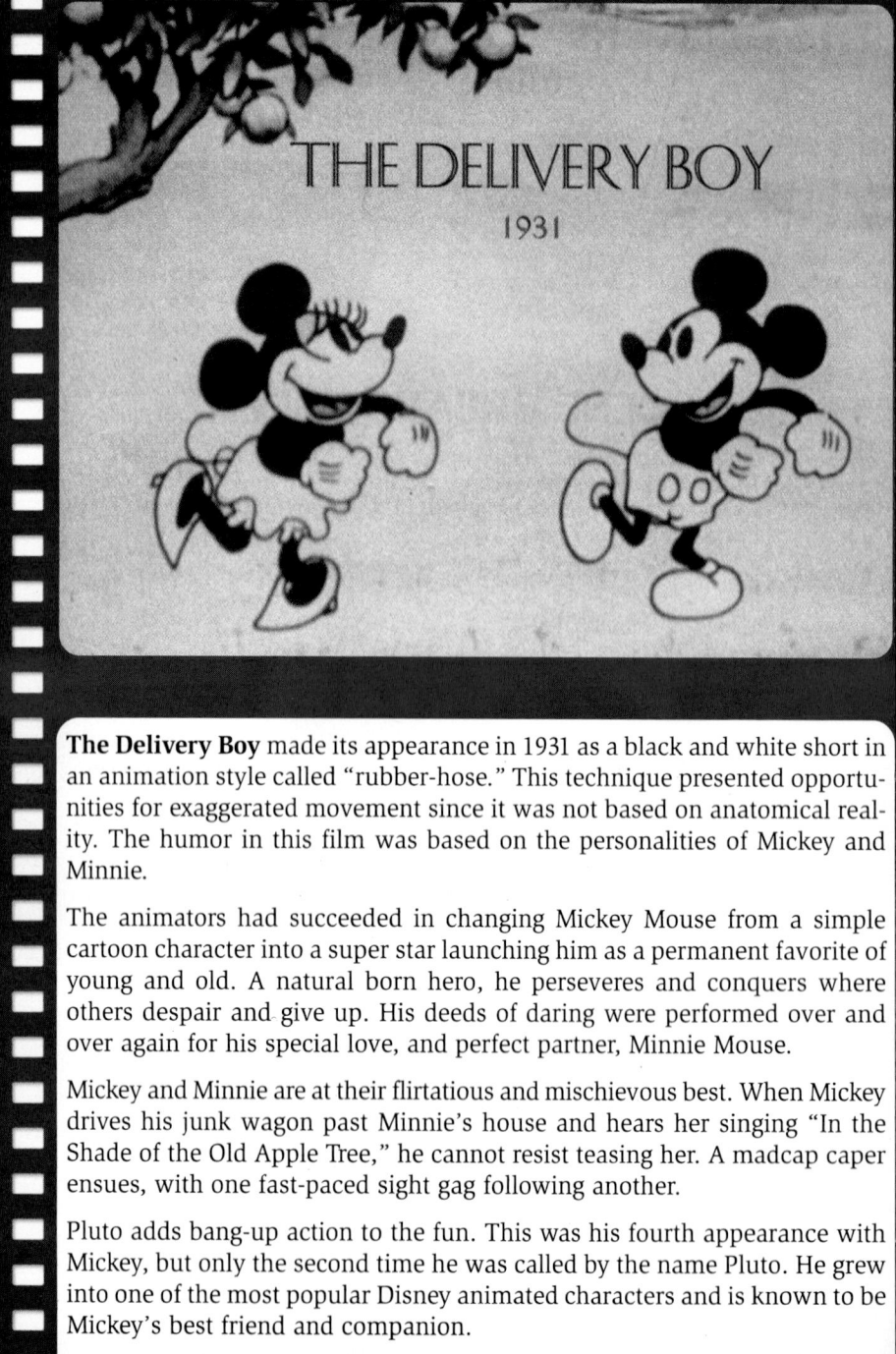

The Delivery Boy made its appearance in 1931 as a black and white short in an animation style called "rubber-hose." This technique presented opportunities for exaggerated movement since it was not based on anatomical reality. The humor in this film was based on the personalities of Mickey and Minnie.

The animators had succeeded in changing Mickey Mouse from a simple cartoon character into a super star launching him as a permanent favorite of young and old. A natural born hero, he perseveres and conquers where others despair and give up. His deeds of daring were performed over and over again for his special love, and perfect partner, Minnie Mouse.

Mickey and Minnie are at their flirtatious and mischievous best. When Mickey drives his junk wagon past Minnie's house and hears her singing "In the Shade of the Old Apple Tree," he cannot resist teasing her. A madcap caper ensues, with one fast-paced sight gag following another.

Pluto adds bang-up action to the fun. This was his fourth appearance with Mickey, but only the second time he was called by the name Pluto. He grew into one of the most popular Disney animated characters and is known to be Mickey's best friend and companion.

THE DELIVERY BOY QUIKREFERENCE

	TITLE	ITEM #	AVAILABLE
RETIRED EDITIONS:			
Scroll	*The Delivery Boy* Opening Title	41019	3/93 - 7/97
Mickey Mouse	"Hey Minnie, Wanna Go Steppin'?"	41020	3/93 - 7/97
Minnie Mouse	"I'm A Jazz Baby!"	41021	7/93 - 7/97
Pluto	Dynamite Dog	41022	7/93 - 7/97

The Delivery Boy Opening Title

TITLE: *The Delivery Boy* Opening Title
SCROLL: Opening Title
ITEM NUMBER: 41019
SIZE: 1.6"
DATE OF ISSUE: 3/93

PLUSSING: Color Palette: Black, white, and shades of gray, to replicate early animation art.
PRODUCTION CHANGES: Annual Production Mark: Added after production began.
PARTICULARS: Certificate of Authenticity. Decal backstamp with WDCC Logo and Annual Production Mark.
STATUS: RETIRED 7/97.

YEAR	MARK	SRP	GBTru
❏ 1992	No Mark	$29	**$85**
❏ 1992	❀	29	**85**
❏ 1993	𝒮	29	**29**
❏ 1994	⚘	29	**29**
❏ 1995	∽	29	**29**
❏ 1996	⌒	29	**29**
❏ 1997	⚘	29	**29**

Delivery Boy, The

"Hey Minnie, Wanna Go Steppin'?"

TITLE: "Hey Minnie, Wanna Go Steppin'?"
FIGURINE: Mickey Mouse
ITEM NUMBER: 41020
SIZE: 6"
DATE OF ISSUE: 3/93

PLUSSING: Arms & Legs: Pewter duplicated "rubber hose" animation style. **Tail:** Crafted of metal to achieve correct scale. **Color Palette:** Black, white, and shades of gray, to replicate early animation art.
PRODUCTION CHANGES: SRP Change: Effective 3/15/94 $125 to $135.
PARTICULARS: Certificate of Authenticity. Incised Annual Production Mark.
STATUS: RETIRED 7/97.

YEAR	MARK	SRP	GBTru
☐ 1992	✹	$125	**$165**
☐ 1993		125	**135**
☐ 1994		135	**135**
☐ 1995		135	**135**
☐ 1996		135	**135**
☐ 1997		135	**135**

"I'm A Jazz Baby"

TITLE: "I'm A Jazz Baby"
FIGURINE: Minnie Mouse
ITEM NUMBER: 41021
SIZE: 6"
DATE OF ISSUE: 7/93

PLUSSING: Arms & Legs: Pewter duplicated "rubber hose" animation style. **Tail:** Crafted of metal to achieve correct scale. **Color Palette:** Black, white, and shades of gray, to replicate early animation art.
PRODUCTION CHANGES: SRP Change: Effective 3/15/94 $125 to $135.
PARTICULARS: Certificate of Authenticity. Incised Annual Production Mark.
STATUS: RETIRED 7/97.

YEAR	MARK	SRP	GBTru
☐ 1992	✹	$125	**$165**
☐ 1993		125	**135**
☐ 1994		135	**135**
☐ 1995		135	**135**
☐ 1996		135	**135**
☐ 1997		135	**135**

Delivery Boy, The

Dynamite Dog

TITLE: Dynamite Dog
FIGURINE: Pluto
ITEM NUMBER: 41022
SIZE: 3.6"
DATE OF ISSUE: 7/93

PLUSSING: Dynamite Wick: Crafted of metal. **Tail:** Crafted of metal to achieve correct scale. **Color Palette:** Black, white, and shades of gray to replicate early animation art.
PRODUCTION CHANGES: 3 Versions Of Danger/Blasting Sign: *Version 1:* Raised wood grain, raised letters, can see wood grain in the painted letters. *Version 2:* Less raised wood grain, smoother painted letters. *Version 3:* Smooth wood, smooth painted letters.
PARTICULARS: Certificate of Authenticity. Incised Annual Production Mark.

STATUS: RETIRED 7/97.

YEAR	MARK	SRP	GBTru
☐ 1992	✹	$125	**$275** *Ver. 1*
☐ 1992	✹	125	**170** *Ver. 2*
☐ 1993		125	**125** *Ver. 3*
☐ 1994		125	**125** *Ver. 3*
☐ 1995		125	**125** *Ver. 3*
☐ 1996		125	**125** *Ver. 3*
☐ 1997		125	**125** *Ver. 3*

Notes: _____

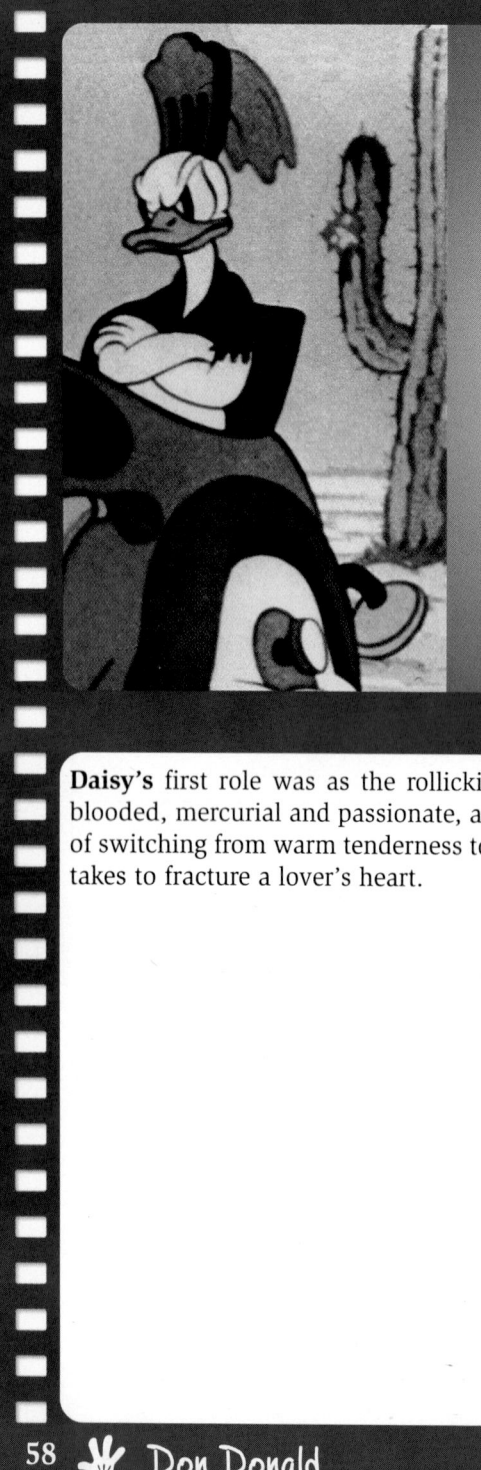

Don Donald
1937

Daisy's first role was as the rollicking Mexican Donna Duck. She is hot blooded, mercurial and passionate, and, as Donald discovers, very capable of switching from warm tenderness to destructive wrath in less time than it takes to fracture a lover's heart.

Don Donald

DON DONALD QUIKREFERENCE

LIMITED EDITION:
Daisy Duck as Donna Duck

TITLE	ITEM #	AVAILABLE
Daisy's Debut	41313	1/99

Daisy's Debut

TITLE: Daisy's Debut
FIGURINE: Daisy Duck
ITEM NUMBER: 41313
SIZE: 5.5"
DATE OF ISSUE: 1/99

PLUSSING: Dress: Fringe on collar is metal. **Bracelets:** Painted with gold. **Backstamp:** Special Gold Circle Dealer backstamp.
PRODUCTION CHANGES: None.
PARTICULARS: Certificate of Authenticity. Incised Annual Production Mark.
STATUS: LIMITED EDITION: 10,000 Pieces. 1999 Gold Circle Exclusive – 3rd Issue.

YEAR	MARK	SRP	GBTru
☐ 1998	⊤	$130	**$130**
☐ 1999	⌂	130	**130**

Don Donald

DONALD'S BETTER SELF
1938

Donald is on his way to school when he meets his Better Self, an Angel, and his Evil Self, a quack-up little Devil. The two spirits battle over whether Donald should continue on to school or find other activities for the day. Despite Donald's mischievous personality, it is his Better Self who shows stronger powers of persuasion.

DONALD'S BETTER SELF QUIKREFERENCE

	TITLE	ITEM #	AVAILABLE
SCROLL:			
Scroll	*Donald's Better Self* Opening Title	41298	6/98
OPEN EDITIONS:			
Donald Duck	Donald's Decision	41296	6/98
Angel Donald	What An Angel	41297	6/98
Devil Donald	Little Devil	41309	6/98

Donald's Better Self Opening Title

TITLE: *Donald's Better Self* Opening Title
SCROLL: Opening Title
ITEM NUMBER: 41298
SIZE: 1.6"
DATE OF ISSUE: 6/98

PLUSSING: None.
PRODUCTION CHANGES: None.
PARTICULARS: Certificate of Authenticity. Decal backstamp with WDCC logo and Annual Production Mark.
STATUS: OPEN EDITION.

YEAR	MARK	SRP	GBTru
❏ 1998	⚒	$29	**$29**
❏ 1999	🎩	29	29

Donald's Better Self 61

Donald's Decision

TITLE: Donald's Decision
FIGURINE: Donald Duck
ITEM NUMBER: 41296
SIZE: 5.25"
DATE OF ISSUE: 6/98

PLUSSING: Books: Held with a pewter strap. **Anniversary Backstamp:** A special gold script message *'60th Anniversary'* was added to the backstamp of sculptures crafted in 1998.
PRODUCTION CHANGES: None.
PARTICULARS: Certificate of Authenticity. Incised Annual Production Mark.
STATUS: OPEN EDITION.

YEAR	MARK	SRP	GBTru
☐ 1998	↥ Anniv. Mark	$145	**$145**
☐ 1999	⛵	145	**145**

What An Angel

TITLE: What An Angel
FIGURINE: Angel Donald
ITEM NUMBER: 41297
SIZE: 6"
DATE OF ISSUE: 6/98

PLUSSING: Halo: Clear plastic with gold paint. **Anniversary Backstamp:** A special gold script message *'60th Anniversary'* was added to the backstamp of sculptures crafted in 1998.
PRODUCTION CHANGES: None.
PARTICULARS: Certificate of Authenticity. Incised Annual Production Mark.
STATUS: OPEN EDITION.

YEAR	MARK	SRP	GBTru
☐ 1998	↥ Anniv. Mark	$145	**$145**
☐ 1999	⛵	145	**145**

Donald's Better Self

TITLE: Little Devil
FIGURINE: Devil Donald
ITEM NUMBER: 41309
SIZE: 4.25"
DATE OF ISSUE: 6/98

PLUSSING: Anniversary Backstamp: A special gold script message '*60th Anniversary*' was added to the backstamp of sculptures crafted in 1998.
PRODUCTION CHANGES: None.
PARTICULARS: Certificate of Authenticity. Incised Annual Production Mark.
STATUS: OPEN EDITION.

YEAR	MARK	SRP	GBTru
❒ 1998	Anniv. Mark	$145	**$145**
❒ 1999		145	**145**

Notes:

Donald's Better Self

Double Dribble
1946

Goofy, in a "how to" demonstration, shows expertise dribbling down court to score points.

DOUBLE DRIBBLE QUIKREFERENCE

	TITLE	ITEM #	AVAILABLE
OPEN EDITION:			
Goofy	Dribbling Down Court	41404	1/99

Dribbling Down Court

TITLE: Dribbling Down Court
FIGURINE: Goofy
ITEM NUMBER: 41404
SIZE: 8.5"
DATE OF ISSUE: 1/99

PLUSSING: Ears: Goofy had no ears in this film.
PRODUCTION CHANGES: None.
PARTICULARS: Certificate of Authenticity. Incised Annual Production Mark.
STATUS: OPEN EDITION.

YEAR	MARK	SRP	GBTru
❏ 1998		$175	**$175**
❏ 1999		175	**175**

Double Dribble 65

DUMBO

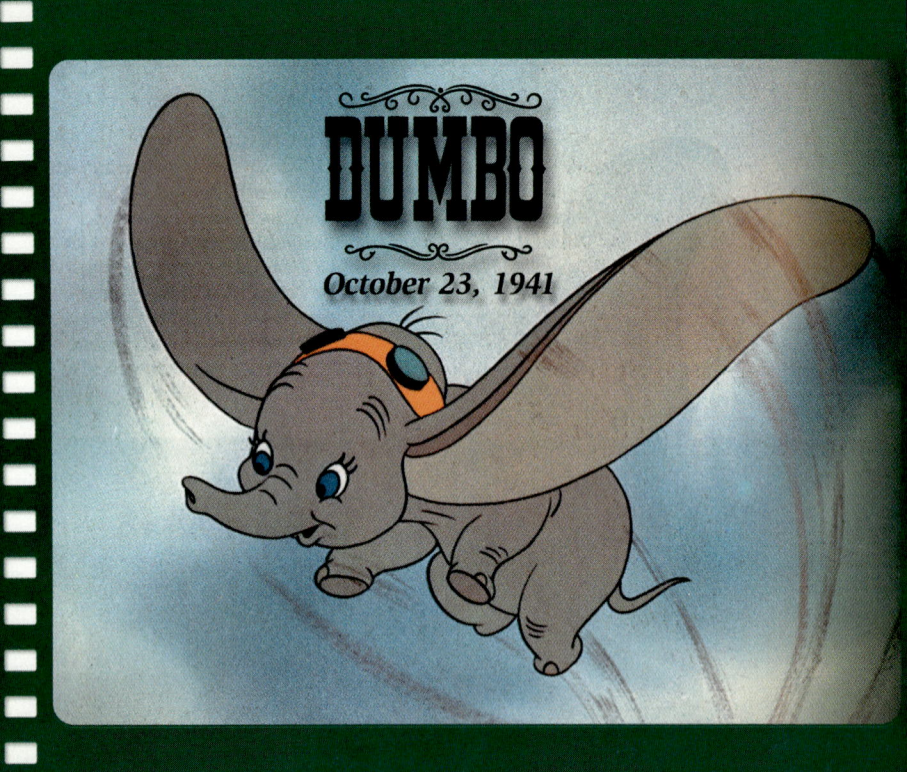

October 23, 1941

Dumbo is a film of great simplicity based on a charming tale held together by the fantasy of an elephant able to fly because of a tremendous set of ears. Unlike earlier animated features, *Dumbo* was in production for a little over a year.

Although Mrs. Jumbo believes her baby is beautiful, the other performers at the circus make fun of his ears and the fact that he stumbles and falls over them. When the abuse turns from verbal to physical, Mrs. Jumbo spanks one of the bullies and is imprisoned. A lonely Dumbo is befriended by Timothy the mouse. All animals must earn their way in the circus but Dumbo just creates chaos and disaster. He becomes a foil for the clowns in a very non-elephant role. The clowns become drunk celebrating their successful new act with Dumbo, and, in their tipsy state, upset champagne into his water bucket. Dumbo hallucinates the most famous scene of the film (regarded as one of the best feats of animation of all time) – the dancing pink elephants. He and Timothy fall asleep and awake high in a tree and Timothy concludes they must have flown there. Passing crows laugh at the idea but give Dumbo a "magic feather" to bolster his confidence so that he can fly home to the circus. Again the clowns force Dumbo to perform a scary high-diving trick and during this plunge from a high platform Dumbo loses the feather and panics. Timothy persuades the baby elephant that he can overcome his fear and fly, and suddenly it happens. Dumbo, with his new and special flying act, becomes the star, Mrs. Jumbo is freed from her prison, his tormentors are humiliated and everyone enjoys the happiest of endings.

DUMBO QUIKREFERENCE

	TITLE	ITEM #	AVAILABLE
OPEN EDITION:			
Dumbo and Stork	Bundle Of Joy	41153	4/97
EVENT PIECE:			
Dumbo Ornament and Cloud	"When I See An Elephant Fly"	41283	9/98

COMPLEMENTARY PIECES:

WALT DISNEY COLLECTORS SOCIETY

MEMBERSHIP GIFT SCULPTURE: (see page 265)

Dumbo	"Simply Adorable"	41082	1995

MEMBERS-ONLY ORNAMENTS: (see page 275)

Dumbo	"Simply Adorable"	41081	1/95 - 3/96
Timothy Mouse	Friendship Offering	41179	1/98 - 3/99

Bundle Of Joy

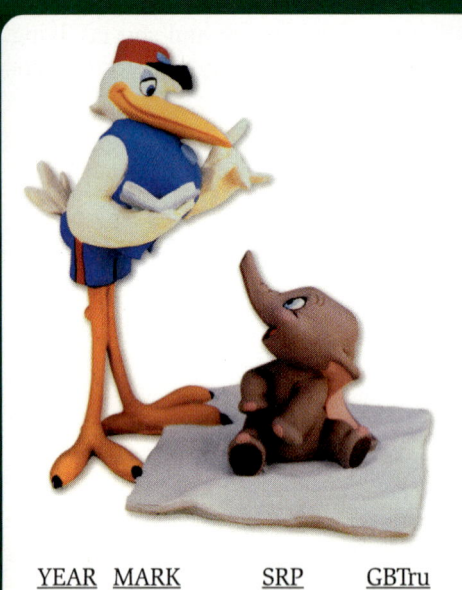

TITLE: Bundle Of Joy
FIGURINE: Dumbo and Mr. Stork
ITEM NUMBER: 41153
SIZE: 5"
DATE OF ISSUE: 4/97

PLUSSING: Stork Legs: Metal.
PRODUCTION CHANGES: None.
PARTICULARS: Two-figure Sculpture. Certificate of Authenticity. Incised Annual Production Mark.
STATUS: OPEN EDITION.

YEAR	MARK	SRP	GBTru
☐ 1997		$125	**$125**
☐ 1998		125	**125**
☐ 1999		125	**125**

"When I See An Elephant Fly"

TITLE: "When I See An Elephant Fly"
ORNAMENT: Dumbo
ITEM NUMBER: 41283
SIZE: Dumbo: 3", Cloud: 1"
DATE OF ISSUE: 9/98

PLUSSING: 2 Piece Set: Dumbo: Hat contains miniature bronze Timothy Mouse. **Base:** Fluffy cloud under Dumbo's front feet is a separate base. Dumbo ornament can be displayed as a figurine leaning against the cloud.
PRODUCTION CHANGES: None.
PARTICULARS: Certificate of Authenticity. Incised Annual Production Mark.
STATUS: EDITION CLOSED. 1998 Fall Open House Event Piece available 9/19 and 9/20/98.

YEAR	MARK	SRP	GBTru
☐ 1998		$50	**$50**

68 Dumbo

FANTASIA
November 13, 1940

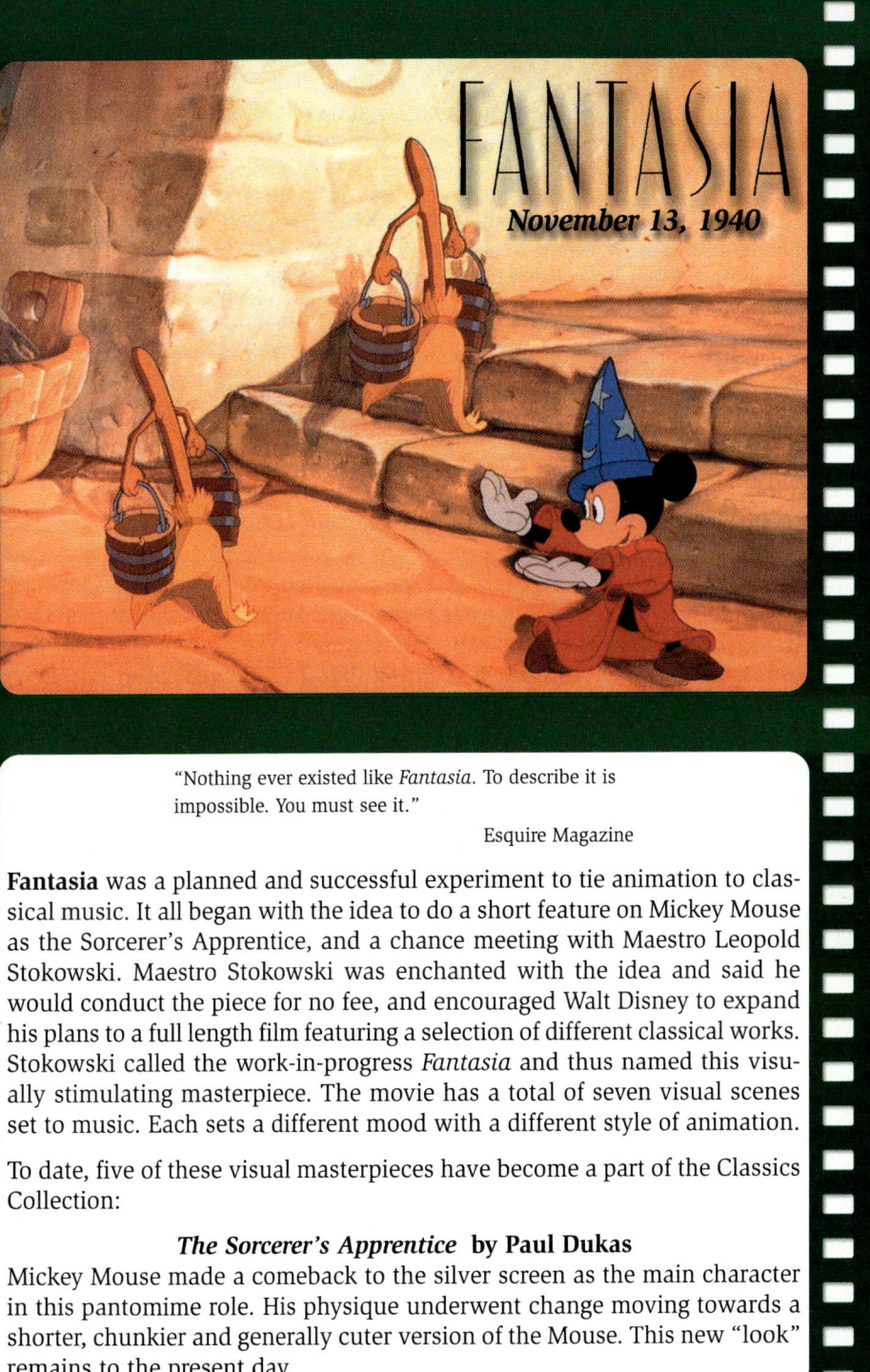

> "Nothing ever existed like *Fantasia*. To describe it is impossible. You must see it."
>
> Esquire Magazine

Fantasia was a planned and successful experiment to tie animation to classical music. It all began with the idea to do a short feature on Mickey Mouse as the Sorcerer's Apprentice, and a chance meeting with Maestro Leopold Stokowski. Maestro Stokowski was enchanted with the idea and said he would conduct the piece for no fee, and encouraged Walt Disney to expand his plans to a full length film featuring a selection of different classical works. Stokowski called the work-in-progress *Fantasia* and thus named this visually stimulating masterpiece. The movie has a total of seven visual scenes set to music. Each sets a different mood with a different style of animation.

To date, five of these visual masterpieces have become a part of the Classics Collection:

The Sorcerer's Apprentice by Paul Dukas

Mickey Mouse made a comeback to the silver screen as the main character in this pantomime role. His physique underwent change moving towards a shorter, chunkier and generally cuter version of the Mouse. This new "look" remains to the present day.

Beethoven's *Sixth Symphony*: The Pastoral

This sequence featured teenage beauties, the Centaurettes, primping, preening and hoping they would soon meet that special someone and fall in love. The cupids become the willing helpers.

Tchaikovsky's *Nutcracker Suite*: The Chinese Dance

Six segments were created based on this classical piece. Mushrooms were featured in The Chinese Dance where the mushroom cap became the Coolie Hat and the stem was transformed into blue robes.

Ponchielli's *Dance Of The Hours*

Hyacinth Hippo, prima ballerina, dances herself to exhaustion, and gracefully reclines on a divan in a dreamy state. Hero Ben Ali Gator comes to her rescue as Lizard Lotharios descends upon the scene hoping to captivate her. She awakens and flees.

Mussorgsky's *Night On Bald Mountain*

This tone poem began life as music for a play called *The Witch* and was originally titled *St. John's Night On The Bare Mountain*. After Mussorgsky's death, Rimsky-Korsakov, acting as musical executor, completed and orchestrated the work. It was retitled and became one of the most popular Russian orchestral works of all time. It is fitting that it is the vehicle to introduce Chernabog. Though it is clearly stated that Chernabog is not the Devil, he is clearly a monstrous demon. He appears at night over a sleeping village and draws ghouls, imps and a ghostly skeletons to him. He forces them to dance the torments of Hades before banishing them back from whence they came as daylight appears.

FANTASIA QUIKREFERENCE

	TITLE	ITEM #	AVAILABLE
SCROLL:			
Scroll	*Fantasia* Opening Title	41018	10/92
OPEN EDITIONS:			
Nutcracker Suite: The Chinese Dance			
Large Mushroom	Mushroom Dancer	41058	9/94
Small Mushroom	Hop Low	41067	9/94
Medium Mushroom	Mushroom Dancer	41068	9/94
The Dance Of The Hours			
Hippopotamus	Hyacinth Hippo	41117	5/96
Alligator	Ben Ali Gator	41118	5/96
Mademoiselle Upanova	Prima Ballerina	41178	8/97

EVENT PIECES:
Sixth Symphony: The Pastoral
  Cupid Ornament   Flight Of Fancy   41051   3/94 - 8/94
  Display Stand   Cupid Ornament Display Stand   41056   3/94

LIMITED EDITION:
Night On Bald Mountain
  Chernabog   Night On Bald Mountain   41180   9/97

RETIRED EDITIONS:
The Sorcerer's Apprentice
  Mickey Mouse   Mischievous Apprentice   41016   10/92 - 2/95
  Broom with Water Pails   Bucket Brigade   41017   10/92 - 2/95

Sixth Symphony: The Pastoral
  Pink Centaurette   Romantic Reflections   41040   9/93 - 7/95
  Blue Centaurette   Beauty In Bloom   41041   9/93 - 7/95
  Cupids on a Pillar   Love's Little Helpers   41042   9/94 - 7/95

COMPLEMENTARY PIECES:

ENCHANTED PLACES

ANNUAL:
Sixth Symphony: The Pastoral
  Miniature   Unicorn   41237   7/97

LIMITED EDITION:
Sixth Symphony: The Pastoral
  Sculpture   Pastoral Gazebo   41232   7/97

MICKEY THROUGH THE YEARS SERIES

The Sorcerer's Apprentice (see page 253)
  Mickey Mouse   Summoning The Stars   41278   8/98

WALT DISNEY COLLECTORS SOCIETY

MEMBERS-ONLY NUMBERED LIMITED EDITION: (see page 283)
Nutcracker Suite: Waltz Of The Flowers
  Autumn Fairy   The Touch Of An Autumn Fairy   41281   6/98 - 7/98

Fantasia

Fantasia Opening Title

TITLE: *Fantasia* Opening Title
SCROLL: Opening Title
ITEM NUMBER: 41018
SIZE: 1.6"
DATE OF ISSUE: 10/92

PLUSSING: None.
PRODUCTION CHANGES: Trademarks: The word 'Technicolor' was removed for trademark protection issues and errors occurred.
1st Version �: *Fantasia* + Technicolor and RKO insignia.
2nd Version §: *Fantasia* only. (Too much was removed.) **3rd Version ⚑ and on):** This is now the correct version and has been available since October 1994.
PARTICULARS: Certificate of Authenticity. Decal with WDCC logo and Annual Production Mark.
STATUS: OPEN EDITION.

YEAR	MARK	SRP	GBTru
☐ 1992	�	$29	$35
☐ 1993	§	29	45
☐ 1994	⚑	29	29
☐ 1995	∽	29	29
☐ 1996	⌒	29	29
☐ 1997	⚑	29	29
☐ 1998	✝	29	29
☐ 1999	⚑	29	29

Mushroom Dancer

TITLE: Mushroom Dancer
FIGURINE: Large Mushroom
ITEM NUMBER: 41058
SEGMENT: *Nutcracker Suite:* The Chinese Dance
SIZE: 4.75"
DATE OF ISSUE: 9/94

PLUSSING: Dewdrops: The dewdrops are genuine Austrian crystal. **Pigtail:** Metal.
PRODUCTION CHANGES: Teal Green Background Logo replaced with revised Boxed-in Logo during 1994. **SRP Change:** $60 to $70 in 1998.
PARTICULARS: Certificate of Authenticity. Incised Annual Production Mark.
STATUS: OPEN EDITION.

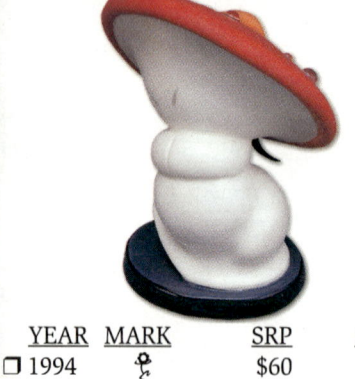

YEAR	MARK	SRP	GBTru
☐ 1994 Teal Green Logo	⚑	$60	$70
☐ 1994 Boxed-in Logo	⚑	60	70
☐ 1995	∽	60	70
☐ 1996	⌒	60	70
☐ 1997	⚑	60	70
☐ 1998	✝	70	70
☐ 1999	⚑	70	70

Hop Low

TITLE: Hop Low
FIGURINE: Small Mushroom
ITEM NUMBER: 41067
SEGMENT: *Nutcracker Suite:* The Chinese Dance
SIZE: 2.75"
DATE OF ISSUE: 9/94

PLUSSING: Dewdrops: The dewdrops are genuine Austrian crystal.
PRODUCTION CHANGES: SRP Change: $35 to $45 in 1998.
PARTICULARS: Only Mushroom not crafted with the Teal Green Logo. Certificate of Authenticity. Incised Annual Production Mark.
STATUS: OPEN EDITION.

YEAR	MARK	SRP	GBTru
❏ 1994		$35	**$45**
❏ 1995		35	**45**
❏ 1996		35	**45**
❏ 1997		35	**45**
❏ 1998		45	**45**
❏ 1999		45	**45**

Mushroom Dancer

TITLE: Mushroom Dancer
FIGURINE: Medium Mushroom
ITEM NUMBER: 41068
SEGMENT: *Nutcracker Suite:* The Chinese Dance
SIZE: 4.75"
DATE OF ISSUE: 9/94

PLUSSING: Dewdrops: The dewdrops are genuine Austrian crystal. **Pigtail:** Metal.
PRODUCTION CHANGES: Teal Green Background Logo replaced with revised Boxed-in Logo during 1994. **SRP Change:** $50 to $60 in 1998.
PARTICULARS: Certificate of Authenticity. Incised Annual Production Mark.
STATUS: OPEN EDITION.

YEAR	MARK	SRP	GBTru
❏ 1994 Teal Green Logo		$50	**$60**
❏ 1994 Boxed-in Logo		50	**60**
❏ 1995		50	**60**
❏ 1996		50	**60**
❏ 1997		50	**60**
❏ 1998		60	**60**
❏ 1999		60	**60**

Fantasia

Hyacinth Hippo

TITLE: Hyacinth Hippo
FIGURINE: Hippopotamus
ITEM NUMBER: 41117
SEGMENT: *The Dance Of The Hours*
SIZE: 5.5"
DATE OF ISSUE: 5/96

PLUSSING: Divan: The divan that Hyacinth is lying on has bronze legs.
PRODUCTION CHANGES: SRP Change: $195 to $200 in 1998.
PARTICULARS: Some pieces were released with backstamp of Ben Ali Gator. Certificate of Authenticity. Incised Annual Production Mark.
STATUS: OPEN EDITION.

YEAR	MARK	SRP	GBTru
☐ 1996		$195	**$215**
☐ 1997		195	**200**
☐ 1998		200	**200**
☐ 1999		200	**200**

Ben Ali Gator

TITLE: Ben Ali Gator
FIGURINE: Alligator
ITEM NUMBER: 41118
SEGMENT: *The Dance Of The Hours*
SIZE: 7.5"
DATE OF ISSUE: 5/96

PLUSSING: Plume: Bronze plume decorates cap.
PRODUCTION CHANGES: SRP Change: $185 to $190 in 1998.
PARTICULARS: Some pieces were issued with backstamp of Hyacinth Hippo. Certificate of Authenticity. Incised Annual Production Mark.
STATUS: OPEN EDITION.

YEAR	MARK	SRP	GBTru
☐ 1996		$185	**$195**
☐ 1997		185	**190**
☐ 1998		190	**190**
☐ 1999		190	**190**

Fantasia

Prima Ballerina

TITLE: Prima Ballerina
FIGURINE: Mademoiselle Upanova
ITEM NUMBER: 41178
SEGMENT: *The Dance Of The Hours*
SIZE: 8.5"
DATE OF ISSUE: 8/97

PLUSSING: Toes: Pink porcelain. **Neck:** Adorned with a metal bow.
PRODUCTION CHANGES: None.
PARTICULARS: Certificate of Authenticity. Incised Annual Production Mark.
STATUS: OPEN EDITION.

YEAR	MARK	SRP	GBTru
☐ 1997		$165	$165
☐ 1998		165	165
☐ 1999		165	165

Flight Of Fancy

TITLE: Flight Of Fancy
ORNAMENT: Cupid
ITEM NUMBER: 41051
SEGMENT: *Sixth Symphony: The Pastoral*
SIZE: 3"
DATE OF ISSUE: 3/94

PLUSSING: Wings: Wings are frosted crystal. **Annual Production Mark:** Frosted symbol, located on the underneath side of wing, with frosted word 'WDCC.' **Hook:** Hook is gold-plated.
PRODUCTION CHANGES: None.
PARTICULARS: Certificate of Authenticity. Incised Annual Production Mark. (This is the same blond Cupid as on Love's Little Helpers figurine, #41042.)
STATUS: EDITION CLOSED. Event piece was available 3/94 to 8/94.

Due to brief time of availability, a special advance offer in 8/93 enabled Society Members to order the ornament for delivery in 1994.

YEAR	MARK	SRP	GBTru
☐ 1993		$35	$50
☐ 1994		35	50

Fantasia

Flight Of Fancy Ornament Display Stand

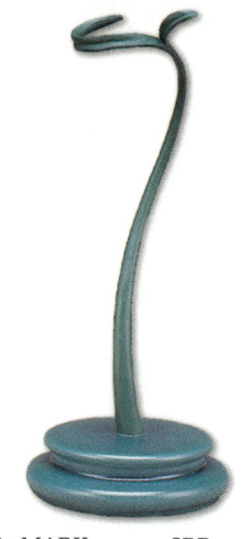

TITLE: Flight Of Fancy Ornament Display Stand
ACCESSORY: Display Stand
ITEM NUMBER: 41056
SEGMENT: *Sixth Symphony: The Pastoral*
SIZE: 7.5"
DATE OF ISSUE: 3/94

PLUSSING: Style: Handcrafted in art deco style. **Paint:** A Fantasia blue.
PRODUCTION CHANGES: None.
PARTICULARS: Certificate of Authenticity. Incised Annual Production Mark.
STATUS: Event Accessory Piece.

YEAR	MARK	SRP	GBTru
☐ 1993		$20	**$55**
☐ 1994		20	**40**
☐ 1995		20	**40**

Night On Bald Mountain

TITLE: Night On Bald Mountain
FIGURINE: Chernabog
ITEM NUMBER: 41180
SEGMENT: *Night On Bald Mountain*
SIZE: 10.5"
DATE OF ISSUE: 9/97

PLUSSING: Special Backstamp: Includes the 1997 Disneyana Convention logo.
PRODUCTION CHANGES: None.
PARTICULARS: As a special Collectors Society Member benefit, 25 Artist Proof sculptures were available for purchase via a special sweepstakes drawing by mail. One entry per person with purchase to be completed by 12/31/97. GBTru$ for Artist Proofs is $1,500. Certificate of Authenticity. Incised Annual Production Mark.
STATUS: LIMITED EDITION: 1,500 Hand Numbered Pieces plus 25 Artist Proofs. Disneyana Convention Event Piece, 9/2 to 9/7/97, Orlando, Florida.

YEAR	MARK	SRP	GBTru
☐ 1997		$750	**$1350**

Fantasia

Mischievous Apprentice

TITLE: Mischievous Apprentice
FIGURINE: Mickey Mouse
ITEM NUMBER: 41016
SEGMENT: *The Sorcerer's Apprentice*
SIZE: 5.13"
DATE OF ISSUE: 10/92

PLUSSING: Platinum Symbols: The stars and moons on Mickey's hat are platinum.
PRODUCTION CHANGES: None.
PARTICULARS: Certificate of Authenticity. Incised Annual Production Mark.
STATUS: RETIRED 2/95.

YEAR	MARK	SRP	GBTru
❒ 1992	✸	$195	**$285**
❒ 1993	◈	195	**265**
❒ 1994	⚘	195	**255**

Bucket Brigade

TITLE: Bucket Brigade
FIGURINE: Broom with Water Pails
ITEM NUMBER: 41017
SEGMENT: *The Sorcerer's Apprentice*
SIZE: 5.8"
DATE OF ISSUE: 10/92

PLUSSING: Water Spots: Early ✸ production had 5 distinct spots — 3 on one side, 2 on the other — to look like splashed-out water.
PRODUCTION CHANGES: Water Spots: Deleted from later ✸ production, following animator's critique.
PARTICULARS: Certificate of Authenticity. Incised Annual Production Mark. 
STATUS: RETIRED 2/95.

YEAR	MARK	SRP	GBTru
❒ 1992	✸	$75	**$220**
w/Water Spots			
❒ 1992	✸	75	**110**
❒ 1993	◈	75	**105**
❒ 1994	⚘	75	**100**

Fantasia

Romantic Reflections

TITLE: Romantic Reflections
FIGURINE: Pink Centaurette
ITEM NUMBER: 41040
SEGMENT: *Sixth Symphony: The Pastoral*
SIZE: 7.5"
DATE OF ISSUE: 9/93

PLUSSING: Mirror: Antique gold-plated hand mirror. High gloss platinum plates reflective face. (Polishing with a soft cloth removes any oxidizing dulling.) **Handmade Flowers:** A delicate blossom graces her hair ribbon.

PRODUCTION CHANGES: Color Variations: § — upper body has bright pink tones. ⚘ and ∽ — upper body has lighter pink tones, grass on the base has a rounder, bumpier appearance.

PARTICULARS: Certificate of Authenticity. Incised Annual Production Mark.
STATUS: RETIRED 7/95.

YEAR	MARK	SRP	GBTru
☐ 1993	§	$175	**$175**
☐ 1994	⚘	175	**175**
☐ 1995	∽	175	**175**

Beauty In Bloom

TITLE: Beauty In Bloom
FIGURINE: Blue Centaurette
ITEM NUMBER: 41041
SEGMENT: *Sixth Symphony: The Pastoral*
SIZE: 7.5"
DATE OF ISSUE: 9/93

PLUSSING: Handmade Flowers: A variety of porcelain blossoms are placed in flowing tail.
PRODUCTION CHANGES: Color Variations: § — upper body has bright blue tone. ⚘ and ∽ — upper body has lighter blue tone, grass on the base has a rounder, bumpier appearance. **SRP Change:** $195 to $215 on 3/15/94.
PARTICULARS: Certificate of Authenticity. Incised Annual Production Mark.
STATUS: RETIRED 7/95.

YEAR	MARK	SRP	GBTru
☐ 1993	§	$195	**$215**
☐ 1994	⚘	215	**215**
☐ 1995	∽	215	**215**

Fantasia

Love's Little Helpers

TITLE: Love's Little Helpers
FIGURINE: Cupids on a Pillar
ITEM NUMBER: 41042
SEGMENT: *Sixth Symphony:* The Pastoral
SIZE: 8"
DATE OF ISSUE: 9/94

PLUSSING: Wings: Each Cupid has its own pair of frosted crystal wings. (6 different wings in total.)
PRODUCTION CHANGES: None.
PARTICULARS: Certificate of Authenticity. Incised Annual Production Mark. NOTE: Some blond Cupids have a frosted 𝄞 on the wing, and a ⚘ on the base. (This is the same blond Cupid as the Flight Of Fancy ornament, #41051.)
STATUS: RETIRED 7/95.

YEAR	MARK	SRP	GBTru
☐ 1994	⚘	$290	**$290**
☐ 1995	〰	290	**290**

Unicorn

TITLE: Unicorn
MINIATURE: Unicorn
ITEM NUMBER: 41237
SEGMENT: *Sixth Symphony:* The Pastoral
SIZE: 1"
DATE OF ISSUE: 7/97

PLUSSING: Miniature: Bronze, hand painted.
PRODUCTION CHANGES: None.
PARTICULARS: Enchanted Places. Green box, picture on box, sticker Annual Production Mark on box and on base of miniature.
STATUS: 1997 ANNUAL.

YEAR	MARK	SRP	GBTru
☐ 1997	⚘	$50	**$50**

Fantasia

Pastoral Setting

TITLE: Pastoral Setting
SCULPTURE: Gazebo
ITEM NUMBER: 41232
SEGMENT: *Sixth Symphony: The Pastoral*
SIZE: 7"
DATE OF ISSUE: 7/97

PLUSSING: Color: Hues tinted to resemble dawn. **Trees:** Pewter trunks.
PRODUCTION CHANGES: None.
PARTICULARS: Enchanted Places. Certificate of Authenticity. Incised Annual Production Mark. Hand Engraved Serial Number. Registration Card redeemable for a deed "signed" by the setting's original "owner," transferring ownership. Sculpture comes with a wood display base with engraved brass nameplate.

STATUS: LIMITED EDITION: 3,000 Hand Numbered Pieces.

YEAR	MARK	SRP	GBTru
☐ 1997	⚲	$195	**$235**

Notes:

Fantasia

HERCULES
June 27, 1997

From Greek mythology comes the story of Hercules, half-god and half-man, caught between two worlds. It is set during the Trojan War, and both sides want the superhero as their secret weapon. While not keeping to every detail of the original Hercules story, it was decided to keep the impulsive, headstrong, resolute part of Hercules and try to fuse it with the innocent hero. The mythical concept of the hero's journey was also followed: immature young man sets off on a quest with the help of a mentor, overcomes impossible obstacles, discovers inside himself the answers he is looking for, and ends up with a maturity that he did not have at the start.

HERCULES QUIKREFERENCE

	TITLE	ITEM #	AVAILABLE
EVENT PIECE:			
Hercules and Pegasus Ornament	A Gift From The Gods	41167	9/6 & 7/97
CLOSED EDITION:			
Hercules	"From Zero To Hero"	41253	3/1 - 5/31/98

COMPLEMENTARY PIECES:

ENCHANTED PLACES

RETIRED EDITIONS:			
Sculpture	Hades' Chariot	41246	8/97 - 1/98
Miniature	Pain	41247	8/97 - 1/98
Miniature	Panic	41250	8/97 - 1/98

A Gift From The Gods

TITLE: A Gift From The Gods
ORNAMENT: Hercules and Pegasus
ITEM NUMBER: 41167
SIZE: 3.5"
DATE OF ISSUE: 9/97

PLUSSING: None.
PRODUCTION CHANGES: None.
PARTICULARS: Certificate of Authenticity. Incised Annual Production Mark.
STATUS: EDITION CLOSED. 1997 Fall Open House Event Ornament available 9/6 & 7/97.

YEAR	MARK	SRP	GBTru
❏ 1997	♀	$55	**$55**

Hercules

"From Zero To Hero"

TITLE: "From Zero To Hero"
FIGURINE: Hercules
ITEM NUMBER: 41253
SERIES: Tribute Series, 1998
Selection: 4th Issue
SIZE: 7.5"
DATE OF ISSUE: 3/98

PLUSSING: Arrow and Arrowhead: Bronze arrow with a pewter arrowhead. **Bow:** Porcelain and pewter. **Sword:** Pewter. **Outfit & Belt:** Gold painted accents. **Backstamp:** Includes special Tribute Series Logo.
PRODUCTION CHANGES: None.
PARTICULARS: The 1998 selection celebrates Disney's 35th animated feature film. Certificate of Authenticity. Incised Annual Production Mark.
STATUS: EDITION CLOSED.

Window for ordering was 3/1/98 to 5/31/98 with Special Commission Authorization Form.

YEAR	MARK	SRP	GBTru
❏ 1997	우	$250	**$265**
❏ 1998	숯	250	**250**

Hades' Chariot

TITLE: Hades' Chariot
SCULPTURE: Hades' Chariot
ITEM NUMBER: 41246
SIZE: 3"
DATE OF ISSUE: 8/97

PLUSSING: Paint: Ghostly gray. **Wheels:** Metal with spike and claw of bronze.
PRODUCTION CHANGES: None.
PARTICULARS: Enchanted Places. Certificate of Authenticity. Incised Annual Production Mark.
STATUS: RETIRED 1/98.

YEAR	MARK	SRP	GBTru
❏ 1997	우	$125	**$125**

Hercules

Pain

TITLE: Pain
MINIATURE: Pain
ITEM NUMBER: 41247
SIZE: .75"
DATE OF ISSUE: 8/97

PLUSSING: Miniature: Bronze, hand painted.
PRODUCTION CHANGES: None.
PARTICULARS: Enchanted Places. Green box, picture on box, sticker Annual Production Mark on box and on base of miniature.
STATUS: RETIRED 1/98.

YEAR	MARK	SRP	GBTru
❏ 1997	♀	$50	**$50**

Panic

TITLE: Panic
MINIATURE: Panic
ITEM NUMBER: 41250
SIZE: .75"
DATE OF ISSUE: 8/97

PLUSSING: Miniature: Bronze, hand painted.
PRODUCTION CHANGES: None.
PARTICULARS: Enchanted Places. Green box, picture on box, sticker Annual Production Mark on box and on base of miniature.
STATUS: RETIRED 1/98.

YEAR	MARK	SRP	GBTru
❏ 1997	♀	$50	**$50**

Hercules

How to Play Baseball 1942

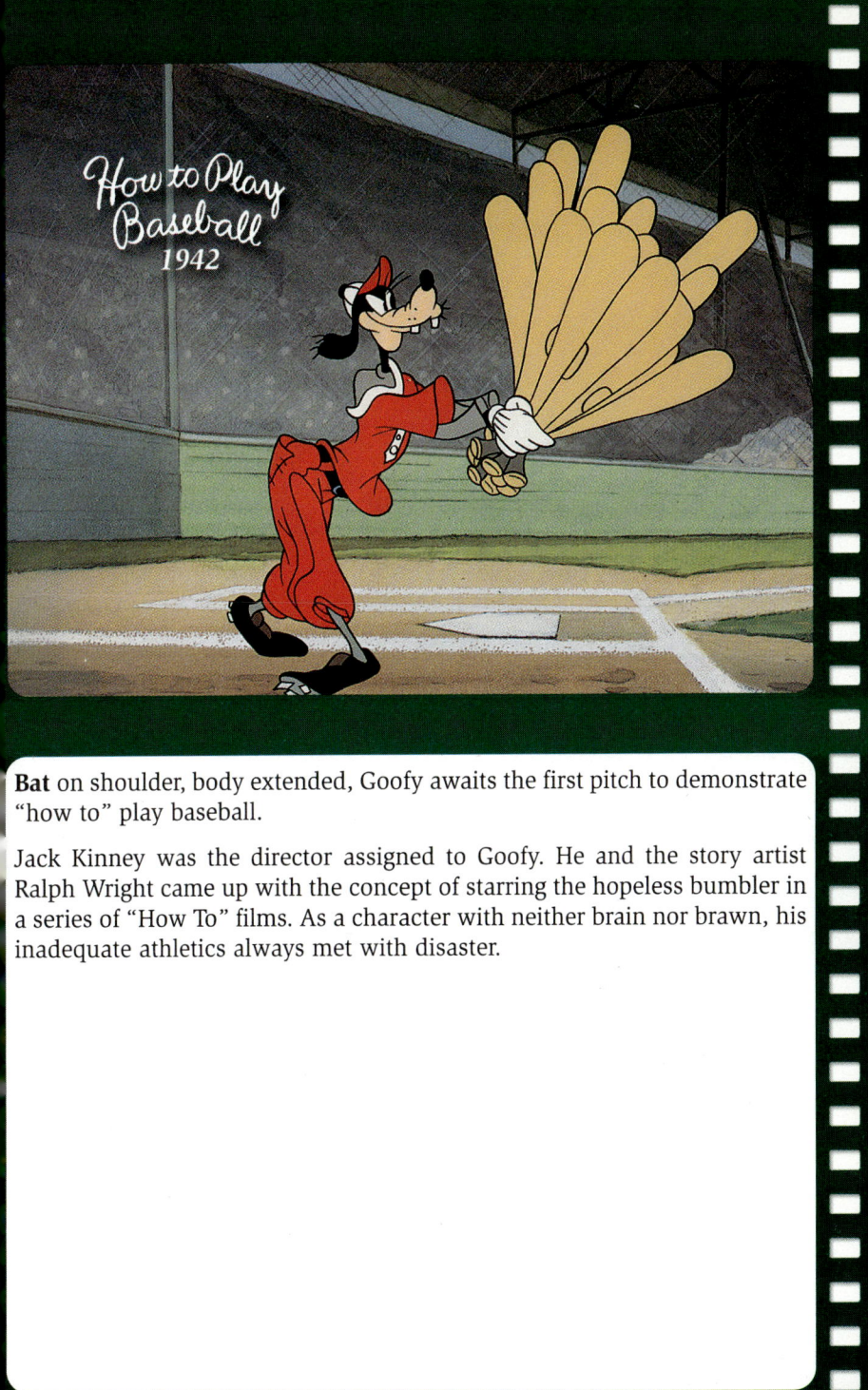

Bat on shoulder, body extended, Goofy awaits the first pitch to demonstrate "how to" play baseball.

Jack Kinney was the director assigned to Goofy. He and the story artist Ralph Wright came up with the concept of starring the hopeless bumbler in a series of "How To" films. As a character with neither brain nor brawn, his inadequate athletics always met with disaster.

How To Play Baseball

HOW TO PLAY BASEBALL QUIKREFERENCE

	TITLE	ITEM #	AVAILABLE
OPEN EDITION:			
Goofy	Batter Up	41266	5/98

Batter Up

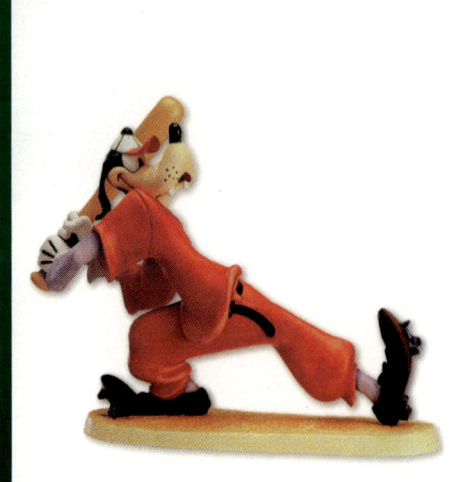

TITLE: Batter Up
FIGURINE: Goofy
ITEM NUMBER: 41266
SIZE: 7.5"
DATE OF ISSUE: 5/98

PLUSSING: Bat: Real wood.
PRODUCTION CHANGES: None.
PARTICULARS: Certificate of Authenticity. Incised Annual Production Mark.
STATUS: OPEN EDITION.

YEAR	MARK	SRP	GBTru
☐ 1998	⊤	$175	**$175**
☐ 1999	⌂	175	175

How To Play Baseball

THE HUNCHBACK OF NOTRE DAME
June 21, 1996

Disney animators had the challenge of transforming a thousand-page, world famous literary classic with a cast of hundreds into an hour-and-a-half animated film. Of course, the title conjures up images everyone knows – Quasimodo, the bell ringer; Esmeralda, the gypsy girl; Frollo, the evil guardian of Quasimodo. One of the first steps in developing the story as an animated feature was a conscious decision to avoid the monster-like characterizations of Quasimodo seen in previous live-action film versions. The animators wanted to focus on the contrast between what you see and what things really are – good and bad, ugly and beautiful, justice and injustice. Even though Quasimodo is ugly and rejected by everyone, he actually has the greatest humanity. He falls in love with the beautiful gypsy dancer, Esmeralda, herself an outcast of society. Unafraid of his looks, she is the only person who shows the gentle bell ringer any kindness, and for the first time in Quasimodo's life he feels accepted for who he is.

With *The Hunchback Of Notre Dame*, classic literature has been melded with classic animation to craft wise and humorous entertainment in keeping with the spirit of Victor Hugo's immortal classic.

THE HUNCHBACK OF NOTRE DAME QUIKREFERENCE

	TITLE	ITEM #	AVAILABLE
CLOSED EDITION:			
Quasimodo and Esmeralda	"Not A Single Monster Line"	41143	3/1/97 - 5/31/97

"Not A Single Monster Line"

TITLE: "Not A Single Monster Line"
FIGURINE: Quasimodo and Esmeralda
ITEM NUMBER: 41143
SERIES: Tribute Series, 1997 Selection: 3rd Issue
SIZE: 5.15"
DATE OF ISSUE: 3/97

PLUSSING: Backstamp: Includes special Tribute Series Logo.
PRODUCTION CHANGES: None.
PARTICULARS: Certificate of Authenticity. Incised Annual Production Mark.
STATUS: EDITION CLOSED. Window for ordering was 3/1/97 to 5/31/97 with Special Commission Authorization Form.

YEAR	MARK	SRP	GBTru
❏ 1997	⚲	$195	**$195**

Hunchback Of Notre Dame, The

THE JUNGLE BOOK
October, 1967

Walt Disney thought that the Rudyard Kipling classic story with its host of colorful animal characters would make a great vehicle for an animated film of high-spirited fun and adventure. The animators were told to concentrate on developing the funny sequences and not to worry about the story line.

The young mancub, Mowgli, was raised in the jungle by a wolf family, so goes the strange tale from India. He wants to stay in the jungle forever but Shere Kahn, the man-hating tiger, returns to hunt again. Mowgli's protector, Bagheera, the black panther, plans to take Mowgli to a man-village and leave him in the safety of his own kind. But Mowgli stubbornly refuses to go along, so Bagheera leaves him on his own. He strikes up a friendship with Baloo, the bear, but then a band of monkeys grab Mowgli and carry him off to the ruins of an ancient temple where their king, Louie, waits. King Louie believes Mowgli can give him the secret of Man's Red Flower – fire! Baloo and Bagheera arrive just in time and the fun begins. Bagheera watches as everyone is caught up in the swinging rhythms of the dancing, singing animals. He waits his chance and finally snatches Mowgli to safety. In the end, Shere Khan is dispatched and Mowgli willingly returns to the man-village.

This was the first of the Disney animated films in which the major characters were based on the personalities of the voice artists. It was the last animated feature to be supervised by Walt himself. Audiences made the movie one of the most popular Disney films ever presented.

Jungle Book, The

THE JUNGLE BOOK QUIKREFERENCE

	TITLE	ITEM #	AVAILABLE
SCROLL:			
Scroll	*The Jungle Book* Opening Title	41171	6/97
OPEN EDITIONS:			
King Louie	King Of The Swingers	41158	6/97
Baloo	Hula Baloo	41160	6/97
Mowgli	Mancub	41161	6/97
Bagheera	Mowgli's Protector	41162	6/97
ANNUAL:			
Flunky Monkey	Monkeying Around	41159	6/97 - 12/97
EVENT PIECE:			
Shere Khan	"Everyone Runs From Shere Khan"	41254	2/27 - 3/29/98

COMPLEMENTARY PIECES:

ENCHANTED PLACES

ANNUAL:			
Sculpture	King Louie's Temple	41241	6/97 - 12/97

The Jungle Book Opening Title

TITLE: *The Jungle Book* Opening Title
SCROLL: Opening Title
ITEM NUMBER: 41171
SIZE: 1.6"
DATE OF ISSUE: 6/97

PLUSSING: None.
PRODUCTION CHANGES: None.
PARTICULARS: Certificate of Authenticity. Decal backstamp with WDCC logo and Annual Production Mark.
STATUS: OPEN EDITION.

YEAR	MARK	SRP	GBTru
☐ 1997		$29	**$29**
☐ 1998		29	**29**
☐ 1999		29	**29**

King Of The Swingers

TITLE: King Of The Swingers
FIGURINE: King Louie
ITEM NUMBER: 41158
SIZE: 6.75"
DATE OF ISSUE: 6/97

PLUSSING: Anniversary Backstamp: A special gold script message '*30th Anniversary*' was added to the backstamp of sculptures crafted in 1997.
PRODUCTION CHANGES: None.
PARTICULARS: Certificate of Authenticity. Incised Annual Production Mark.
STATUS: OPEN EDITION.

YEAR	MARK	SRP	GBTru
☐ 1997	Anniv. Mark	$175	**$175**
☐ 1998		175	**175**
☐ 1999		175	**175**

Jungle Book, The

Hula Baloo

TITLE: Hula Baloo
FIGURINE: Baloo
ITEM NUMBER: 41160
SIZE: 7"
DATE OF ISSUE: 6/97

PLUSSING: Anniversary
Backstamp: A special gold script message '*30th Anniversary*' was added to the backstamp of sculptures crafted in 1997.
PRODUCTION CHANGES: None.
PARTICULARS: Certificate of Authenticity. Incised Annual Production Mark.
STATUS: OPEN EDITION.

YEAR	MARK	SRP	GBTru
☐ 1997	⚚ Anniv. Mark	$185	**$185**
☐ 1998	⊤	185	**185**
☐ 1999	◬	185	**185**

Mancub

TITLE: Mancub
FIGURINE: Mowgli
ITEM NUMBER: 41161
SIZE: 4.75"
DATE OF ISSUE: 6/97

PLUSSING: Anniversary
Backstamp: A special gold script message '*30th Anniversary*' was added to the backstamp of sculptures crafted in 1997.
PRODUCTION CHANGES: None.
PARTICULARS: Certificate of Authenticity. Incised Annual Production Mark.
STATUS: OPEN EDITION.

YEAR	MARK	SRP	GBTru
☐ 1997	⚚ Anniv. Mark	$115	**$115**
☐ 1998	⊤	115	**115**
☐ 1999	◬	115	**115**

Jungle Book, The

Mowgli's Protector

TITLE: Mowgli's Protector
FIGURINE: Bagheera
ITEM NUMBER: 41162
SIZE: 4.6"
DATE OF ISSUE: 6/97

PLUSSING: Tail: Painted metal.
Anniversary Backstamp: A special gold script message '*30th Anniversary*' was added to the backstamp of sculptures crafted in 1997.
PRODUCTION CHANGES: None.
PARTICULARS: Certificate of Authenticity. Incised Annual Production Mark.
STATUS: OPEN EDITION.

YEAR	MARK	SRP	GBTru
❏ 1997	Anniv. Mark	$135	**$135**
❏ 1998		135	**135**
❏ 1999		135	**135**

Monkeying Around

TITLE: Monkeying Around
FIGURINE: Flunky Monkey
ITEM NUMBER: 41159
SIZE: 4.75"
DATE OF ISSUE: 6/97

PLUSSING: Tail: Painted metal.
Leaf: Metal. **Anniversary Backstamp:** A special gold script message '*30th Anniversary*' was added to the backstamp of sculptures crafted in 1997.
PRODUCTION CHANGES: None.
PARTICULARS: Certificate of Authenticity. Incised Annual Production Mark.
STATUS: 1997 ANNUAL.

YEAR	MARK	SRP	GBTru
❏ 1997	Anniv. Mark	$135	**$135**

Jungle Book, The

"Everyone Runs From Shere Khan"

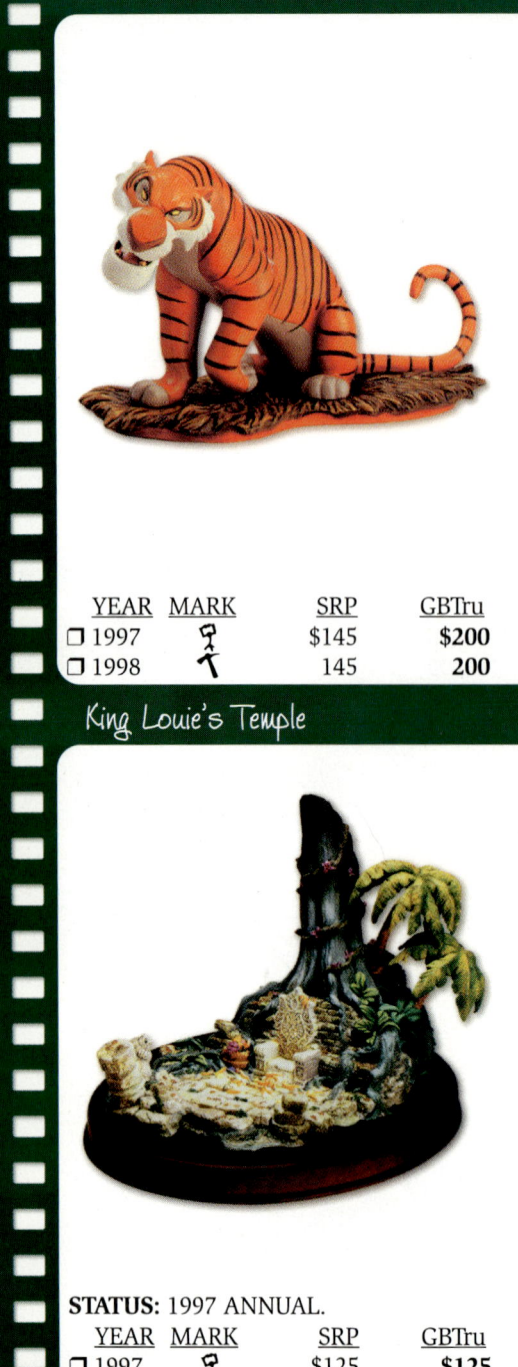

TITLE: "Everyone Runs From Shere Khan"
FIGURINE: Shere Khan
ITEM NUMBER: 41254
SIZE: 4.67"
DATE OF ISSUE: 2/98

PLUSSING: None. (NOTE: Shere Khan did not receive the special 30th Anniversary Backstamp.)
PRODUCTION CHANGES: None.
PARTICULARS: Certificate of Authenticity. Incised Annual Production Mark.
STATUS: EDITION CLOSED. Hand Numbered, Spring 1998 Special Event Piece was available 2/27/98 to 3/29/98.

YEAR	MARK	SRP	GBTru
☐ 1997		$145	**$200**
☐ 1998		145	**200**

King Louie's Temple

TITLE: King Louie's Temple
SCULPTURE: King Louie's Temple
ITEM NUMBER: 41241
SIZE: 9"
DATE OF ISSUE: 6/97

PLUSSING: Anniversary Backstamp: A special gold script message '*30th Anniversary*' was added to the backstamp of sculptures crafted in 1997.
PRODUCTION CHANGES: None.
PARTICULARS: Enchanted Places. Certificate of Authenticity. Incised Annual Production Mark. Hand Engraved Serial Number. Registration Card redeemable for a deed "signed" by the setting's original "owner," transferring ownership. Sculpture comes with a wood display base with engraved brass nameplate.

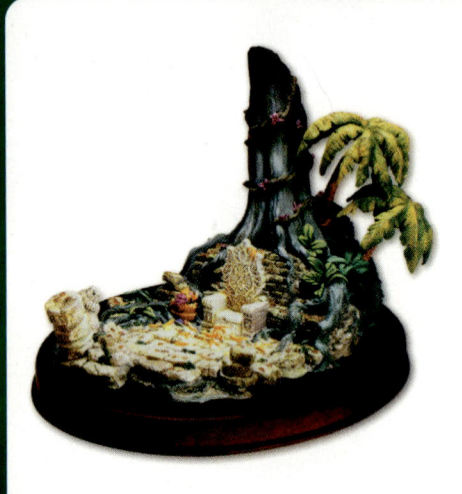

STATUS: 1997 ANNUAL.

YEAR	MARK	SRP	GBTru
☐ 1997	Anniv. Mark	$125	**$125**

Jungle Book, The

LADY and THE TRAMP
June 16, 1955

Lady And The Tramp is noteworthy for two firsts; it was the first full-length animated feature not based on a published novel or story; and it was the first animated film to be made in Cinemascope.

The opening sequence, when Darling opens up a hat box to discover a Christmas puppy, had its origins in Walt's own life. After forgetting a dinner engagement with his wife, he presented her with a hat box containing a cuddly pup as a peace offering.

The use of Cinemascope meant that, because of the much wider screen, the *characters* moved around rather than the *backgrounds*. This had the effect of making the film more realistic but was panned by critics who claimed audiences wanted cartoons as an escape from reality.

Lady And The Tramp is classic Disney. Like all great film sweethearts, movie goers were captivated by the romance, gentle tenderness and caring between two perfectly suited canines.

LADY AND THE TRAMP QUIKREFERENCE

	TITLE	ITEM #	AVAILABLE
SCROLL:			
Scroll	*Lady And The Tramp* Opening Title	41099	1/96
LIMITED EDITIONS:			
Lady, Tramp, Tony and Joe	"Bella Notte"	41284	8/98 - 12/98
Bella Notte Base	Lady and the Tramp Base	41403	9/98 - 12/98
RETIRED EDITIONS:			
Lady	Lady In Love	41089	1/96 - 4/97
Tramp	Tramp In Love	41090	1/96 - 4/97

COMPLEMENTARY PIECE:

WALT DISNEY COLLECTORS SOCIETY
MEMBERSHIP GIFT SCULPTURE: (see page 267)
Lady   "A Perfectly Beautiful Little Lady" 41327   1999

Lady And The Tramp Opening Title

TITLE: *Lady And The Tramp* Opening Title
SCROLL: Opening Title
ITEM NUMBER: 41099
SIZE: 1.6"
DATE OF ISSUE: 1/96

PLUSSING: None.
PRODUCTION CHANGES: Original Backstamp Decal had Annual Production Mark flopped.
PARTICULARS: Certificate of Authenticity. Decal backstamp with WDCC logo and Annual Production Mark.
STATUS: OPEN EDITION.

YEAR	MARK	SRP	GBTru
☐ 1995		$29	**$45**
☐ 1996		29	**29**
☐ 1997		29	**29**
☐ 1998		29	**29**
☐ 1999		29	**29**

Lady And The Tramp

"Bella Notte"

TITLE: "Bella Notte"
FIGURINE: Lady, Tramp, Tony and Joe
ITEM NUMBER: 41284
SIZE: 7.25"
DATE OF ISSUE: 8/98

PLUSSING: License: Made of gold-plated metal with a brass wire hook. **Spaghetti:** Brass wire. **Mandolin:** Has metal strings. **Barrel & Accordion Trim:** Painted with silver metallic paint. **Joe's Shirt Buttons:** Painted with gold metallic paint.
PRODUCTION CHANGES: None.
PARTICULARS: 3 Piece Set. Certificate of Authenticity. Incised Annual Production Mark.
STATUS: LIMITED EDITION: 5,000 Hand Numbered, Matched Sets. (Each piece is individually numbered.)

YEAR	MARK	SRP	GBTru
❒ 1998	⟁	$795	**$795**

"Bella Notte" Base

TITLE: "Bella Notte" Base
ACCESSORY BASE: Display Base
ITEM NUMBER: 41403
SIZE: 5" tall x 9" wide x 12.5" long
DATE OF ISSUE: 9/98

PLUSSING: None.
PRODUCTION CHANGES: None.
PARTICULARS: Base for the Limited Edition Set, "Bella Notte". Incised Annual Production Mark.
STATUS: EDITION CLOSED.

YEAR	MARK	SRP	GBTru
❒ 1998	⟁	$75	**$75**
❒ 1999	🪨	75	**75**

Lady And The Tramp

Lady In Love

TITLE: Lady In Love
FIGURINE: Lady
ITEM NUMBER: 41089
SIZE: 4.5"
DATE OF ISSUE: 1/96

PLUSSING: Dog Tag: Cocker Spaniel Lady wears a gold-tone metal license around her neck.
PRODUCTION CHANGES: None.
PARTICULARS: Certificate of Authenticity. Incised Annual Production Mark.
STATUS: RETIRED 4/97.

YEAR	MARK	SRP	GBTru
☐ 1995	⌒	$120	**$180**
☐ 1996	⌒	120	**120**
☐ 1997	웃	120	**120**

Tramp In Love

TITLE: Tramp In Love
FIGURINE: Tramp
ITEM NUMBER: 41090
SIZE: 5.5"
DATE OF ISSUE: 1/96

PLUSSING: None.
PRODUCTION CHANGES: None.
PARTICULARS: Certificate of Authenticity. Incised Annual Production Mark.
STATUS: RETIRED 4/97.

YEAR	MARK	SRP	GBTru
☐ 1995	⌒	$100	**$140**
☐ 1996	⌒	100	**120**
☐ 1997	웃	100	**110**

Lady And The Tramp

The Lion King
June 24, 1994

The Lion King is different from other Disney features in that it is entirely original material crafted from storyboards and plotting sessions by studio artists and writers.

Not since *Bambi* had Disney artists been faced with the challenge of animating animals in the wild whose movements needed to be lifelike. Producer Don Hahn explained the difficulty, "I remember the directors being frustrated because they had characters with no opposable thumb; they couldn't pick up anything. You've got no props, no costumes, no architecture, no doors to slam, no stairs to walk down. You don't realize how much you rely on those things for business, for acting, for staging. You have all these naked animals on the Serengeti. What do you do?"

The artists visited zoos, watched animal footage on nature programs, trainers brought animals to the studio, a biology professor lectured on animal movement and six members of the company toured East Africa.

Computer imagery accomplished something that never could have been possible by animators alone: the stampede of a giant herd of wildebeests. In one scene there were a thousand.

All is not well in the Pride Lands when King Mufasa's brother, Scar, is consumed by jealously and plots to take over the throne. Scar succeeds in his plans to kill the King, and attempts to murder Simba, the heir to the throne. Simba, persuaded that it was his fault that Mufasa died, leaves the Pride Lands. Scar takes over and the result of his greed for power devastates the Land. Meanwhile, Simba makes friends with a meercat and a warthog and the three share adventures as the cub grows to be a young adult. The warthog is attacked by a lioness one day and thus Simba's old playmate, Nala, finds her old friend, Simba, and convinces him that he must return to save the Lands and claim his kingship. The two fall in love and Simba, now the image of his father, returns home to dispatch the evil Scar. The circle of life is illustrated as the Land recovers, and Simba and Nala present their firstborn cub, gently held by wise old Rafiki, to the kingdom.

The Lion King surpassed all expectations with a worldwide gross of $435 million and an industry record of 30 million videocassette sales. It became the fifth biggest money-maker in film history. Elton John's "Can You Feel The Love Tonight" won the Academy Award as best song of 1994.

THE LION KING QUIKREFERENCE

	TITLE	ITEM #	AVAILABLE
SCROLL:			
Scroll	*The Lion King* Opening Title	41356	5/99
OPEN EDITIONS:			
Simba	Simba's Pride	41357	5/99
Rafiki with Cub	The Circle Continues	41358	5/99
Nala	Nala's Joy	41359	5/99
ANNUAL:			
Zazu	Major Domo	41360	5/99 - 12/99
EVENT PIECE:			
Simba Ornament	Simba	41256	4/24 - 26/98
CLOSED EDITION:			
Mufasa & Simba	Pals Forever	41085	3/1/95 - 4/28/95

COMPLEMENTARY PIECES:

WALT DISNEY COLLECTORS SOCIETY

MEMBERSHIP GIFT SCULPTURE: (see page 267)
| Timon | "Luau!" | 41197 | 1998 |

MEMBERS-ONLY ORNAMENT: (see page 277)
| Timon Ornament | "Luau!" | 41262 | 1/98 - 3/99 |

MEMBERS-ONLY SCENE COMPLETER: (see page 284)
| Pumbaa and Timon | Double Trouble | 41416 | 5/99 |

The Lion King Opening Title

TITLE: *The Lion King* Opening Title
SCROLL: Opening Title
ITEM NUMBER: 41356
SIZE: 1.6"
DATE OF ISSUE: 5/99

PLUSSING: None.
PRODUCTION CHANGES: None.
PARTICULARS: Certificate of Authenticity. Decal backstamp with WDCC logo and Annual Production Mark.
STATUS: OPEN EDITION.

YEAR	MARK	SRP	GBTru
☐ 1999	🎩	$29	**$29**

Simba's Pride

TITLE: Simba's Pride
FIGURINE: Simba
ITEM NUMBER: 41357
SIZE: 6.75"
DATE OF ISSUE: 5/99

PLUSSING: Anniversary Backstamp: Special *'5th Anniversary'* backstamp on sculptures crafted in 1999.
PRODUCTION CHANGES: None.
PARTICULARS: Certificate of Authenticity. Incised Annual Production Mark.
STATUS: OPEN EDITION.

YEAR	MARK	SRP	GBTru
☐ 1999	🎩 Anniv. Mark	$175	**$175**

Lion King, The 101

The Circle Continues

TITLE: The Circle Continues
FIGURINE: Rafiki with Cub
ITEM NUMBER: 41358
SIZE: 5.75"
DATE OF ISSUE: 5/99

PLUSSING: Rafiki: Plussed with pewter tail. **Anniversary Backstamp:** Special *'5th Anniversary'* backstamp on sculptures crafted in 1999.
PRODUCTION CHANGES: None.
PARTICULARS: Certificate of Authenticity. Incised Annual Production Mark.
STATUS: OPEN EDITION.

YEAR	MARK	SRP	GBTru
☐ 1999	Anniv. Mark	$150	**$150**

Nala's Joy

TITLE: Nala's Joy
FIGURINE: Nala
ITEM NUMBER: 41359
SIZE: 6"
DATE OF ISSUE: 5/99

PLUSSING: Anniversary Backstamp: Special *'5th Anniversary'* backstamp on sculptures crafted in 1999.
PRODUCTION CHANGES: None.
PARTICULARS: Certificate of Authenticity. Incised Annual Production Mark.
STATUS: OPEN EDITION.

YEAR	MARK	SRP	GBTru
☐ 1999	Anniv. Mark	$165	**$165**

Lion King, The

Major Domo

TITLE: Major Domo
FIGURINE: Zazu
ITEM NUMBER: 41360
SIZE: 3.5"
DATE OF ISSUE: 5/99

PLUSSING: Anniversary Backstamp: Special *'5th Anniversary'* backstamp on sculptures crafted in 1999.
PRODUCTION CHANGES: None.
PARTICULARS: Certificate of Authenticity. Incised Annual Production Mark.
STATUS: 1999 ANNUAL.

YEAR	MARK	SRP	GBTru
☐ 1999	Anniv. Mark	$75	**$75**

Simba

TITLE: Simba
ORNAMENT: Simba
ITEM NUMBER: 41256
SIZE: 2.75"
DATE OF ISSUE: 4/98

PLUSSING: None.
PRODUCTION CHANGES: None.
PARTICULARS: Certificate of Authenticity. Incised Annual Production Mark.
STATUS: EDITION CLOSED. 1998 Spring Open House Event Piece available 4/24 - 26/98.

YEAR	MARK	SRP	GBTru
☐ 1997		$49	$50
☐ 1998		49	50

Lion King, The

Pals Forever

TITLE: Pals Forever
FIGURINE: Mufasa and Simba
ITEM NUMBER: 41085
SERIES: Tribute Series, 1995
Selection: 1st Issue
SIZE: 10"
DATE OF ISSUE: 3/1/95

PLUSSING: Backstamp: Includes special Tribute Series Logo.
PRODUCTION CHANGES: None.
PARTICULARS: Certificate of Authenticity. Incised Annual Production Mark. This piece was in such high demand that even though it closed 4/95 they were still being produced in 1996.
STATUS: EDITION CLOSED. Window for ordering was 3/1/95 to 4/28/95 with Special Commission Authorization Form.

YEAR	MARK	SRP	GBTru
❏ 1995	∾	$175	**$175**
❏ 1996	⌒	175	**175**

Notes:

Lion King, The

THE LITTLE MERMAID

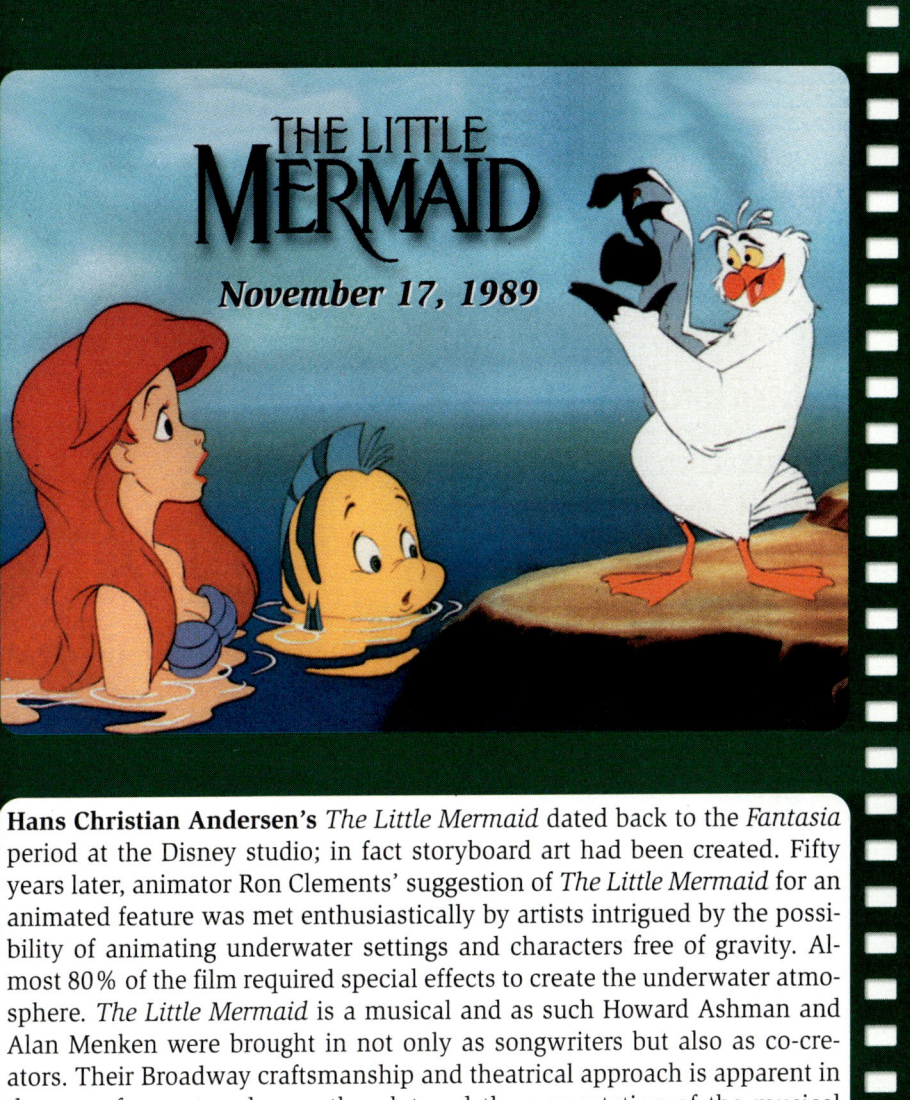

November 17, 1989

Hans Christian Andersen's *The Little Mermaid* dated back to the *Fantasia* period at the Disney studio; in fact storyboard art had been created. Fifty years later, animator Ron Clements' suggestion of *The Little Mermaid* for an animated feature was met enthusiastically by artists intrigued by the possibility of animating underwater settings and characters free of gravity. Almost 80% of the film required special effects to create the underwater atmosphere. *The Little Mermaid* is a musical and as such Howard Ashman and Alan Menken were brought in not only as songwriters but also as co-creators. Their Broadway craftsmanship and theatrical approach is apparent in the use of song to advance the plot and the presentation of the musical numbers.

It is the story of a beautiful spirited young mermaid, Ariel, who yearns for adventure and romance. Although a Princess in an undersea kingdom, she longs for life on land in the human world. Sebastian, the sea kingdom's musical maestro, has been sent by King Triton to watch Ariel. He learns of her secret wish. Sebastian tries to show Ariel the greatest jam session of music and merriment to prove that real excitement is in a calypso jam session. In this film the villain takes the form of Ursula, the Sea Witch. As an octopus with an attitude she slithers and audiences shiver.

The Little Mermaid was a milestone in the rebirth of Disney animation.

THE LITTLE MERMAID QUIKREFERENCE

	TITLE	ITEM #	AVAILABLE
SCROLL:			
Scroll	*The Little Mermaid* Opening Title	41188	11/97
EVENT PIECE:			
Ursula	"We Made A Deal"	41285	10/98 - 11/98
LIMITED EDITION:			
Carp with Harp	Classical Carp	41194	1/98
RETIRED EDITIONS:			
Ariel	Seahorse Surprise	41184	11/97 - 3/99
Sebastian	Calypso Crustacean	41187	5/98 - 3/99
Fluke	Duke Of Soul	41191	5/98 - 3/99
Turtle	Twistin' Turtle	41192	11/97 - 3/99
Newt	Newt's Nautical Note	41193	5/98 - 3/99
Blackfish	Deep Sea Diva	41195	11/97 - 3/99
Snails	Sing-Along Snails	41196	5/98 - 3/99
Flounder	Flounder's Fandango	41198	11/97 - 3/99

COMPLEMENTARY PIECES:

ENCHANTED PLACES

RETIRED EDITIONS:			
Sculpture	Ariel's Secret Grotto	41235	11/97 - 3/99
Miniature	Ariel	41240	11/97 - 3/99

The Little Mermaid Opening Title

TITLE: *The Little Mermaid* Opening Title
SCROLL: Opening Title
ITEM NUMBER: 41188
SIZE: 1.6"
DATE OF ISSUE: 11/97

PLUSSING: None.
PRODUCTION CHANGES: None.
PARTICULARS: Certificate of Authenticity. Decal backstamp with WDCC logo and Annual Production Mark.
STATUS: OPEN EDITION.

YEAR	MARK	SRP	GBTru
☐ 1997	🦀	$29	$29
☐ 1998	🍴	29	29
☐ 1999	🎩	29	29

"We Made A Deal"

TITLE: "We Made A Deal"
FIGURINE: Ursula
ITEM NUMBER: 41285
SIZE: 7.5"
DATE OF ISSUE: 10/98

PLUSSING: Contract: Ursula's contract is finished with gold paint.
PRODUCTION CHANGES: None.
PARTICULARS: Certificate of Authenticity. Incised Annual Production Mark. Piece came with a silver seashell charm, Item Number 11K-42666-0.
STATUS: EDITION CLOSED. Hand Numbered, Fall 1998 Special Event Piece was available 10/16/98 to 11/1/98.

YEAR	MARK	SRP	GBTru
☐ 1998	🍴	$165	$165

Classical Carp

TITLE: Classical Carp
FIGURINE: Carp with Harp
ITEM NUMBER: 41194
SIZE: 4.5"
DATE OF ISSUE: 1/98

PLUSSING: Harpstrings: Metal wire. **Fins & Tail:** Accented with opalescent paint. **Backstamp:** Special Gold Circle Dealer backstamp.
PRODUCTION CHANGES: None.
PARTICULARS: Certificate of Authenticity. Incised Annual Production Mark.
STATUS: LIMITED EDITION: 10,000 Pieces. 1998 Gold Circle Exclusive – 2nd Issue.

YEAR	MARK	SRP	GBTru
☐ 1997	웃	$150	**$198**
☐ 1998	주	150	**198**

Seahorse Surprise

TITLE: Seahorse Surprise
FIGURINE: Ariel
ITEM NUMBER: 41184
SIZE: 6.5"
DATE OF ISSUE: 11/97

PLUSSING: Clam Shell: Shell is bronze and contains a real pearl. **Seahorses:** Olszewski bronze miniatures. **Fins:** Opalescent paint highlights on fin.
PRODUCTION CHANGES: Fins: *Version 1* – Early 웃 production had opalescent paint highlighting edges and end of fin. *Version 2* – Later 웃 and all subsequent production has opalescent paint covering complete fin.
PARTICULARS: Certificate of Authenticity. Incised Annual Production Mark.
STATUS: RETIRED 3/19/99.

YEAR	MARK	SRP	GBTru
☐ 1997	웃	$275	**$400** *Ver. 1*
☐ 1997	웃	275	**275** *Ver. 2*
☐ 1998	주	275	**275** *Ver. 2*
☐ 1999	♗	275	**275** *Ver. 2*

Little Mermaid, The

Calypso Crustacean

TITLE: Calypso Crustacean
FIGURINE: Sebastian
ITEM NUMBER: 41187
SIZE: 4"
DATE OF ISSUE: 5/98

PLUSSING: Arms: Metal "arms" hold Sebastian's heavy porcelain claws.
PRODUCTION CHANGES: None.
PARTICULARS: Certificate of Authenticity. Incised Annual Production Mark.
STATUS: RETIRED 3/19/99.

YEAR	MARK	SRP	GBTru
☐ 1997	🜲	$130	**$130**
☐ 1998	🝊	130	**130**
☐ 1999	🜋	130	**130**

Duke Of Soul

TITLE: Duke Of Soul
FIGURINE: Fluke
ITEM NUMBER: 41191
SIZE: 4.5"
DATE OF ISSUE: 5/98

PLUSSING: None.
PRODUCTION CHANGES: None.
PARTICULARS: Certificate of Authenticity. Incised Annual Production Mark.
STATUS: RETIRED 3/19/99.

YEAR	MARK	SRP	GBTru
☐ 1998	🝊	$120	**$120**
☐ 1999	🜋	120	**120**

Little Mermaid, The

Twistin' Turtle

TITLE: Twistin' Turtle
FIGURINE: Turtle
ITEM NUMBER: 41192
SIZE: 5.25"
DATE OF ISSUE: 11/97

PLUSSING: None.
PRODUCTION CHANGES: None.
PARTICULARS: Certificate of Authenticity. Incised Annual Production Mark.
STATUS: RETIRED 3/19/99.

YEAR	MARK	SRP	GBTru
☐ 1997		$85	$85
☐ 1998		85	85
☐ 1999		85	85

Newt's Nautical Note

TITLE: Newt's Nautical Note
FIGURINE: Newt
ITEM NUMBER: 41193
SIZE: 5.5"
DATE OF ISSUE: 5/98

PLUSSING: Bubble: A blown glass bubble emerges from Newt's horn.
PRODUCTION CHANGES: None.
PARTICULARS: Certificate of Authenticity. Incised Annual Production Mark.
STATUS: RETIRED 3/19/99.

YEAR	MARK	SRP	GBTru
☐ 1997		$135	$135
☐ 1998		135	135
☐ 1999		135	135

Little Mermaid, The

Deep Sea Diva

TITLE: Deep Sea Diva
FIGURINE: Blackfish
ITEM NUMBER: 41195
SIZE: 3.5"
DATE OF ISSUE: 11/97

PLUSSING: Fins: Opalescent paint.
PRODUCTION CHANGES: None.
PARTICULARS: Certificate of Authenticity. Incised Annual Production Mark.
STATUS: RETIRED 3/19/99.

YEAR	MARK	SRP	GBTru
☐ 1997		$95	**$95**
☐ 1998		95	**95**
☐ 1999		95	**95**

Sing-Along Snails

TITLE: Sing-Along Snails
FIGURINE: Snails
ITEM NUMBER: 41196
SIZE: 3.25"
DATE OF ISSUE: 5/98

PLUSSING: None.
PRODUCTION CHANGES: None.
PARTICULARS: Certificate of Authenticity. Incised Annual Production Mark.
STATUS: RETIRED 3/19/99.

YEAR	MARK	SRP	GBTru
☐ 1997		$135	**$135**
☐ 1998		135	**135**
☐ 1999		135	**135**

Little Mermaid, The

Flounder's Fandango

TITLE: Flounder's Fandango
FIGURINE: Flounder
ITEM NUMBER: 41198
SIZE: 4.75"
DATE OF ISSUE: 11/97

PLUSSING: Treasure: Real bronze earring and metal seaweed.
PRODUCTION CHANGES: None.
PARTICULARS: Certificate of Authenticity. Incised Annual Production Mark.
STATUS: RETIRED 3/19/99.

YEAR	MARK	SRP	GBTru
☐ 1997	𓁹	$150	**$150**
☐ 1998	𓏤	150	**150**
☐ 1999	𓊪	150	**150**

Ariel's Secret Grotto

TITLE: Ariel's Secret Grotto
SCULPTURE: Ariel's Secret Grotto
ITEM NUMBER: 41235
SIZE: 5.25"
DATE OF ISSUE: 11/97

PLUSSING: Clam Shell: Real mother-of-pearl decorates shell.
Candelabra Gadget: Pewter.
PRODUCTION CHANGES: Candelabra: *Version 1:* Error, some early pieces had two candelabras.
Version 2: Current sculpture has one candelabra.
PARTICULARS: Enchanted Places. Certificate of Authenticity. Incised Annual Production Mark. Hand Engraved Serial Number. Registration Card redeemable for a deed "signed" by the setting's original "owner," transferring ownership. Sculpture comes with a wood display base with engraved brass nameplate.
STATUS: RETIRED 3/19/99.

YEAR	MARK	SRP	GBTru
☐ 1997	𓁹	$175	**$175** *Ver. 1, 2*
☐ 1998	𓏤	175	**175** *Ver. 2*
☐ 1999	𓊪	175	**175** *Ver. 2*

Little Mermaid, The

Ariel

TITLE: Ariel
MINIATURE: Ariel
ITEM NUMBER: 41240
SIZE: 1"
DATE OF ISSUE: 11/97

PLUSSING: Miniature: Bronze, hand painted.
PRODUCTION CHANGES: None.
PARTICULARS: Enchanted Places. Green box, picture on box, sticker Annual Production Mark on box and on base of miniature.
STATUS: RETIRED 3/19/99.

YEAR	MARK	SRP	GBTru
❐ 1997		$50	**$50**
❐ 1998		50	**50**
❐ 1999		50	**50**

Notes: _____

Little Mermaid, The 113

The Little Whirlwind
1941

It is a beautiful fall day and Minnie happily sings in her kitchen. She's just put a cake to cool on the windowsill when Mickey happens along. After the cake is iced and properly finished with a cherry on top, she'll share it with Mickey if he can clean up her yard. Little does she know, Mickey will get into big trouble with a little whirlwind and her beautiful cake is about to wind up all over Mickey.

THE LITTLE WHIRLWIND QUIKREFERENCE

	TITLE	ITEM #	AVAILABLE
OPEN EDITION: Minnie Mouse with Cake	For My Sweetie	41402	6/99

For My Sweetie

TITLE: For My Sweetie
FIGURINE: Minnie Mouse with Cake
ITEM NUMBER: 41402
SIZE: 5.75"
DATE OF ISSUE: 6/99

PLUSSING: None.
PRODUCTION CHANGES: None.
PARTICULARS: Certificate of Authenticity. Incised Annual Production Mark.
STATUS: OPEN EDITION.

YEAR	MARK	SRP	GBTru
☐ 1999	⌂	$95	**$95**

Little Whirlwind, The

Make Mine Music
April 20, 1946

Peter And The Wolf, Sergei Prokofiev's famous 1936 composition for voice and orchestra was deemed by many to be one of those works that simply could not be interpreted on the cinema screen. The narration had to be largely rewritten for this musical segment and even the order of the introduction of the principal characters presented something of a problem. In the original work the Wolf is the first to appear, but in Disney's version the order is shuffled for potential dramatic impact, and he is introduced after the opening words. He was one of the scariest monsters Disney ever produced. He terrorizes the neighborhood, but young Peter, unlike the adults, is not the slightest bit frightened. From Grandpa's house, nestled deep in the snowy countryside of Russia, he treks away to hunt the beast down, taking along his friends, Sasha the bird, Sonia the duck, and Ivan the cat.

MAKE MINE MUSIC QUIKREFERENCE

	TITLE	ITEM #	AVAILABLE
	ENCHANTED PLACES		
ANNUALS:			
Background	Grandpa's House	41211	7/96 - 12/96
Miniature	Peter	41221	7/96 - 12/96
Ornament	Grandpa's House	41222	7/96 - 12/96

Nestled In The Snow...

TITLE: Nestled In The Snow…
SCULPTURE: Grandpa's House
ITEM NUMBER: 41211
SEGMENT: *Peter And The Wolf*
SIZE: 6"
DATE OF ISSUE: 7/96

PLUSSING: Backstamp: Dated.
PRODUCTION CHANGES: None.
PARTICULARS: Enchanted Places. Certificate of Authenticity. Incised Annual Production Mark.
STATUS: DATED 1996 ANNUAL.

YEAR	MARK	SRP	GBTru
❏ 1996	ꝏ	$125	**$125**

Make Mine Music

Peter

TITLE: Peter
MINIATURE: Peter
ITEM NUMBER: 41221
SEGMENT: *Peter And The Wolf*
SIZE: 1"
DATE OF ISSUE: 7/96

PLUSSING: Miniature: Bronze, hand painted.
PRODUCTION CHANGES: None.
PARTICULARS: Enchanted Places. Green box, no picture on box, no Annual Production Mark.
STATUS: 1996 ANNUAL.

YEAR	MARK	SRP	GBTru
❏ 1996	No Mark	$50	**$50**

Nestled In The Snow…

TITLE: Nestled In The Snow…
ORNAMENT: Grandpa's House
ITEM NUMBER: 41222
SEGMENT: *Peter And The Wolf*
SIZE: 2.5"
DATE OF ISSUE: 7/96

PLUSSING: Backstamp: Brass, Dated 1996.
PRODUCTION CHANGES: None.
PARTICULARS: Enchanted Places.
STATUS: DATED 1996 ANNUAL.

YEAR	MARK	SRP	GBTru
❏ 1996		$35	**$35**

Make Mine Music

Mickey Cuts Up
1931

It is spring cleaning time in the garden and Minnie takes a few minutes to water her flower garden. Her green thumb tells her that whistling a happy tune will help the flowers grow. Mickey and Pluto are having problems with their spring garden chores. Mayhem ensues as Pluto pulls a lawnmower chaotically around the garden.

MICKEY CUTS UP QUIKREFERENCE

	TITLE	ITEM#	AVAILABLE
SCROLL:			
Scroll	*Mickey Cuts Up* Opening Title	1203580	9/99
OPEN EDITION:			
Minnie Mouse	Minnie's Garden	41397	3/99
LIMITED EDITION:			
Mickey Mouse	A Little Off The Top	1023578	9/99

Mickey Cuts Up Opening Title

TITLE: *Mickey Cuts Up* Opening Title
SCROLL: Opening Title
ITEM NUMBER: 1203580
SIZE: 1.6"
DATE OF ISSUE: 9/99

PLUSSING: None.
PRODUCTION CHANGES: None.
PARTICULARS: Certificate of Authenticity. Decal backstamp with WDCC logo and Annual Production Mark.
STATUS: OPEN EDITION.

Photo not available at press time.

YEAR	MARK	SRP	GBTru
☐ 1999	🎩	$29	**$29**

Minnie's Garden

TITLE: Minnie's Garden
FIGURINE: Minnie Mouse
ITEM NUMBER: 41397
SIZE: 5.5"
DATE OF ISSUE: 3/99

PLUSSING: Hat: Wire stem on flower. **Tail:** Metal wire. **Watering Can:** Clear resin to simulate water with droplets.
PRODUCTION CHANGES: None.
PARTICULARS: Sculpture is in color although cartoon is in black and white because many of the early Disney cartoons were colorized once the technology was available. Certificate of Authenticity. Incised Annual Production Mark.
STATUS: OPEN EDITION.

YEAR	MARK	SRP	GBTru
☐ 1999	🎩	$120	**$120**

A Little Off The Top

TITLE: A Little Off The Top
FIGURINE: Mickey Mouse
ITEM NUMBER: 1023578
SIZE: 6.5"
DATE OF ISSUE: 9/99
PARTICULARS: Sculpture is in color although cartoon is in black and white because many of the early Disney cartoons were colorized once the technology was available. Certificate of Authenticity. Incised Annual Production Mark.
STATUS: LIMITED EDITION: 3,500 Numbered Pieces. Syndicated Catalog Exclusive.

YEAR	MARK	SRP	GBTru
☐ 1999	🎩	$150	**$150**

Mickey Cuts Up

MICKEY'S BIRTHDAY PARTY
1942

Mickey's friends decide to throw a surprise birthday party for him. Goofy volunteers to bake a cake and runs into nothing but trouble. Finally, his solution is a store-bought cake, but as he presents it he trips and Mickey gets cake, SPLAT, right in the face.

MICKEY'S BIRTHDAY PARTY QUIKREFERENCE

	TITLE	ITEM #	AVAILABLE
OPEN EDITION:			
Mickey Mouse	"Happy Birthday!"	41170	4/97

"Happy Birthday!"

TITLE: "Happy Birthday!"
FIGURINE: Mickey Mouse
ITEM NUMBER: 41170
SIZE: 4.5"
DATE OF ISSUE: 4/97

PLUSSING: Candles: Wicks are made of metal wire. **Ears:** Shaded paint makes ears look three-dimensional.
PRODUCTION CHANGES: None.
PARTICULARS: Certificate of Authenticity. Incised Annual Production Mark.
STATUS: OPEN EDITION.

YEAR	MARK	SRP	GBTru
☐ 1997		$95	**$95**
☐ 1998		95	95
☐ 1999		95	95

Mickey's Birthday Party

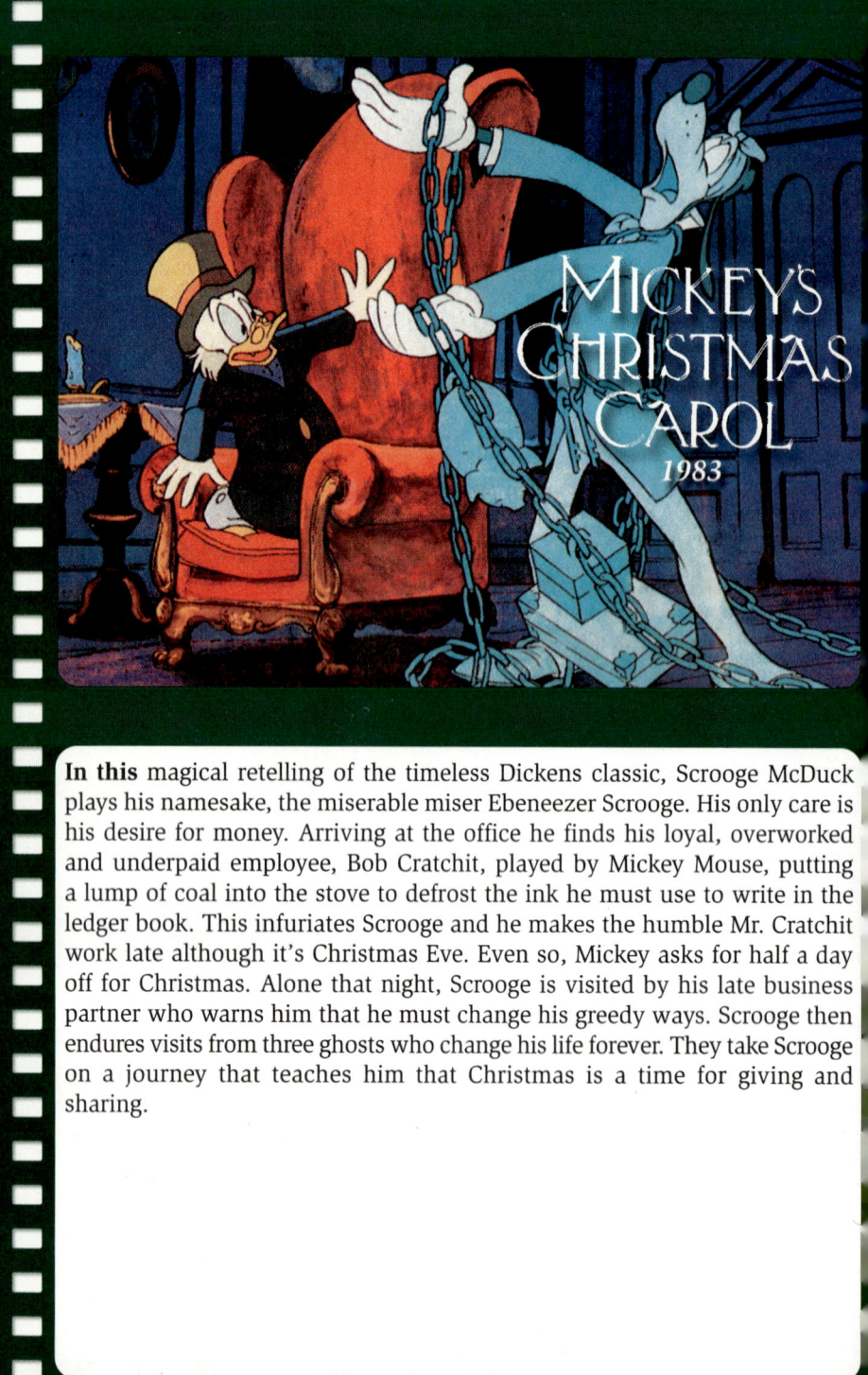

In this magical retelling of the timeless Dickens classic, Scrooge McDuck plays his namesake, the miserable miser Ebeneezer Scrooge. His only care is his desire for money. Arriving at the office he finds his loyal, overworked and underpaid employee, Bob Cratchit, played by Mickey Mouse, putting a lump of coal into the stove to defrost the ink he must use to write in the ledger book. This infuriates Scrooge and he makes the humble Mr. Cratchit work late although it's Christmas Eve. Even so, Mickey asks for half a day off for Christmas. Alone that night, Scrooge is visited by his late business partner who warns him that he must change his greedy ways. Scrooge then endures visits from three ghosts who change his life forever. They take Scrooge on a journey that teaches him that Christmas is a time for giving and sharing.

MICKEY'S CHRISTMAS CAROL QUIKREFERENCE

	TITLE	ITEM #	AVAILABLE
OPEN EDITIONS:			
Mickey Ornament	"And A Merry Christmas To You…"	41144	7/97
Minnie Ornament	Mrs. Cratchit	41145	7/97
Scrooge McDuck Ornament	"Bah-Humbug!"	41146	7/97
Jiminy Cricket Ornament	The Ghost Of Christmas Past	41251	7/98

"And A Merry Christmas To You…"

TITLE: "And A Merry Christmas To You…"
ORNAMENT: Mickey Mouse
ITEM NUMBER: 41144
SIZE: 4"
DATE OF ISSUE: 7/97

PLUSSING: None.
PRODUCTION CHANGES: None.
PARTICULARS: Animated adaptation of Charles Dickens' 1843 novel, *A Christmas Carol*. Film was nominated for an Academy Award. Certificate of Authenticity. Incised Annual Production Mark.
STATUS: OPEN EDITION.

YEAR	MARK	SRP	GBTru
❏ 1997		$50	**$50**
❏ 1998		50	**50**
❏ 1999		50	**50**

Mickey's Christmas Carol   125

Mrs. Cratchit

TITLE: Mrs. Cratchit
ORNAMENT: Minnie Mouse
ITEM NUMBER: 41145
SIZE: 3.25"
DATE OF ISSUE: 7/97

PLUSSING: None.
PRODUCTION CHANGES: None.
PARTICULARS: Animated adaptation of Charles Dickens' 1843 novel, *A Christmas Carol*. Film was nominated for an Academy Award. Certificate of Authenticity. Incised Annual Production Mark.
STATUS: OPEN EDITION.

YEAR	MARK	SRP	GBTru
☐ 1997		$50	**$50**
☐ 1998		50	**50**
☐ 1999		50	**50**

"Bah-Humbug!"

TITLE: "Bah-Humbug!"
ORNAMENT: Scrooge McDuck
ITEM NUMBER: 41146
SIZE: 3.75"
DATE OF ISSUE: 7/97

PLUSSING: Spectacles: Wire-rimmed with real glass lenses.
PRODUCTION CHANGES: None.
PARTICULARS: Animated adaptation of Charles Dickens' 1843 novel, *A Christmas Carol*. Film was nominated for an Academy Award. Certificate of Authenticity. Incised Annual Production Mark.
STATUS: OPEN EDITION.

YEAR	MARK	SRP	GBTru
☐ 1997		$50	**$50**
☐ 1998		50	**50**
☐ 1999		50	**50**

Mickey's Christmas Carol

The Ghost Of Christmas Past

TITLE: The Ghost Of Christmas Past
ORNAMENT: Jiminy Cricket
ITEM NUMBER: 41251
SIZE: 3.75"
DATE OF ISSUE: 7/98

PLUSSING: Umbrella: Shaft is metal.
PRODUCTION CHANGES: None.
PARTICULARS: Animated adaptation of Charles Dickens' 1843 novel, *A Christmas Carol*. Film was nominated for an Academy Award. Certificate of Authenticity. Incised Annual Production Mark.
STATUS: OPEN EDITION.

YEAR	MARK	SRP	GBTru
☐ 1998	⊤	$50	**$50**
☐ 1999	◮	50	50

Notes: _____

Mickey's Christmas Carol

Mr. Duck Steps Out 1940

The 1940 Cartoon Classic *Mr. Duck Steps Out* was chosen to commemorate the 60th Birthday of a Disney character that began as a voice in search of the animator's artistic creation.

Donald Duck, it seems, started out as a voice. The voice was so unusual that Walt Disney decided to create a character to go with it. And so, a monumental event took place in a modest film short entitled *The Wise Little Hen*. Donald Duck, the high-energy, volatile, passionate, bouncy-yet-lazy rascal emerged to capture and delight audiences. A favorite in 76 countries, his escapades and exploits allow us to catch vicarious thrills as he bends all the rules.

Daisy, his one true love made her second appearance in this film, and it was here that she received her name. She has been the object of Donald's affection and fidelity for more than fifty years.

The trio of nephews debuted in 1938 and reappeared in this film to be triple terrors, creating obstacles to test the perseverance and agility of Uncle Donald jitterbugging with his beloved Daisy. True love wins out. Daisy showers Donald with kisses and the nephews have to wait for a different cartoon to try once again to best their favorite Uncle.

MR. DUCK STEPS OUT QUIKREFERENCE

	TITLE	ITEM #	AVAILABLE
LIMITED EDITION:			
Donald and Daisy	"Oh Boy, What A Jitterbug!"	41024	3/93 - 12/93
RETIRED EDITIONS:			
Nephew Dewey	"I Got Something For Ya"	41025	3/93 - 6/96
Scroll	*Mr. Duck Steps Out* Opening Title	41032	3/93 - 6/96
Nephew Huey	Tag-Along Trouble	41049	10/93 - 6/96
Nephew Louie	Tag-Along Trouble	41050	10/93 - 6/96
Uncle Donald	"With Love From Daisy"	41060	8/94 - 6/96

"Oh Boy, What A Jitterbug!"

TITLE: "Oh Boy, What A Jitterbug!"
FIGURINE: Donald and Daisy
ITEM NUMBER: 41024
SIZE: 6.6"
DATE OF ISSUE: 3/93

PLUSSING: Jacket: Required two firings to make Donald's plaid jacket. **Limited Edition Backstamp:** Each piece is crafted with a gold backstamp.
PRODUCTION CHANGES: Edition Limit: Limit was dropped from 7,500 to 5,000 Numbered Pieces due to production difficulties. **Rug Variations:** 1) Smooth and painted two shades of green; 2) Textured and painted as if braided. **Donald's Left Hand Variations:** 1) 3rd finger sticks out; 2) 3rd finger does not stick out.

PARTICULARS: Hand Numbered Certificate of Authenticity. Incised Annual Production Mark.
STATUS: LIMITED EDITION: 5,000 Hand Numbered Pieces. EDITION CLOSED 12/93.

YEAR	MARK	SRP	GBTru
❏ 1992	✺	$295	**$600**
❏ 1993	ℽ	295	**500**

Mr. Duck Steps Out

"I Got Somethin' For Ya"

TITLE: "I Got Somethin' For Ya"
FIGURINE: Nephew Dewey
ITEM NUMBER: 41025
SIZE: 4"
DATE OF ISSUE: 3/93

PLUSSING: None.
PRODUCTION CHANGES: None.
PARTICULARS: Certificate of Authenticity. Incised Annual Production Mark.
STATUS: RETIRED 6/96.

YEAR	MARK	SRP	GBTru
☐ 1992	✲	$65	**$65**
☐ 1993		65	**65**
☐ 1994		65	**65**
☐ 1995		65	**65**
☐ 1996		65	**65**

Mr. Duck Steps Out Opening Title

TITLE: *Mr. Duck Steps Out* Opening Title
SCROLL: Opening Title
ITEM NUMBER: 41032
SIZE: 1.6"
DATE OF ISSUE: 3/93

PLUSSING: None.
PRODUCTION CHANGES: None.
PARTICULARS: Certificate of Authenticity. Decal backstamp with WDCC logo and Annual Production Mark.
STATUS: RETIRED 6/96.

YEAR	MARK	SRP	GBTru
☐ 1993		$29	**$29**
☐ 1994		29	**29**
☐ 1995		29	**29**
☐ 1996		29	**29**

Mr. Duck Steps Out

Tag-Along Trouble

TITLE: Tag-Along Trouble
FIGURINE: Nephew Huey
ITEM NUMBER: 41049
SIZE: 4"
DATE OF ISSUE: 10/93

PLUSSING: Details: Huey and Louie look identical, however Huey's jacket is green. Louie's jacket is yellow. Also note opposite placement of tail and hat ribbons.
PRODUCTION CHANGES:
Backstamp: Initially, a small quantity was produced with Louie's backstamp. Add $75 to GBTru$ for this variation.
PARTICULARS: Certificate of Authenticity. Incised Annual Production Mark.
STATUS: RETIRED 6/96.

YEAR	MARK	SRP	GBTru
☐ 1993		$65	**$65**
☐ 1994		65	**65**
☐ 1995		65	**65**
☐ 1996		65	**65**

Tag-Along Trouble

TITLE: Tag-Along Trouble
FIGURINE: Nephew Louie
ITEM NUMBER: 41050
SIZE: 4"
DATE OF ISSUE: 10/93

PLUSSING: Details: Louie and Huey look identical, however Louie's jacket is yellow. Huey's jacket is green. Also note opposite placement of tail and hat ribbons.
PRODUCTION CHANGES:
Backstamp: Initially, a small quantity was produced with Huey's backstamp. Add $75 to GBTru$ for this variation.
PARTICULARS: Certificate of Authenticity. Incised Annual Production Mark.
STATUS: RETIRED 6/96.

YEAR	MARK	SRP	GBTru
☐ 1993		$65	**$65**
☐ 1994		65	**65**
☐ 1995		65	**65**
☐ 1996		65	**65**

Mr. Duck Steps Out

"With Love From Daisy"

TITLE: "With Love From Daisy"
FIGURINE: Uncle Donald
ITEM NUMBER: 41060
SIZE: 6.25"
DATE OF ISSUE: 8/94

PLUSSING: Donald's Jacket: Two firings make it plaid. **Daisy's Photo:** A miniature replica of the original including the message "With Love From Daisy." **Anniversary Backstamp:** *'Donald's 60th Birthday'* appears on all pieces produced in 1994. **Backstamp:** There are two versions of Collection Backstamp — Teal Green Background Logo and Boxed-in Logo. No specific date is associated with the change, both were used in 1994.

PRODUCTION CHANGES:
Backstamp: *'Donald's 60th Birthday'* done in green in error. (There are none in gold.)

PARTICULARS: Certificate of Authenticity. Incised Annual Production Mark.
STATUS: RETIRED 6/96.

YEAR	MARK	SRP	GBTru
❏ 1994 Anniv. Mark & Teal Green Logo	♀	$180	**$190**
❏ 1994 Anniv. Mark & Boxed-in Logo	♀	180	190
❏ 1995	∞	180	180
❏ 1996	~	180	180

Notes:

Mr. Duck Steps Out

Mulan
June 19, 1998

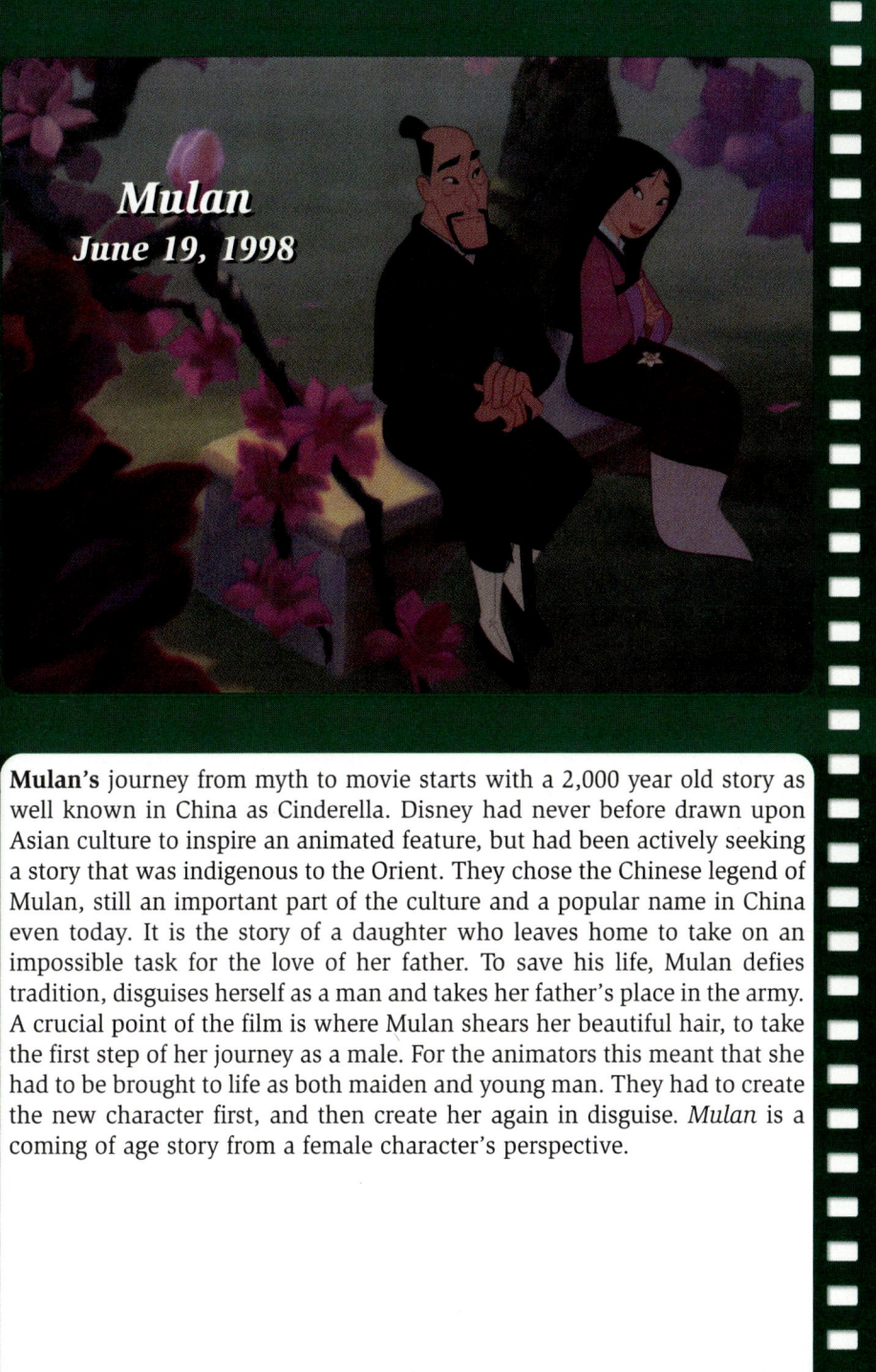

Mulan's journey from myth to movie starts with a 2,000 year old story as well known in China as Cinderella. Disney had never before drawn upon Asian culture to inspire an animated feature, but had been actively seeking a story that was indigenous to the Orient. They chose the Chinese legend of Mulan, still an important part of the culture and a popular name in China even today. It is the story of a daughter who leaves home to take on an impossible task for the love of her father. To save his life, Mulan defies tradition, disguises herself as a man and takes her father's place in the army. A crucial point of the film is where Mulan shears her beautiful hair, to take the first step of her journey as a male. For the animators this meant that she had to be brought to life as both maiden and young man. They had to create the new character first, and then create her again in disguise. *Mulan* is a coming of age story from a female character's perspective.

MULAN QUIKREFERENCE

	TITLE	ITEM #	AVAILABLE
OPEN EDITION:			
Mulan	Honorable Decision	41374	3/1/99 - 5/31/99

Honorable Decision

with Special Commission Authorization Form.

YEAR	MARK	SRP	GBTru
☐ 1998	⊤	$175	**$175**
☐ 1999	♟	175	**175**

TITLE: Honorable Decision
FIGURINE: Mulan
ITEM NUMBER: 41374
SERIES: Tribute Series, 1999
Selection: 5th & Final Issue
SIZE: 6"
DATE OF ISSUE: 3/99

PLUSSING: Sword: Pewter.
Backstamp: Includes special Tribute Series Logo.
PRODUCTION CHANGES: None.
PARTICULARS: Certificate of Authenticity. Incised Annual Production Mark. A certain amount of production will have a special "Cast Member" backstamp, Item Number 1201747, available by redemption certificate to all Cast Members.
STATUS: OPEN EDITION. Window for ordering is 3/1/99 to 5/31/99

Mulan

ON ICE
1935

On a brisk winter afternoon, Mickey proudly says, "Watch me!" and gives a dazzling display of skating expertise that has him leaping and turning all over the frozen pond. Some might even say he's showing off, but why not? His sweetheart Minnie is looking to be impressed as she tries to keep her balance. Meanwhile, Donald decides to play a trick on Pluto by placing skates on Pluto's paws. Donald gets a huge laugh as he watches Pluto fall all over the ice.

ON ICE QUIKREFERENCE

	TITLE	ITEM #	AVAILABLE
SCROLL:			
Scroll	*On Ice* Opening Title	41261	2/98
OPEN EDITIONS:			
Minnie Mouse	"Whee!"	41151	10/97
Mickey Mouse	"Watch Me!"	41270	2/98
Donald Duck	"Away We Go"	41396	8/99
Display Base	*On Ice* Base	41433	8/99

On Ice Opening Title

TITLE: *On Ice* Opening Title
SCROLL: Opening Title
ITEM NUMBER: 41261
SIZE: 1.6"
DATE OF ISSUE: 2/98

PLUSSING: None.
PRODUCTION CHANGES: None.
PARTICULARS: Certificate of Authenticity. Decal backstamp with WDCC logo and Annual Production Mark.
STATUS: OPEN EDITION.

YEAR	MARK	SRP	GBTru
☐ 1997		$29	**$29**
☐ 1998		29	**29**
☐ 1999		29	**29**

"Whee!"

TITLE: "Whee!"
FIGURINE: Minnie Mouse
ITEM NUMBER: 41151
SIZE: 6"
DATE OF ISSUE: 10/97

PLUSSING: Skates: Polished metal blades. **Hat:** Painted metal flower stem on hat.
PRODUCTION CHANGES: None.
PARTICULARS: Certificate of Authenticity. Incised Annual Production Mark.
STATUS: OPEN EDITION.

YEAR	MARK	SRP	GBTru
❑ 1997	윷	$165	**$165**
❑ 1998	⊤	165	**165**
❑ 1999	♙	165	**165**

"Watch Me!"

TITLE: "Watch Me!"
FIGURINE: Mickey Mouse
ITEM NUMBER: 41270
SIZE: 5"
DATE OF ISSUE: 2/98

PLUSSING: Skates: Polished metal blades. **Scarf:** Painted metal.
Birthday Backstamp: A special teal block print message *'Mickey's 70th Birthday'* was added to the backstamp of sculptures crafted in 1998.
PRODUCTION CHANGES: None.
PARTICULARS: Certificate of Authenticity. Incised Annual Production Mark. Some ⊤ sculptures were released in 1998 without the 70th Birthday backstamp.
STATUS: OPEN EDITION.

YEAR	MARK	SRP	GBTru
❑ 1997	윷	$165	**$165**
❑ 1998	⊤	165	**165**
w/70th Birthday Backstamp			
❑ 1998	⊤	165	**165**
w/o 70th Birthday Backstamp			
❑ 1999	♙	165	**165**

On Ice — 137

"Away We Go!"

TITLE: "Away We Go!"
FIGURINE: Donald Duck
ITEM NUMBER: 41396
SIZE: 4.75"
DATE OF ISSUE: 8/99

PLUSSING: Skates: Donald has metal skates.
PRODUCTION CHANGES: None.
PARTICULARS: Certificate of Authenticity. Incised Annual Production Mark.
STATUS: OPEN EDITION.

YEAR	MARK	SRP	GBTru
☐ 1999	🎩	$150	**$150**

On Ice Base

TITLE: *On Ice* Base
ACCESSORY BASE: Display Base
ITEM NUMBER: 41433
SIZE: 1.75"
DATE OF ISSUE: 8/99

PLUSSING: None.
PRODUCTION CHANGES: None.
PARTICULARS: Certificate of Authenticity. No Annual Production Mark.
STATUS: OPEN EDITION.

YEAR	MARK	SRP	GBTru
☐ 1999	No Mark	$50	**$50**

On Ice

One Hundred and One Dalmatians
January 25, 1961

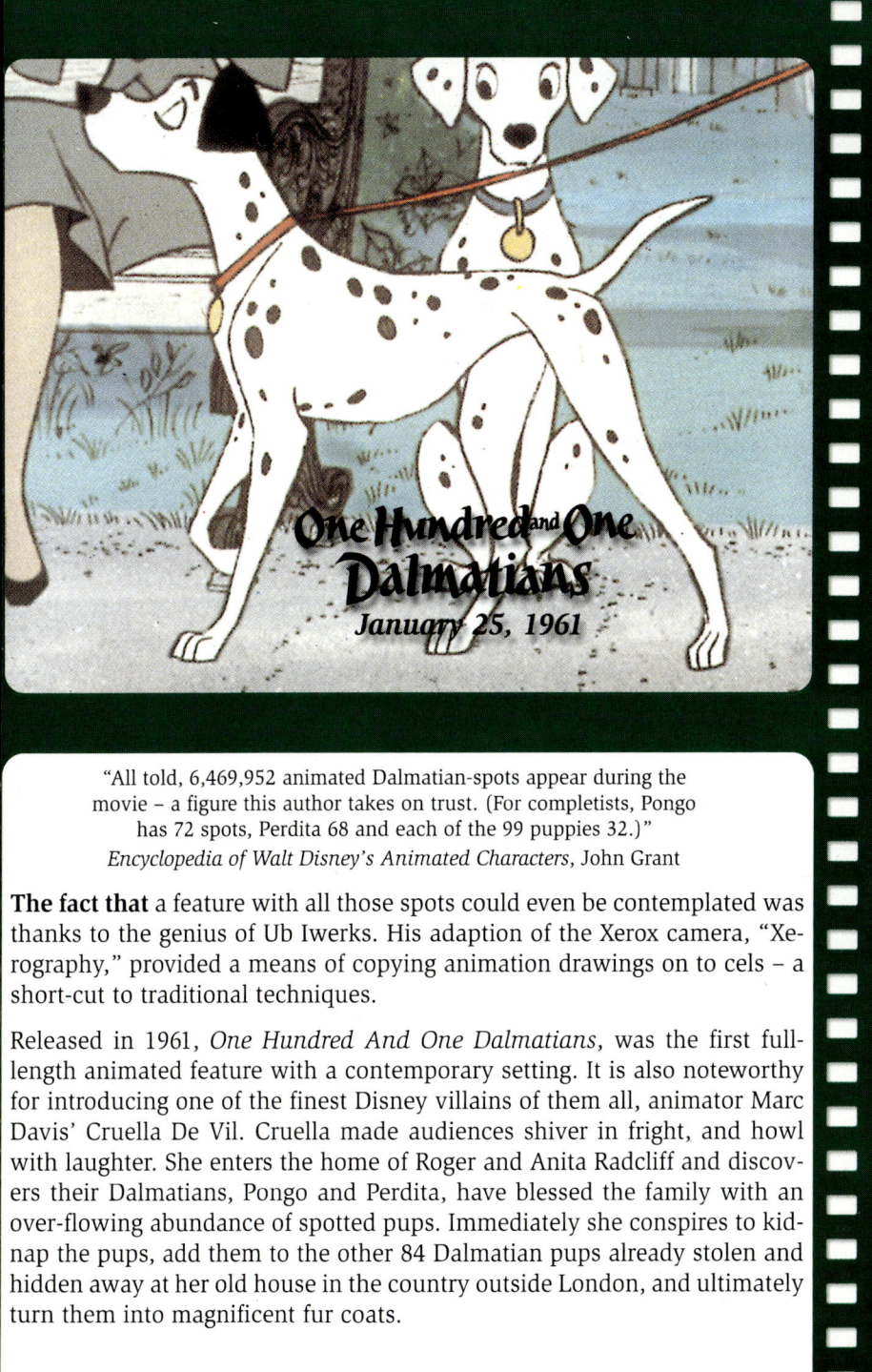

> "All told, 6,469,952 animated Dalmatian-spots appear during the movie – a figure this author takes on trust. (For completists, Pongo has 72 spots, Perdita 68 and each of the 99 puppies 32.)"
> *Encyclopedia of Walt Disney's Animated Characters*, John Grant

The fact that a feature with all those spots could even be contemplated was thanks to the genius of Ub Iwerks. His adaption of the Xerox camera, "Xerography," provided a means of copying animation drawings on to cels – a short-cut to traditional techniques.

Released in 1961, *One Hundred And One Dalmatians*, was the first full-length animated feature with a contemporary setting. It is also noteworthy for introducing one of the finest Disney villains of them all, animator Marc Davis' Cruella De Vil. Cruella made audiences shiver in fright, and howl with laughter. She enters the home of Roger and Anita Radcliff and discovers their Dalmatians, Pongo and Perdita, have blessed the family with an over-flowing abundance of spotted pups. Immediately she conspires to kidnap the pups, add them to the other 84 Dalmatian pups already stolen and hidden away at her old house in the country outside London, and ultimately turn them into magnificent fur coats.

The capture, escape, and chase is on. Cruella bullies the Radcliffs, collides with everyone she meets, and has two nefarious henchmen to assist her in her wicked plans. The dogs of London band together with Pongo and Perdita to rescue the kidnapped pups.

With great relief, good triumphs over evil. The pups, their mom Perdita, their dad Pongo, and Roger and Anita defeat Cruella's plans. Roger and Anita adopt the additional 84 pups, and with Nanny's help they plan to buy a Dalmatian farm and live happily ever after. Imagine the fun they had naming all those spotted pups!

ONE HUNDRED AND ONE DALMATIANS QUIKREFERENCE

	TITLE	ITEM #	AVAILABLE
SCROLL:			
Scroll	One Hundred And One Dalmatians Opening Title	41169	11/96
OPEN EDITIONS:			
Two Puppies on Newspaper	"Go Get Him, Thunder!"	41129	11/96
Rolly the Puppy	"I'm Hungry, Mother!"	41130	11/96
Lucky and Television	"Come On, Lucky..."	41131	11/96
Pongo with Pepper and Penny	Proud Pongo	41132	11/96
Perdita with Patch and Puppy	Patient Perdita	41133	11/96
EVENT PIECE:			
Lucky Ornament and Ottoman	Lucky	41080	10/21 & 22/95

COMPLEMENTARY PIECES:

ENCHANTED PLACES

OPEN EDITIONS:			
Sculpture	Cruella's Car	41230	11/96
Ornament	Cruella's Car	41245	7/97

WALT DISNEY COLLECTORS SOCIETY

ANIMATORS' CHOICE: (see page 269)
Cruella De Vil	"Anita Daahling!"	41088	3/95 - 3/96

DISNEY VILLAIN SERIES: (see page 281)
Cruella De Vil	"It's That De Vil Woman!"	41405	5/23/99 - 8/31/99

One Hundred And One Dalmatians Opening Title

TITLE: *One Hundred And One Dalmatians* Opening Title
SCROLL: Opening Title
ITEM NUMBER: 41169
SIZE: 1.6"
DATE OF ISSUE: 11/96

PLUSSING: None.
PRODUCTION CHANGES: None.
PARTICULARS: Certificate of Authenticity. Decal backstamp with WDCC logo and Annual Production Mark.
STATUS: OPEN EDITION.

YEAR	MARK	SRP	GBTru
❒ 1996		$29	$29
❒ 1997		29	29
❒ 1998		29	29
❒ 1999		29	29

"Go Get Him, Thunder!"

TITLE: "Go Get Him, Thunder!"
FIGURINE: Two Puppies on Newspaper
ITEM NUMBER: 41129
SIZE: 2.5"
DATE OF ISSUE: 11/96

PLUSSING: None.
PRODUCTION CHANGES: None.
PARTICULARS: Certificate of Authenticity. Incised Annual Production Mark.
STATUS: OPEN EDITION.

YEAR	MARK	SRP	GBTru
❒ 1996		$120	$120
❒ 1997		120	120
❒ 1998		120	120
❒ 1999		120	120

"I'm Hungry, Mother!"

TITLE: "I'm Hungry, Mother!"
FIGURINE: Rolly the Puppy
ITEM NUMBER: 41130
SIZE: 3"
DATE OF ISSUE: 11/96

PLUSSING: None.
PRODUCTION CHANGES: None.
PARTICULARS: Certificate of Authenticity. Incised Annual Production Mark.
STATUS: OPEN EDITION.

YEAR	MARK	SRP	GBTru
☐ 1996	〜	$65	$65
☐ 1997	只	65	65
☐ 1998	亻	65	65
☐ 1999	♙	65	65

"Come On, Lucky…"

TITLE: "Come On, Lucky…"
FIGURINE: Lucky and Television
ITEM NUMBER: 41131
SIZE: Puppy: 2.5", TV: 8"
DATE OF ISSUE: 11/96

PLUSSING: 2 Piece Set: TV is separate resin piece with decal of Lucky's favorite TV personality, *Thunderbolt*. **Real Metal Attachments:** Books, pipe, ashtray and tobacco pouch on top of TV. Chewed slipper attached to leg.
PRODUCTION CHANGES: Early Dealer Display TV: Picture in sepia tones. Other pieces were gray and white.
PARTICULARS: Certificate of Authenticity. Incised Annual Production Mark.
STATUS: OPEN EDITION.

YEAR	MARK	SRP	GBTru
☐ 1996	〜	$150	$150
☐ 1997	只	150	150
☐ 1998	亻	150	150
☐ 1999	♙	150	150

Proud Pongo

TITLE: Proud Pongo
FIGURINE: Pongo with Pepper and Penny
ITEM NUMBER: 41132
SIZE: 6.75"
DATE OF ISSUE: 11/96

PLUSSING: Dog Tag: Metal dog tag on Pongo. **Disneyana Convention Piece:** Special Backstamp on approximately 1,000 to 1,200 pieces includes the 9/3 to 9/7/96 Convention Logo.
PRODUCTION CHANGES: None.
PARTICULARS: Certificate of Authenticity. Incised Annual Production Mark.
STATUS: OPEN EDITION.

YEAR	MARK	SRP	GBTru
❏ 1996		$175	$350
❏ 1997		175	175
❏ 1998		175	175
❏ 1999		175	175

Patient Perdita

TITLE: Patient Perdita
FIGURINE: Perdita with Patch and Puppy
ITEM NUMBER: 41133
SIZE: 5"
DATE OF ISSUE: 11/96

PLUSSING: Dog Tag: Metal dog tag on Perdita.
PRODUCTION CHANGES: None.
PARTICULARS: Certificate of Authenticity. Incised Annual Production Mark.
STATUS: OPEN EDITION.

YEAR	MARK	SRP	GBTru
❏ 1996		$175	$175
❏ 1997		175	175
❏ 1998		175	175
❏ 1999		175	175

One Hundred And One Dalmatians

Lucky

TITLE: Lucky
ORNAMENT: Lucky and Ottoman
ITEM NUMBER: 41080
SIZE: Lucky: 3", Ottoman: 1"
DATE OF ISSUE: 10/95

PLUSSING: Spots: Horseshoe-shaped pattern of spots. **2 Piece Set:** Pup ornament can be displayed as a figurine leaning against the ottoman.
PRODUCTION CHANGES: None.
PARTICULARS: Certificate of Authenticity. Incised Annual Production Mark.
STATUS: EDITION CLOSED. Available exclusively at Fall Open House Events, 10/21 and 10/22/95.

YEAR	MARK	SRP	GBTru
❏ 1995	∽	$40	**$45**

Cruella's Car

TITLE: Cruella's Car
SCULPTURE: Cruella's Car
ITEM NUMBER: 41230
SIZE: 9"
DATE OF ISSUE: 11/96

PLUSSING: Door: Driver's side door opens. **Car Trim:** Grill, horn and bumpers are chrome-plated. **Wheels:** Wheels turn and hubcaps are monogrammed.
PRODUCTION CHANGES: None.
PARTICULARS: Enchanted Places. Certificate of Authenticity. Incised Annual Production Mark.
STATUS: OPEN EDITION.

YEAR	MARK	SRP	GBTru
❏ 1996	◡	$165	**$165**
❏ 1997	우	165	**165**
❏ 1998	大	165	**165**
❏ 1999	♟	165	**165**

One Hundred And One Dalmatians

Cruella's Car

TITLE: Cruella's Car
ORNAMENT: Cruella's Car
ITEM NUMBER: 41245
SIZE: 3.5"
DATE OF ISSUE: 7/97

PLUSSING: None.
PRODUCTION CHANGES: None.
PARTICULARS: Enchanted Places. Certificate of Authenticity. Sticker Annual Production Mark.
STATUS: OPEN EDITION.

YEAR	MARK	SRP	GBTru
☐ 1997	🜉	$45	**$45**
☐ 1998	🜋	45	**45**
☐ 1999	🜍	45	**45**

Notes: _____

One Hundred And One Dalmatians

Peter Pan
February 5, 1953

Not quite exactly as expected.

Those few words sum up the genius of Walt Disney in transferring Sir James M. Barrie's play and books to the screen. Most people were very familiar with the popular story and anticipated the Disney version to recreate the stage effects.

Disney made Peter Pan his own. Walt was very concerned with Peter's depiction. Working closely with animator Milt Kahl, Pan came to life as an impish, willful, funny, exasperating, lovable twelve year old boy. It is said that Disney's personality was injected into the animator's pen to be captured forever in a boy and story that delights the audience by wrapping them in a land of fable, enchantment, adventure and magic.

Originally seen on the stage as a beam of light, Tinker Bell came to the screen as a sprightly, flirtatious, sometimes hot-tempered, petite fairy. Today she often represents Disney in a range of appearances from television to theme parks.

Captain Hook, the pirate, was a menacing, vain, scheming braggart. An excellent villain, he worked hard at pursuing Peter. After his unlucky encounter with the crocodile, Hook was forever peering over his shoulder to check on the location of the snapping jaws.

Peter Pan

The Crocodile, with large snapping jaws and offstage tick-tock, kept his focus on Captain Hook, determined to complete a pirate dinner.

PETER PAN QUIKREFERENCE

	TITLE	ITEM #	AVAILABLE
EVENT PIECES:			
Mr. Smee	"Oh dear, dear, dear."	41062	9/94 - 8/95
Tinker Bell Ornament	Tinker Bell	41119	5/4 & 5/5/96
Display Stand	Tinker Bell Ornament Display Stand	41127	5/4 & 5/5/96
LIMITED EDITION:			
Tinker Bell	"A Firefly! A Pixie! Amazing!"	41045	6/94 - 9/94
SUSPENDED EDITIONS:			
Peter Pan	"Nobody Calls Pan A Coward!"	41043	6/94 - 3/98
Captain Hook	"I've Got You This Time!"	41044	6/94 - 3/98
Scroll	*Peter Pan* Opening Title	41047	6/94 - 3/98
Crocodile	"Tick-Tock, Tick-Tock"	41054	6/94 - 3/98

COMPLEMENTARY PIECES:

ENCHANTED PLACES

OPEN EDITION:			
Ornament	Captain Hook's Ship	41243	7/97
LIMITED EDITION:			
Sculpture	Captain Hook's Ship	41209	8/96
RETIRED:			
Miniature	Captain Hook	41219	8/96

WALT DISNEY COLLECTORS SOCIETY

ANIMATORS' CHOICE: (see page 271)			
Tinker Bell	"Tinker Bell Pauses To Reflect"	41366	1999

Peter Pan 147

"Oh dear, dear, dear."

TITLE: "Oh dear, dear, dear."
FIGURINE: Mr. Smee
ITEM NUMBER: 41062
SIZE: 5"
DATE OF ISSUE: 9/94

PLUSSING: Backstamp: A special backstamp was designed for the Events-Only Sculpture. **Eyeglasses:** Real glass lenses and gold wire frames.
PRODUCTION CHANGES: Teal Green Background Logo replaced with revised Boxed-in Logo during 1994. *Newsflash* 2/95 issue stated half of the sculptures were crafted with the Teal Green Background Logo and half with the Boxed-in Logo.
PARTICULARS: Certificate of Authenticity. Incised Annual Production Mark.
STATUS: EDITION CLOSED. Was available 9/94 to 8/95 at Special Events.

YEAR	MARK	SRP	GBTru
❒ 1994	♀	$90	**$100**
Teal Green Logo			
❒ 1994	♀	90	90
Boxed-in Logo			

Tinker Bell

TITLE: Tinker Bell
ORNAMENT: Tinker Bell
ITEM NUMBER: 41119
SIZE: 4"
DATE OF ISSUE: 5/96

PLUSSING: Wings: Opalescent paint on wings.
PRODUCTION CHANGES: None.
PARTICULARS: Certificate of Authenticity. Incised Annual Production Mark.
STATUS: EDITION CLOSED. Was available 5/4 and 5/5/96 at Spring Open House Events.

YEAR	MARK	SRP	GBTru
❒ 1996	ᗢ	$50	**$77**

Peter Pan

Tinker Bell Ornament Display Stand

TITLE: Tinker Bell Ornament Display Stand
ACCESSORY: Display Stand
ITEM NUMBER: 41127
SIZE: 7.5"
DATE OF ISSUE: 5/96

PLUSSING: Paint: A Peter Pan green.
PRODUCTION CHANGES: None.
PARTICULARS: No Certificate of Authenticity. Incised Annual Production Mark.
STATUS: EDITION CLOSED 5/96. Spring 1996 Open House Event Accessory Piece.

YEAR	MARK	SRP	GBTru
❏ 1996	⌒	$25	**$42**

"A Firefly! A Pixie! Amazing!"

TITLE: "A Firefly! A Pixie! Amazing!"
FIGURINE: Tinker Bell
ITEM NUMBER: 41045
SIZE: 5"
DATE OF ISSUE: 6/94

PLUSSING: Anniversary Backstamp: A special gold message '40th Anniversary' was added to the backstamp of sculptures crafted in 1993.
PRODUCTION CHANGES: Edition Limit: Originally announced at 10,000, changed to 12,500.
Backstamp: Two variations have been noted: 1) § with '40th Anniversary' missing, and, 2) ⚘ with 'Limited Edition' missing.
PARTICULARS: Hand Numbered Certificate of Authenticity. Incised Annual Production Mark.
STATUS: LIMITED EDITION: 12,500 Hand Numbered Pieces.

YEAR	MARK	SRP	GBTru
❏ 1993	§ Anniv. Mark	$215	**$500**
❏ 1994	⚘	215	380

Peter Pan 149

"Nobody Calls Pan A Coward!"

TITLE: "Nobody Calls Pan A Coward!"
FIGURINE: Peter Pan
ITEM NUMBER: 41043
SIZE: 7.5"
DATE OF ISSUE: 6/94

PLUSSING: Anniversary Backstamp: A special gold message '40th Anniversary' was added to the backstamp of sculptures crafted in 1993. **Peter's Knife:** Handle is gold-plated, blade is silver-plated, sheath is bronze-colored.

PRODUCTION CHANGES: SRP Change: $165 to $175 in 1998.
PARTICULARS: Certificate of Authenticity. Incised Annual Production Mark.
STATUS: SUSPENDED 3/98.

YEAR	MARK	SRP	GBTru
☐ 1993	§ Anniv. Mark	$165	$220
☐ 1994		165	175
☐ 1995		165	175
☐ 1996		165	175
☐ 1997		165	175
☐ 1998		175	175

"I've Got You This Time!"

TITLE: "I've Got You This Time!"
FIGURINE: Captain Hook
ITEM NUMBER: 41044
SIZE: 8"
DATE OF ISSUE: 6/94

PLUSSING: Anniversary Backstamp: A special gold message '40th Anniversary' was added to the backstamp of sculptures crafted in 1993. **Scabbard & Sword:** Metal sword, with bronzed scabbard, silver-plated blade, gold-plated handle. **Shoe Buckles:** Gold-plated. **Hook:** Platinum-plated metal.
PRODUCTION CHANGES: Mold Change: Initially, Hook's hook hand was cast in two pieces. **SRP Change:** $275 to $290 in 1998.
PARTICULARS: Certificate of Authenticity. Incised Annual Production Mark.
STATUS: SUSPENDED 3/98.

YEAR	MARK	SRP	GBTru
☐ 1993	§ Anniv. Mark	$275	$600
☐ 1994		275	290
☐ 1995		275	290
☐ 1996		275	290
☐ 1997		275	290
☐ 1998		290	290

Peter Pan Opening Title

TITLE: *Peter Pan* Opening Title
SCROLL: Opening Title
ITEM NUMBER: 41047
SIZE: 1.6"
DATE OF ISSUE: 6/94

PLUSSING: None.
PRODUCTION CHANGES: None.
PARTICULARS: Certificate of Authenticity. Decal backstamp with WDCC logo and Annual Production Mark.
STATUS: SUSPENDED 3/98.

YEAR	MARK	SRP	GBTru
❒ 1993	🎵	$29	**$35**
❒ 1994	🎵	29	**29**
❒ 1995	〰	29	**29**
❒ 1996	〰	29	**29**
❒ 1997	🎵	29	**29**
❒ 1998	✝	29	**29**

"Tick-Tock, Tick-Tock"

TITLE: "Tick-Tock, Tick-Tock"
FIGURINE: Crocodile
ITEM NUMBER: 41054
SIZE: 6.25"
DATE OF ISSUE: 6/94

PLUSSING: Tick-Tock: A mechanism inside the body creates the sound of the clock.
PRODUCTION CHANGES: None.
PARTICULARS: Certificate of Authenticity. Incised Annual Production Mark.
STATUS: SUSPENDED 3/98.

YEAR	MARK	SRP	GBTru
❒ 1994	🎵	$315	**$315**
❒ 1995	〰	315	**315**
❒ 1996	〰	315	**315**
❒ 1997	🎵	315	**315**
❒ 1998	✝	315	**315**

Peter Pan 151

The Jolly Roger

TITLE: The Jolly Roger
ORNAMENT: Captain Hook's Ship
ITEM NUMBER: 41243
SIZE: 3.15"
DATE OF ISSUE: 7/97

PLUSSING: Rigging: Black Thread.
PRODUCTION CHANGES: None.
PARTICULARS: Enchanted Places. Certificate of Authenticity. Incised Annual Production Mark.
STATUS: OPEN EDITION.

YEAR	MARK	SRP	GBTru
☐ 1997		$45	**$45**
☐ 1998		45	**45**
☐ 1999		45	**45**

The Jolly Roger

TITLE: The Jolly Roger
SCULPTURE: Captain Hook's Ship
ITEM NUMBER: 41209
SIZE: 9.5"
DATE OF ISSUE: 8/96

PLUSSING: Props: Ship body cast in pewter. Ropes and rigging are handtied. Ship's wheel rotates.
PRODUCTION CHANGES: None.
PARTICULARS: Enchanted Places. Certificate of Authenticity. Incised Annual Production Mark. Hand Engraved Serial Number. Registration Card redeemable for a deed "signed" by the setting's original "owner," transferring ownership. Sculpture comes with a wood display base with engraved brass nameplate.
STATUS: LIMITED EDITION: 10,000 Hand Numbered Pieces.

YEAR	MARK	SRP	GBTru
☐ 1996		$475	**$485**
☐ 1997		475	**475**

Peter Pan

NO POSTAGE
NECESSARY
IF MAILED
IN THE
UNITED STATES

BUSINESS REPLY MAIL
FIRST-CLASS MAIL PERMIT 9640 PACIFIC GROVE, CALIFORNIA

POSTAGE WILL BE PAID BY ADDRESSEE

GREENBOOK

Collectors' Information Services
P.O. Box 645
Pacific Grove CA 93950-9989

Thank You for purchasing this GREENBOOK Guide. We'd like to let you know when updates are published and to learn a little bit more about you and how we can help you. Please return this postage-paid card to us and we'll also enter your name in our **Quarterly GREENBOOK Guide and Collectible Thank You Giveaway Drawing.** We'll be giving away a Guide and a current piece from the Collection covered four times a year…at the end of March, June, September and December. All responses received that quarter will go into the drawing.

Please visit our website at: www.greenbooks.com

NAME:

COMPLETE STREET ADDRESS:

TOWN & ZIP:

TELEPHONE: _____ EMAIL ADDRESS:

☐ I own a computer w/CD drive & would like information on GREENBOOK Contemporary Collectible CD Roms.

I purchased/received the GREENBOOK Guide to: *(Check All That Apply)*
☐ Beanie Babies ☐ Department 56® Villages ☐ Harbour Lights ☐ Precious Moments Company Dolls
☐ Boyds Collectibles ☐ Department 56® Snowbabies™ ☐ Precious Moments® Collection
☐ Charming Tails ☐ Hallmark Keepsake Ornaments ☐ Walt Disney Classics Collections
☐ Cherished Teddies™ ☐ Hallmark Kiddie Cars

I collect: *(Check All That Apply)*
☐ Annalee Dolls ☐ Christopher Radko Ornaments ☐ Harbour Lights ☐ Precious Moments Company Dolls
☐ Armani Figurines ☐ Coca Cola Collectibles ☐ Harmony Kingdom ☐ Precious Moments® Collection
☐ Barbie ☐ Department 56® Villages ☐ Hummel Figurines by Goebel ☐ Sarah's Attic
☐ Beanie Babies ☐ Department 56® Snowbabies™ ☐ Berta Hummel Collectibles ☐ Seraphim Angels by Roman
☐ Thomas Blackshear Sculptures ☐ Dreamsicles ☐ Emmet Kelly, Jr. ☐ Shelia's Collectibles
☐ Boyds Collectibles ☐ Fenton Glass ☐ Thomas Kinkaide ☐ Steiff
☐ Cat's Meow ☐ Greenwich Workshop ☐ Sandra Kuck Figurines ☐ Swarovski Silver Crystal
☐ Charming Tails ☐ Hallmark Keepsake Ornaments ☐ Lefton Carousel Collection ☐ Walt Disney Classics Collection
☐ Cherished Teddies™ ☐ Hallmark Kiddie Cars ☐ Lladro ☐ Other _____

Captain Hook

TITLE: Captain Hook
MINIATURE: Captain Hook
ITEM NUMBER: 41219
SIZE: 1"
DATE OF ISSUE: 8/96

PLUSSING: Miniature: Bronze, hand painted.
PRODUCTION CHANGES: None.
PARTICULARS: Enchanted Places. Green box, no picture on box, no Annual Production Mark.
STATUS: CLOSED EDITION.

YEAR	MARK	SRP	GBTru
☐ 1996	No Mark	$50	**$50**

Notes: _____
_____
_____
_____
_____
_____
_____
_____
_____
_____
_____
_____

Peter Pan

Walt Disney's Pinocchio
February 7, 1940

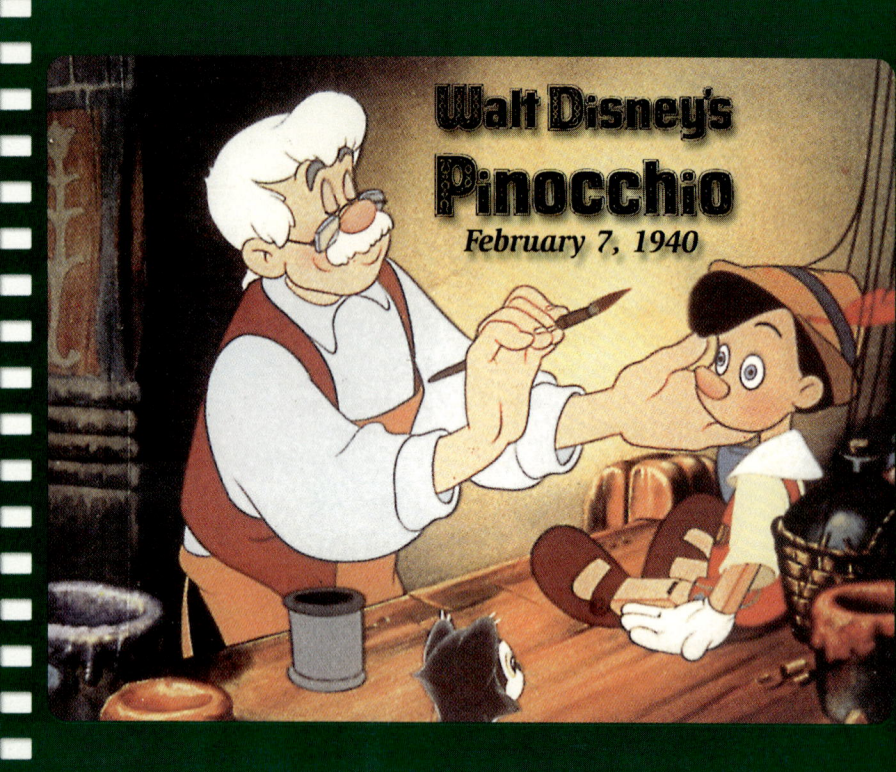

Pinocchio, Disney's "first and only FULL LENGTH FEATURE since *Snow White*," premiered on February 7, 1940. Widely regarded as the best cartoon ever made, some say its technical advances and depth and definition of character have never been surpassed.

It is the story of Geppetto, carpenter and puppet-maker, who wishes that the puppet, Pinocchio, would become a real boy. The Wishing Star hears Geppetto's words. Descending from the sky, the Blue Fairy brings life to the puppet but tells him he will remain an animated marionette until he proves himself brave, truthful and unselfish. Thus begins an odyssey that will test Pinocchio's virtue and end with him becoming a real boy when he is reunited with his father and his home. Jiminy Cricket, appointed Pinocchio's conscience by the Blue Fairy, and our narrator, does his best to protect, teach and guide Pinocchio along the way.

Pinocchio is not just another fairy tale but a great fable that examines the conflicts of right and wrong and the choices involved in good over evil. What small child hasn't been threatened with the thought that their nose would grow longer like Pinocchio's if they told a lie?

"When You Wish Upon A Star" won the Academy Award as Best Song of 1940. The entire Pinocchio score including the lesser known "Give A Little Whistle" and "Hi-Diddle-Dee-Dee, An Actor's Life For Me" was honored with another Oscar that same year.

PINOCCHIO QUIKREFERENCE

	TITLE	ITEM #	AVAILABLE
SCROLL:			
Scroll	*Pinocchio* Opening Title	41116	9/96
EVENT PIECE:			
Blue Fairy	Making Dreams Come True	41139	9/97 - 11/97
RETIRED EDITIONS:			
Jiminy Cricket	"Wait For Me, Pinoke!"	41109	9/96 - 11/98
Pinocchio	"Good-bye, Father"	41110	9/96 - 11/98
Figaro	"Say Hello To Figaro"	41111	9/96 - 11/98
Geppetto	"Good-bye, Son"	41114	9/96 - 11/98

COMPLEMENTARY PIECES:

ENCHANTED PLACES

ANNUALS:			
Sculpture	Geppetto's Toy Creations (Hutch)	41315	10/98 - 12/98
Miniature	Jiminy Cricket	41335	10/98 - 12/98
RETIRED EDITIONS:			
Sculpture	Geppetto's Toy Shop	41207	3/96 - 11/98
Miniature	Pinocchio	41217	6/96 - 11/98

WALT DISNEY COLLECTORS SOCIETY

MEMBERSHIP GIFT SCULPTURE: (see page 264)
| Jiminy Cricket | "Cricket's The Name, Jiminy Cricket" | 41035 | 1993 |

Pinocchio Opening Title

TITLE: *Pinocchio* Opening Title
SCROLL: Opening Title
ITEM NUMBER: 41116
SIZE: 1.6"
DATE OF ISSUE: 9/96

PLUSSING: None.
PRODUCTION CHANGES: None.
PARTICULARS: Certificate of Authenticity. Decal backstamp with WDCC logo and Annual Production Mark.
STATUS: OPEN EDITION.

YEAR	MARK	SRP	GBTru
☐ 1996		$29	**$29**
☐ 1997		29	29
☐ 1998		29	29
☐ 1999		29	29

Making Dreams Come True

TITLE: Making Dreams Come True
FIGURINE: Blue Fairy
ITEM NUMBER: 41139
SIZE: 9.5"
DATE OF ISSUE: 9/97

PLUSSING: Wand: Metal. **Gown:** Opalescent paint.
PRODUCTION CHANGES: None.
PARTICULARS: Certificate of Authenticity. Incised Annual Production Mark. A pin duplicating the "Official Conscience" badge given to Jiminy Cricket by the Blue Fairy was a gift with purchase.
STATUS: EDITION CLOSED 11/97. 1997 Fall Event Piece.

YEAR	MARK	SRP	GBTru
☐ 1997		$150	**$150**

"Wait For Me, Pinoke!"

TITLE: "Wait For Me, Pinoke!"
FIGURINE: Jiminy Cricket
ITEM NUMBER: 41109
SIZE: 3"
DATE OF ISSUE: 9/96

PLUSSING: None.
PRODUCTION CHANGES: SRP Change: $85 to $90 in 1998.
PARTICULARS: Certificate of Authenticity. Incised Annual Production Mark.
STATUS: RETIRED 11/98.

YEAR	MARK	SRP	GBTru
☐ 1996		$85	**$90**
☐ 1997		85	**90**
☐ 1998		90	**90**

"Good-bye, Father"

TITLE: "Good-bye, Father"
FIGURINE: Pinocchio
ITEM NUMBER: 41110
SIZE: 5.5"
DATE OF ISSUE: 9/96

PLUSSING: Apple: Has a pewter stem.
PRODUCTION CHANGES: SRP Change: $125 to $135 in 1998.
PARTICULARS: Certificate of Authenticity. Incised Annual Production Mark.
STATUS: RETIRED 11/98.

YEAR	MARK	SRP	GBTru
☐ 1996		$125	**$135**
☐ 1997		125	**135**
☐ 1998		135	**135**

Pinocchio

"Say Hello To Figaro"

TITLE: "Say Hello To Figaro"
FIGURINE: Figaro
ITEM NUMBER: 41111
SIZE: 2.5"
DATE OF ISSUE: 9/96

PLUSSING: None.
PRODUCTION CHANGES: None.
PARTICULARS: Certificate of Authenticity. Incised Annual Production Mark.
STATUS: RETIRED 11/98.

YEAR	MARK	SRP	GBTru
☐ 1996		$65	**$65**
☐ 1997		65	**65**
☐ 1998		65	**65**

"Good-bye, Son"

TITLE: "Good-bye, Son"
FIGURINE: Geppetto
ITEM NUMBER: 41114
SIZE: 8.25"
DATE OF ISSUE: 9/96

PLUSSING: Eyeglasses: Brass wire with glass lenses. **Shoes:** Gold-colored paint used to highlight the buckles.
PRODUCTION CHANGES: SRP Change: $145 to $155 in 1998.
PARTICULARS: Certificate of Authenticity. Incised Annual Production Mark.
STATUS: RETIRED 11/98.

YEAR	MARK	SRP	GBTru
☐ 1996		$145	**$155**
☐ 1997		145	**155**
☐ 1998		155	**155**

Pinocchio

Geppetto's Toy Creations

TITLE: Geppetto's Toy Creations
SCULPTURE: Geppetto's Toy Hutch
ITEM NUMBER: 41315
SIZE: 8.75"
DATE OF ISSUE: 10/98

PLUSSING: Hutch: Thirty attachments added to hutch. **Duck:** Pewter wind-up key. **Music Box:** Sterling Silver wind-up key. **Elephant Roller Toy:** Real string hangs over edge of hutch. **Hutch Door:** Hinged and opens to reveal more toys. **Paint:** Original color palettes from film were used to create the colors.
PRODUCTION CHANGES: None.
PARTICULARS: Enchanted Places. Certificate of Authenticity. Incised Annual Production Mark.
STATUS: 1998 ANNUAL.

YEAR	MARK	SRP	GBTru
☐ 1998	⊤	$125	**$125**

Jiminy Cricket

TITLE: Jiminy Cricket
MINIATURE: Jiminy Cricket
ITEM NUMBER: 41335
SIZE: 1"
DATE OF ISSUE: 10/98

PLUSSING: Miniature: Bronze, hand painted.
PRODUCTION CHANGES: None.
PARTICULARS: Enchanted Places. Green box, picture on box, sticker Annual Production Mark on box and on base of miniature.
STATUS: 1998 ANNUAL.

YEAR	MARK	SRP	GBTru
☐ 1998	⊤	$50	**$50**

Pinocchio

Geppetto's Toy Shop

TITLE: Geppetto's Toy Shop
SCULPTURE: Geppetto's Toy Shop
ITEM NUMBER: 41207
SIZE: 6"
DATE OF ISSUE: 3/96

PLUSSING: Props: Pewter toys in window, lantern at back door, pewter water trough with clear resin water, pewter water pump, chimney, mailbox, signboards.
PRODUCTION CHANGES: New logo and **backstamp** mid-1996. **Annual Production Mark** added mid-1996.
PARTICULARS: Enchanted Places. Certificate of Authenticity. Incised Annual Production Mark. Hand Engraved Serial Number. Registration Card redeemable for a deed "signed" by the setting's original "owner," transferring ownership.

Sculpture comes with a wood display base with engraved brass nameplate.
STATUS: RETIRED 11/98.

YEAR	MARK	SRP	GBTru
☐ 1996	No Mark	$150	**$175**
☐ 1996	〜	150	**150**
☐ 1997	早	150	**150**
☐ 1998	木	150	**150**

Pinocchio

TITLE: Pinocchio
MINIATURE: Pinocchio
ITEM NUMBER: 41217
SIZE: 1"
DATE OF ISSUE: 6/96

PLUSSING: Miniature: Bronze, hand painted.
PRODUCTION CHANGES: None.
PARTICULARS: Enchanted Places. Burgundy box, no picture on box, no Annual Production Mark.
STATUS: RETIRED 11/98.

YEAR	MARK	SRP	GBTru
☐ 1996	No Mark	$50	**$50**

Pluto's CHRISTMAS TREE 1952

In 1995, the Walt Disney Classics Collection introduced a new annual dated Holiday Series. Each year a sculpture and special matching ornament are planned to celebrate the Christmas season.

Mickey and Pluto bring in a tree to decorate with a little "help" from Chip and Dale hiding inside. After Pluto destroys the tree in his quest for the errant chipmunks, Mickey discovers the pair. As Goofy, Minnie and Donald sing "Deck The Halls" outside, Mickey tells Pluto to make friends. "After all," says Mickey "it is Christmas." Soon everyone is getting into the holiday spirit and all is well on a fine winter's evening.

PLUTO'S CHRISTMAS TREE
(Holiday Series)
QUIKREFERENCE

	TITLE	ITEM #	AVAILABLE
ANNUAL FIGURINES:			
Mickey Mouse	"Presents For My Pals"	41086	9/95 - 12/95
Pluto	Pluto Helps Decorate	41112	8/96 - 12/96
Chip 'N Dale with a Santa Candle	Little Mischief Makers	41163	7/97 - 12/97
Santa Candle	Santa Candle	41172	7/97 - 12/97
Minnie Mouse	Caroler Minnie	41308	7/98 - 12/98
Goofy	"'Tis The Season To Be Jolly"	41367	7/99 - 12/99
ANNUAL ORNAMENTS:			
Mickey Mouse	"Presents For My Pals"	41087	9/95 - 12/95
Pluto	Pluto Helps Decorate	41113	8/96 - 12/96
Chip 'N Dale	Little Mischief Makers	41190	7/97 - 12/97
Minnie Mouse	Caroler Minnie	41311	7/98 - 12/98
Goofy	"'Tis The Season To Be Jolly"	41368	7/99 - 12/99
ANNUAL DISC ORNAMENTS:			
Pluto	Pluto Helps Decorate	41142	8/96 - 12/96
Chip 'N Dale	Little Mischief Makers	41141	7/97 - 12/97
DISPLAY BASE:			
Display Base	Holiday Series	41140	7/97

"Presents For My Pals"

TITLE: "Presents For My Pals"
FIGURINE: Mickey Mouse
ITEM NUMBER: 41086
SERIES: Holiday Figurine Series, 1995 Selection: 1st Issue
SIZE: 5.5"
DATE OF ISSUE: 9/95

PLUSSING: Backstamp: Includes special Holiday Series Logo.
PRODUCTION CHANGES: None.
PARTICULARS: Certificate of Authenticity. Incised Annual Production Mark.
STATUS: DATED 1995 ANNUAL. Was available 9/95 to 12/95.

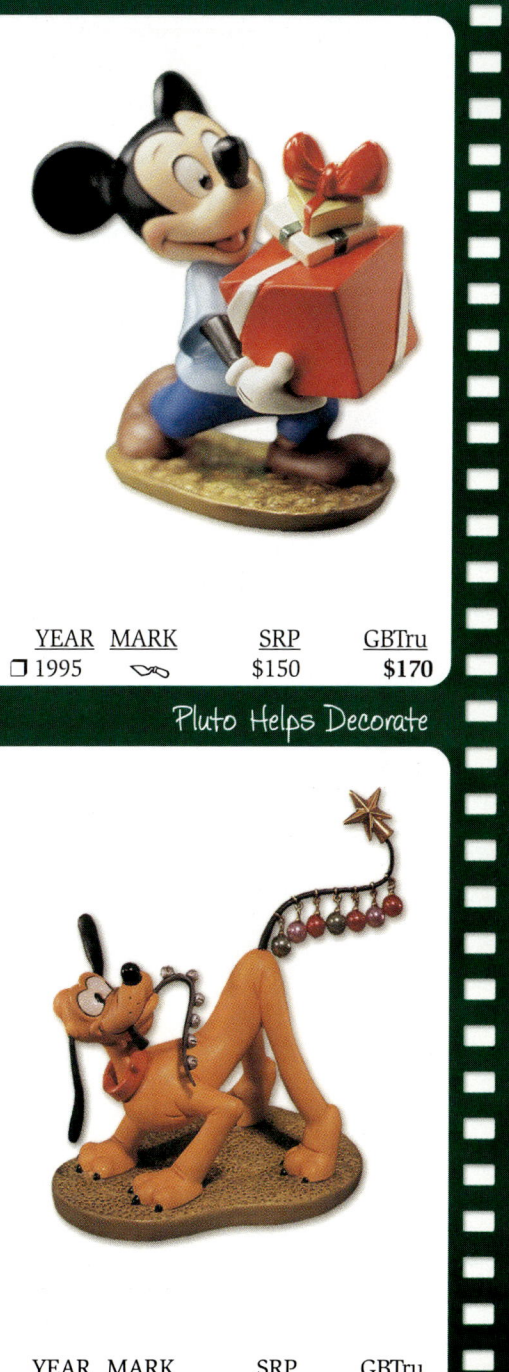

YEAR	MARK	SRP	GBTru
❑ 1995	∞	$150	**$170**

Pluto Helps Decorate

TITLE: Pluto Helps Decorate
FIGURINE: Pluto
ITEM NUMBER: 41112
SERIES: Holiday Figurine Series, 1996 Selection: 2nd Issue
SIZE: 5.5"
DATE OF ISSUE: 8/96

PLUSSING: Pluto's Ears, Tail, Bells, Bell Strap: Bronze. **Bead Ornaments:** Real glass. **Backstamp:** Includes special Holiday Series Logo.
PRODUCTION CHANGES: None.
PARTICULARS: Certificate of Authenticity. Incised Annual Production Mark.
STATUS: DATED 1996 ANNUAL. Was available 8/96 to 12/96.

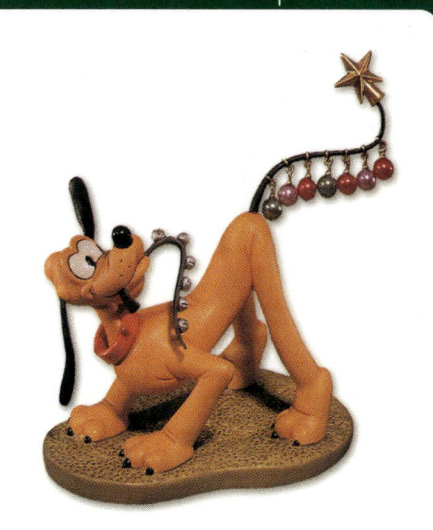

YEAR	MARK	SRP	GBTru
❑ 1996	⌒	$150	**$150**

Pluto's Christmas Tree

Little Mischief Makers

TITLE: Little Mischief Makers
FIGURINE: Chip 'N Dale & Santa Candle
ITEM NUMBER: 41163
SERIES: Holiday Figurine Series, 1997 Selection: 3rd Issue
SIZE: 4.18"
DATE OF ISSUE: 7/97

PLUSSING: Candle Snuffer: Real metal. **Backstamp:** Includes special Holiday Series Logo.
PRODUCTION CHANGES: None.
PARTICULARS: Certificate of Authenticity. Incised Annual Production Mark. Includes one Santa Candle figurine (not shown here), Item Number 41172, also available separately.
STATUS: DATED 1997 ANNUAL. Was available 7/97 to 12/97.

YEAR	MARK	SRP	GBTru
☐ 1997	⚲	$150	**$150**

Santa Candle

TITLE: Santa Candle
FIGURINE: Santa Candle
ITEM NUMBER: 41172
SERIES: Holiday Figurine Series, 1997 Selection: Part of 3rd Issue
SIZE: 4"
DATE OF ISSUE: 7/97

PLUSSING: Backstamp: Includes special Holiday Series Logo.
PRODUCTION CHANGES: None.
PARTICULARS: Certificate of Authenticity. Incised Annual Production Mark. Also was included in Item Number 41163, *Little Mischief Makers* above.
STATUS: DATED 1997 ANNUAL.

YEAR	MARK	SRP	GBTru
☐ 1997	⚲	$40	**$40**

Pluto's Christmas Tree

Caroler Minnie

TITLE: Caroler Minnie
FIGURINE: Minnie Mouse
ITEM NUMBER: 41308
SERIES: Holiday Figurine Series, 1998 Selection: 4th Issue
SIZE: 6"
DATE OF ISSUE: 7/98

PLUSSING: Backstamp: Includes special Holiday Series Logo.
PRODUCTION CHANGES: None.
PARTICULARS: Certificate of Authenticity. Incised Annual Production Mark.
STATUS: DATED 1998 ANNUAL. Was available 7/98 to 12/98.

YEAR	MARK	SRP	GBTru
❐ 1998	➇	$150	**$150**

"'Tis The Season To Be Jolly"

TITLE: "'Tis The Season To Be Jolly"
FIGURINE: Goofy
ITEM NUMBER: 41367
SERIES: Holiday Figurine Series, 1999 Selection: 5th Issue
SIZE: 7.75"
DATE OF ISSUE: 7/99

PLUSSING: Backstamp: Includes special Holiday Series Logo.
PRODUCTION CHANGES: None.
PARTICULARS: Certificate of Authenticity. Incised Annual Production Mark.
STATUS: DATED 1999 ANNUAL. Available 7/99 to 12/99.

YEAR	MARK	SRP	GBTru
❐ 1999	⌂	$175	**$175**

"Presents For My Pals"

TITLE: "Presents For My Pals"
ORNAMENT: Mickey Mouse
ITEM NUMBER: 41087
SERIES: Holiday Ornament Series, 1995 Selection: 1st Issue
SIZE: 2.75"
DATE OF ISSUE: 9/95

PLUSSING: Backstamp: Includes special Holiday Series Logo.
PRODUCTION CHANGES: None.
PARTICULARS: Certificate of Authenticity. Incised Annual Production Mark.
STATUS: DATED 1995 ANNUAL. Was available 9/95 to 12/95.

YEAR	MARK	SRP	GBTru
☐ 1995		$40	**$60**

Pluto Helps Decorate

TITLE: Pluto Helps Decorate
ORNAMENT: Pluto
ITEM NUMBER: 41113
SERIES: Holiday Ornament Series, 1996 Selection: 2nd Issue
SIZE: 3.75"
DATE OF ISSUE: 8/96

PLUSSING: Pluto's Ears, Tail, Bells, Bell Strap: Bronze. **Bead Ornaments:** Real glass. **Backstamp:** Includes special Holiday Series Logo.
PRODUCTION CHANGES: None.
PARTICULARS: Certificate of Authenticity. Incised Annual Production Mark.
STATUS: DATED 1996 ANNUAL. Was available 8/96 to 12/96.

YEAR	MARK	SRP	GBTru
☐ 1996		$50	**$50**

Pluto's Christmas Tree

Little Mischief Makers

TITLE: Little Mischief Makers
ORNAMENT: Chip 'N Dale
ITEM NUMBER: 41190
SERIES: Holiday Ornament Series, 1997 Selection: 3rd Issue
SIZE: 3.18"
DATE OF ISSUE: 7/97

PLUSSING: Candle Snuffer: Real metal. **Backstamp:** Includes special Holiday Series Logo.
PRODUCTION CHANGES: None.
PARTICULARS: Certificate of Authenticity. Incised Annual Production Mark.
STATUS: DATED 1997 ANNUAL. Was available 7/97 to 12/97.

YEAR	MARK	SRP	GBTru
❏ 1997	⚒	$50	**$50**

Caroler Minnie

TITLE: Caroler Minnie
ORNAMENT: Minnie Mouse
ITEM NUMBER: 41311
SERIES: Holiday Ornament Series, 1998 Selection: 4th Issue
SIZE: 3.25"
DATE OF ISSUE: 7/98

PLUSSING: Backstamp: Includes special Holiday Series Logo.
PRODUCTION CHANGES: None.
PARTICULARS: Certificate of Authenticity. Incised Annual Production Mark.
STATUS: DATED 1998 ANNUAL. Was available 7/98 to 12/98.

YEAR	MARK	SRP	GBTru
❏ 1998	⊤	$50	**$50**

Pluto's Christmas Tree

"'Tis The Season To Be Jolly"

TITLE: "'Tis The Season To Be Jolly"
ORNAMENT: Goofy
ITEM NUMBER: 41368
SERIES: Holiday Ornament Series, 1999 Selection: 5th Issue
SIZE: 4"
DATE OF ISSUE: 7/99

PLUSSING: Backstamp: Includes special Holiday Series Logo.
PRODUCTION CHANGES: None.
PARTICULARS: Certificate of Authenticity. Incised Annual Production Mark.
STATUS: DATED 1999 ANNUAL. Available 7/99 to 12/99.

YEAR	MARK	SRP	GBTru
❏ 1999	🎩	$50	**$50**

Pluto Helps Decorate

TITLE: Pluto Helps Decorate
ORNAMENT – DISC: Pluto
ITEM NUMBER: 41142
SERIES: Holiday Series Disc Ornament
SIZE: 3"
DATE OF ISSUE: 8/96

PLUSSING: Material: Flat porcelain circle. **Decal:** Portrays Pluto helping Mickey decorate the tree.
PRODUCTION CHANGES: None.
PARTICULARS: Designed to complement the "Pluto Helps Decorate" figurine and ornament. Certificate of Authenticity. Incised Annual Production Mark.
STATUS: Syndicated Catalog Exclusive.

YEAR	MARK	SRP	GBTru
❏ 1996	👟	$25	**$35**

168 Pluto's Christmas Tree

Little Mischief Makers

TITLE: Little Mischief Makers
ORNAMENT – DISC: Chip 'N Dale with Santa Candle
ITEM NUMBER: 41141
SERIES: Holiday Series Disc Ornament
SIZE: 3"
DATE OF ISSUE: 7/97

PLUSSING: Material: Flat porcelain circle. **Decal:** Portrays Dale disguising himself as a candle. Chip arrives in time to put out the light.
PRODUCTION CHANGES: None.
PARTICULARS: Designed to complement the "Little Mischief Makers" figurine and ornament. Certificate of Authenticity. Incised Annual Production Mark.
STATUS: Syndicated Catalog Exclusive.

YEAR	MARK	SRP	GBTru
❏ 1997	♀	$16	**$25**

Holiday Series Base

TITLE: Holiday Series Base
ACCESSORY BASE: Display Base
ITEM NUMBER: 41140
SERIES:
SIZE: 6.5" x 4" x 1"
DATE OF ISSUE: 7/97

PLUSSING: None.
PRODUCTION CHANGES: None.
PARTICULARS: Base is oval. No Annual Production Mark.
STATUS: OPEN EDITION.

YEAR	MARK	SRP	GBTru
❏ 1997	No Mark	$25	**$25**

Pluto's Christmas Tree

Pocahontas
June 23, 1995

For this romanticized tale of the beautiful Indian princess who falls in love with Captain John Smith, the film's creators found inspiration in the striking prominence of vertical and horizontal in the Virginia landscape. This helped define a general look for the film's landscape as well as for the characters themselves. Virginia's re-creation of the Jamestown colony and the Indian village was a further enhancement of the filmmakers' artistic take. Another influence was the clear, definite shapes and rich style of American illustration.

Pocahontas' tall, proud look is central to her personality. She is by design a celebration of the regal elegance of the Native American heroine. She is torn between her father's wish to destroy the settlers from across the water and her own wish to help them. There is a pivotal moment in the film when Pocahontas, accompanied by her companions, Meeko and Flit, holds John Smith's compass and realizes that it points to the path she must follow. One sees the beauty that captivated a soldier and the boundless spirit and courage that changed history and made Pocahontas a legend.

POCAHONTAS QUIKREFERENCE

	TITLE	ITEM #	AVAILABLE
CLOSED EDITION:			
Pocahontas	"Listen With Your Heart"	41098	3/1/96 - 4/28/96

"Listen With Your Heart"

TITLE: "Listen With Your Heart"
FIGURINE: Pocahontas
ITEM NUMBER: 41098
SERIES: Tribute Series, 1996
Selection: 2nd Issue
SIZE: 6.5"
DATE OF ISSUE: 3/96

PLUSSING: Compass: Gold paint highlights John Smith's compass held by Pocahontas. **Flit:** Bronze miniature Flit perches on Pocahontas' windblown hair.
Backstamp: Includes special Tribute Series Logo.
PRODUCTION CHANGES: Prototypes were shipped to retailers. Prototypes are Item Number 11098, have thinner bases and are marked "Pre-production."
PARTICULARS: Certificate of Authenticity. Incised Annual Production Mark.
STATUS: EDITION CLOSED. Window for ordering was 3/1/96 to 4/28/96 with Special Commission Authorization Form.

YEAR	MARK	SRP	GBTru
☐ 1996	〜	$225	**$375**
	Prototype		
☐ 1996	〜	225	**225**
	Regular Edition		

Pocahontas 171

Puppy Love
1933

Pluto has forgotten to buy a gift for his sweetheart Fifi. He knows that Mickey has bought gifts for Minnie and Fifi so he pulls a switch-a-roo and takes Mickey's gift for Minnie and pretends it is his gift to Fifi. Fifi now receives a beautiful box of candy. Minnie suddenly finds herself receiving a gift-wrapped bone. Mickey has to figure it all out and undo the mix-up. Luckily they all have a good laugh over the mischievous Pluto.

Mickey and Minnie are back in a nostalgic black and white in this cartoon.

PUPPY LOVE QUIKREFERENCE

	TITLE	ITEM #	AVAILABLE
SCROLL:			
Scroll	*Puppy Love* Opening Title	41326	11/98
OPEN EDITIONS:			
Mickey Mouse	"Brought You Something."	41324	11/98
Minnie Mouse	"Oh, It's Swell!"	41325	11/98
Fifi	Flirtatious Fifi	41336	11/98

Puppy Love Opening Title

TITLE: *Puppy Love* Opening Title
SCROLL: Opening Title
ITEM NUMBER: 41326
SIZE: 1.6"
DATE OF ISSUE: 11/98

PLUSSING: Paint: Done in the nostalgic black and white tones of the film's original palette.
PRODUCTION CHANGES: None.
PARTICULARS: Certificate of Authenticity. Decal backstamp with WDCC logo and Annual Production Mark.
STATUS: OPEN EDITION.

YEAR	MARK	SRP	GBTru
❏ 1998	🧙	$29	**$29**
❏ 1999	🎩	29	**29**

Puppy Love

"Brought You Something."

TITLE: "Brought You Something."
FIGURINE: Mickey Mouse
ITEM NUMBER: 41324
SIZE: 5.75"
DATE OF ISSUE: 11/98

PLUSSING: Tail: Metal. **Paint:** Done in the nostalgic black and white tones of the film's original palette. **Birthday Backstamp:** A special teal block print message *'Mickey's 70th Birthday'* was added to the backstamp of sculptures crafted in 1998.
PRODUCTION CHANGES: None.
PARTICULARS: Certificate of Authenticity. Incised Annual Production Mark.
STATUS: OPEN EDITION.

YEAR	MARK	SRP	GBTru
☐ 1998	⛏	$135	**$135**
☐ 1999	♟	135	**135**

"Oh, It's Swell!"

TITLE: "Oh, It's Swell!"
FIGURINE: Minnie Mouse
ITEM NUMBER: 41325
SIZE: 5.5"
DATE OF ISSUE: 11/98

PLUSSING: Tail: Metal. **Paint:** Done in the nostalgic black and white tones of the film's original palette.
PRODUCTION CHANGES: None.
PARTICULARS: Certificate of Authenticity. Incised Annual Production Mark.
STATUS: OPEN EDITION.

YEAR	MARK	SRP	GBTru
☐ 1998	⛏	$135	**$135**
☐ 1999	♟	135	**135**

Puppy Love

Flirtatious Fifi

TITLE: Flirtatious Fifi
FIGURINE: Fifi
ITEM NUMBER: 41336
SIZE: 3.25"
DATE OF ISSUE: 11/98

PLUSSING: Paint: Done in the nostalgic black and white tones of the film's original palette.
PRODUCTION CHANGES: None.
PARTICULARS: Certificate of Authenticity. Incised Annual Production Mark.
STATUS: OPEN EDITION.

YEAR	MARK	SRP	GBTru
❏ 1998	🎩	$95	**$95**
❏ 1999	🎩	95	**95**

Notes: _____

_____
_____
_____
_____
_____
_____
_____
_____
_____
_____
_____

Puppy Love

the Reluctant Dragon

June 20, 1941

In 1941, a whimsical tale, *The Reluctant Dragon*, was introduced as an animated short film.

Long ago, in a faraway land, when fire-breathing dragons menaced towns and countrysides, dragon-slaying knights helped protect the villagers. A dragon is sighted. Searching for the dragon, a young boy, slingshot in hand, finds a creature spouting pretentious poetry, not fire. The happy dragon enjoys company, notes the boy's curiosity and invites the boy to join him for a tea party.

Meanwhile, believing that the dragon will harm them, the villagers summon the knight, Sir Giles, to slay the fearful dragon. The boy introduces Sir Giles to the dragon to demonstrate his gentleness hoping to protect his new friend. Sir Giles, a gentle soul and a writer of bad poetry himself, recognizes that this is a good dragon. The dragon and the knight agree to engage in a comical, and wild make-believe battle where the grand finale is a "staged" dragon death scene. Sir Giles then ceremoniously raises the dragon from the dead, announces that he has "reformed" it from its assumed earlier habit of scourging the countryside, and watches as the Dragon is welcomed by the villagers as a new friend.

The End.

THE RELUCTANT DRAGON QUIKREFERENCE

	TITLE	ITEM #	AVAILABLE
LIMITED EDITION:			
Dragon	"The More The Merrier"	41072	2/96

"The More The Merrier"

TITLE: "The More The Merrier"
FIGURINE: Dragon
ITEM NUMBER: 41072
SIZE: 7"
DATE OF ISSUE: 2/96

PLUSSING: Dragon's Ears: Floppy ears are bronze. **Boy:** Boy sitting on Dragon's tummy is bronze. **Shakers:** Tiny salt and pepper shakers are pewter. **Bread Basket:** Cold cast resin. **Drop of Tea:** Drop at end of teapot spout is glass. **Ear Imprints:** Imprints of Mickey Mouse's ears can be found on Dragon's left knee and elbow.
PRODUCTION CHANGES: None.
PARTICULARS: Artist Proof: Item Number 31072. Hand Numbered Certificate of Authenticity. Incised Annual Production Mark.

STATUS: LIMITED EDITION: 7,500 Hand Numbered Pieces.

YEAR	MARK	SRP	GBTru
❏ 1995		$695	**$695**
❏ 1996		695	**695**

Reluctant Dragon, The 177

Scrooge McDuck and Money
March 23, 1967

Donald Duck's Uncle Scrooge is one of the world's superheroes. He doesn't fly through the air, wear a cape, or see through walls. What he is best at doing is making money and pinching pennies until they Quack. Carl Barks, the Disney "Duck Man," wanted to provide Donald with a cast of supporting players who would prod him on and into more misadventures. Scrooge's temper rivals Donald's so he became a foil and a sparring partner in many films. Every time Scrooge appeared in films he made money until he was impossibly rich. This movie became a film about economics. It shows Scrooge indulging in his favorite pleasure, playing in his stash of cash.

SCROOGE McDUCK AND MONEY QUIKREFERENCE

OPEN EDITION:

	TITLE	ITEM#	AVAILABLE
Scrooge McDuck	Money! Money! Money!	41152	5/97

Money! Money! Money!

TITLE: Money! Money! Money!
FIGURINE: Scrooge McDuck
ITEM NUMBER: 41152
SIZE: 6"
DATE OF ISSUE: 5/97

PLUSSING: Spectacles: Brass wire with glass lenses. **Coins:** Treated with a special metallic paint.
Anniversary Backstamp: A special gold script message '*30th Anniversary*' was added to the backstamp of sculptures crafted in 1997.
PRODUCTION CHANGES: None.
PARTICULARS: Certificate of Authenticity. Incised Annual Production Mark.
STATUS: OPEN EDITION.

YEAR	MARK	SRP	GBTru
❒ 1997	♀ Anniv. Mark	$175	**$175**
❒ 1998	⊤	175	**175**
❒ 1999	◮	175	**175**

Scrooge McDuck And Money

The Simple Things
1953

Mickey tries to have a relaxing day of fishing but it soon goes wrong when Pluto gets into mischief and a seagull chases them away.

THE SIMPLE THINGS QUIKREFERENCE

	TITLE	ITEM #	AVAILABLE
OPEN EDITION:			
Mickey Mouse	Somethin' Fishy	41363	3/99

Somethin' Fishy

TITLE: Somethin' Fishy
FIGURINE: Mickey Mouse
ITEM NUMBER: 41363
SIZE: 5.5"
DATE OF ISSUE: 3/99

PLUSSING: Pail: Real metal handle. **Fishing Pole:** Metal with fishing line. **Hook:** Real metal.
PRODUCTION CHANGES: None.
PARTICULARS: This was Mickey's last film appearance until the premier of *Mickey's Christmas Carol* in 1983. Certificate of Authenticity. Incised Annual Production Mark.
STATUS: OPEN EDITION.

YEAR	MARK	SRP	GBTru
❑ 1999	⌂	$150	**$150**

Sleeping Beauty

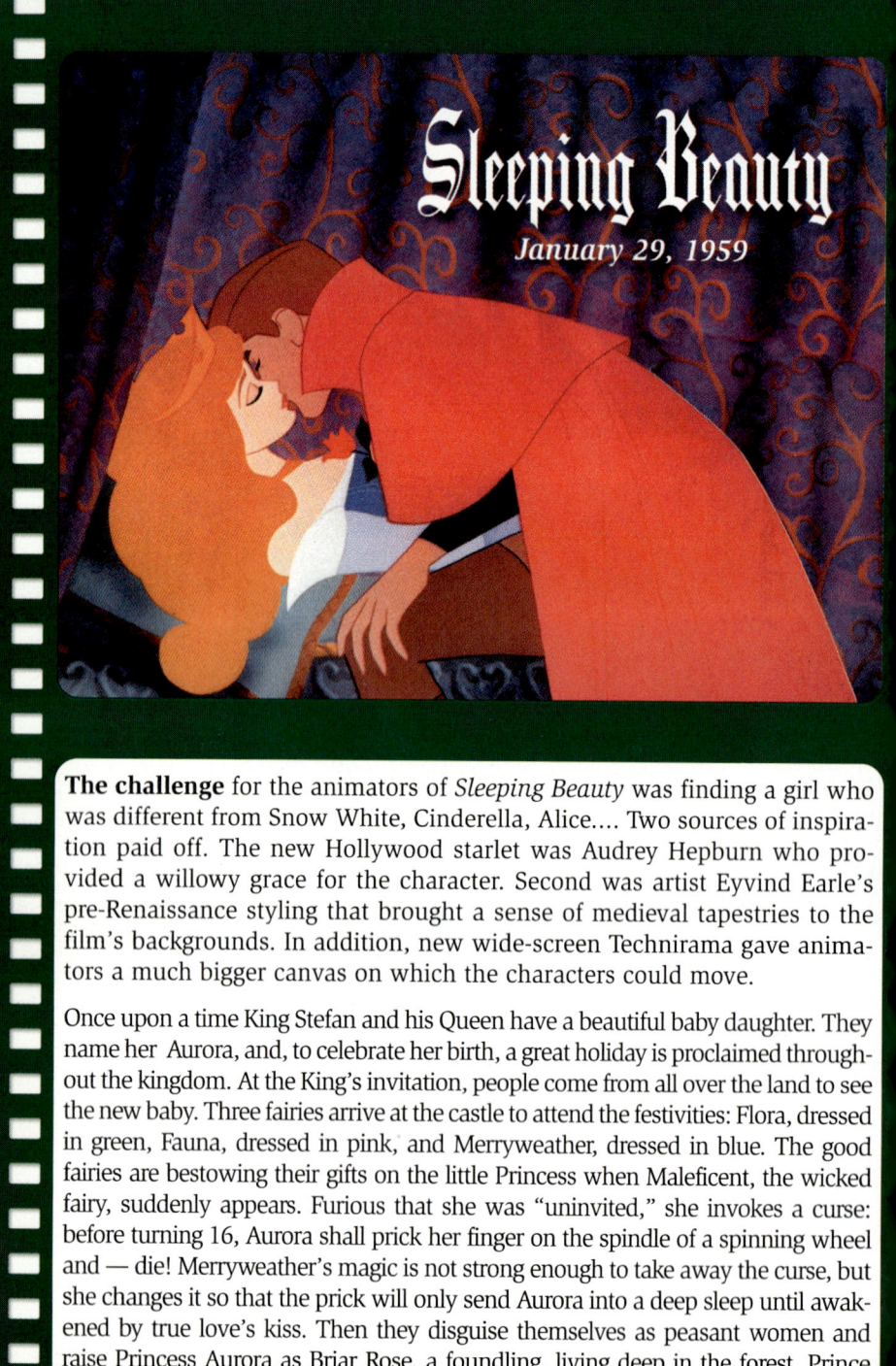

January 29, 1959

The challenge for the animators of *Sleeping Beauty* was finding a girl who was different from Snow White, Cinderella, Alice.... Two sources of inspiration paid off. The new Hollywood starlet was Audrey Hepburn who provided a willowy grace for the character. Second was artist Eyvind Earle's pre-Renaissance styling that brought a sense of medieval tapestries to the film's backgrounds. In addition, new wide-screen Technirama gave animators a much bigger canvas on which the characters could move.

Once upon a time King Stefan and his Queen have a beautiful baby daughter. They name her Aurora, and, to celebrate her birth, a great holiday is proclaimed throughout the kingdom. At the King's invitation, people come from all over the land to see the new baby. Three fairies arrive at the castle to attend the festivities: Flora, dressed in green, Fauna, dressed in pink, and Merryweather, dressed in blue. The good fairies are bestowing their gifts on the little Princess when Maleficent, the wicked fairy, suddenly appears. Furious that she was "uninvited," she invokes a curse: before turning 16, Aurora shall prick her finger on the spindle of a spinning wheel and — die! Merryweather's magic is not strong enough to take away the curse, but she changes it so that the prick will only send Aurora into a deep sleep until awakened by true love's kiss. Then they disguise themselves as peasant women and raise Princess Aurora as Briar Rose, a foundling, living deep in the forest. Prince Phillip, Aurora's betrothed, is riding through the woods one day, sees Briar Rose

Sleeping Beauty

and falls in love with her. While preparing for Aurora's sixteenth birthday, the domestically-challenged fairies resort to the use of magic to make a beautiful dress for the party. An argument breaks out between Fauna and Merryweather over whether the dress should be pink or blue and sparks begin to fly. Maleficent's raven, Diablo, who had been out hunting for the Princess, sees colored blasts of magic from their wands escaping out of the chimney of the cottage and tells his mistress. Maleficent finds Aurora, now back at King Stefan's castle, casts a spell on her and then leads her to the last spinning wheel in the entire land. She pricks her finger and falls into a deep sleep. But Prince Phillip's enchanted sword slays the fire-breathing dragon – Maleficent in disguise – and Aurora is awakened by his gentle kiss. The movie ends as the two young lovers dance to the tune of "Once Upon A Dream," with Aurora's dress changing back and forth between pink and blue.

SLEEPING BEAUTY QUIKREFERENCE

	TITLE	ITEM #	AVAILABLE
SCROLL:			
Scroll	*Sleeping Beauty* Opening Title	41275	4/98
OPEN EDITIONS:			
Aurora and Philip (Blue Gown)	A Dance In The Clouds	41257	4/98
Flora	A Little Bit Of Pink	41258	4/98
Fauna	A Little Bit Of Both	41259	4/98
Merryweather	A Little Bit Of Blue	41260	4/98
EVENT PIECE:			
Maleficent	Evil Enchantress	41345	9/18-10/17/99
LIMITED EDITIONS:			
Aurora and Phillip (Pink Gown)	A Dance In The Clouds	41093	4/98
Briar Rose	"Once Upon A Dream"	41157	3/97
Sleeping Beauty's Dress	"A Dress A Princess Can Be Proud Of"	41344	6/99

COMPLEMENTARY PIECES:

ENCHANTED PLACES

OPEN EDITIONS:			
Sculpture	The Woodcutter's Cottage	41201	7/95
Miniature	Briar Rose	41214	5/96
Sculpture	Sleeping Beauty's Castle	41263	4/98
Ornament	Sleeping Beauty's Castle	41391	6/99

WALT DISNEY COLLECTORS SOCIETY

DISNEY VILLAIN SERIES: (see page 280)			
Maleficent	"The Mistress Of All Evil"	41177	1997

Sleeping Beauty Opening Title

TITLE: *Sleeping Beauty* Opening Title
SCROLL: Opening Title
ITEM NUMBER: 41275
SIZE: 1.6"
DATE OF ISSUE: 4/98

PLUSSING: None.
PRODUCTION CHANGES: None.
PARTICULARS: Certificate of Authenticity. Decal backstamp with WDCC logo and Annual Production Mark.
STATUS: OPEN EDITION.

YEAR	MARK	SRP	GBTru
☐ 1998	⚭	$29	**$29**
☐ 1999	⚮	29	**29**

A Dance In The Clouds

TITLE: A Dance In The Clouds
FIGURINE: Aurora and Philip
ITEM NUMBER: 41257
SIZE: 9.5"
DATE OF ISSUE: 4/98

PLUSSING: Dress: Blue gown shines with opalescent paint. **Crown, Necklace, Brooch & Belt Buckle:** Gold-plated.
PRODUCTION CHANGES: Two dress color versions, blue and pink. This blue gown version was distributed to regular WDCC dealers.
PARTICULARS: Certificate of Authenticity. Incised Annual Production Mark.
STATUS: OPEN EDITION.

YEAR	MARK	SRP	GBTru
☐ 1997	⚬	$295	**$295**
☐ 1998	⚭	295	**295**
☐ 1999	⚮	295	**295**

Sleeping Beauty

A Little Bit Of Pink

TITLE: A Little Bit Of Pink
FIGURINE: Flora
ITEM NUMBER: 41258
SIZE: 7"
DATE OF ISSUE: 4/98

PLUSSING: Wings: Shine with opalescent paint. **Wand:** Metal.
PRODUCTION CHANGES: None.
PARTICULARS: Certificate of Authenticity. Incised Annual Production Mark.
STATUS: OPEN EDITION.

YEAR	MARK	SRP	GBTru
☐ 1997	只	$100	**$100**
☐ 1998	下	100	**100**
☐ 1999	🔔	100	**100**

A Little Bit Of Both

TITLE: A Little Bit Of Both
FIGURINE: Fauna
ITEM NUMBER: 41259
SIZE: 6.75"
DATE OF ISSUE: 4/98

PLUSSING: Wings: Shine with opalescent paint.
PRODUCTION CHANGES: None.
PARTICULARS: Certificate of Authenticity. Incised Annual Production Mark.
STATUS: OPEN EDITION.

YEAR	MARK	SRP	GBTru
☐ 1997	只	$100	**$100**
☐ 1998	下	100	**100**
☐ 1999	🔔	100	**100**

Sleeping Beauty

A Little Bit Of Blue

TITLE: A Little Bit Of Blue
FIGURINE: Merryweather
ITEM NUMBER: 41260
SIZE: 5.75"
DATE OF ISSUE: 4/98

PLUSSING: Wings: Shine with opalescent paint. **Wand:** Metal.
PRODUCTION CHANGES: None.
PARTICULARS: Certificate of Authenticity. Incised Annual Production Mark.
STATUS: OPEN EDITION.

YEAR	MARK	SRP	GBTru
☐ 1997		$95	**$95**
☐ 1998		95	**95**
☐ 1999		95	**95**

Evil Enchantress

TITLE: Evil Enchantress
FIGURINE: Maleficent
ITEM NUMBER: 41345
SIZE: 10"
DATE OF ISSUE: 9/99

PLUSSING: Anniversary Backstamp: A special gold script message '40th Anniversary' is added to the backstamp. **Staff:** Topped by an adventurine stone.
PARTICULARS: A special gift-with-purchase sterling silver spinning wheel charm accompanies every sculpture. Special in-store drawing for whiteware of Maleficent with base – one per dealer, two per Gold Circle Dealer. "Purchase with Purchase" Sleeping Beauty Lenticular. Certificate of Authenticity. Incised Annual Production Mark.
STATUS: Event piece available 9/18 - 10/17/99.

YEAR	MARK	SRP	GBTru
☐ 1999		$185	**$185**

Sleeping Beauty

A Dance In The Clouds

TITLE: A Dance In The Clouds
FIGURINE: Aurora and Philip
ITEM NUMBER: 41093
SIZE: 9.5"
DATE OF ISSUE: 4/98

PLUSSING: Dress: Pink gown shines with opalescent paint. **Crown, Necklace, Brooch & Belt Buckle:** Gold-plated.
PRODUCTION CHANGES: Two dress color versions, blue and pink. This pink gown version was distributed as follows: 2 pieces to each Gold Circle dealer and 1 piece each to full-line WDCC dealers.
PARTICULARS: Certificate of Authenticity. Incised Annual Production Mark.
STATUS: LIMITED EDITION: 2,000 Pieces Pink Gown.

YEAR	MARK	SRP	GBTru
☐ 1998	T	$295	**$800**

"Once Upon A Dream"

TITLE: "Once Upon A Dream"
FIGURINE: Briar Rose
ITEM NUMBER: 41157
SIZE: 10"
DATE OF ISSUE: 3/97

PLUSSING: None.
PRODUCTION CHANGES: None.
PARTICULARS: Certificate of Authenticity. Incised Annual Production Mark.
STATUS: LIMITED EDITION: 12,500 Hand Numbered Pieces.

YEAR	MARK	SRP	GBTru
☐ 1996	◡	$345	**$350**
☐ 1997	♀	345	350

Sleeping Beauty

"A Dress A Princess Can Be Proud Of"

TITLE: "A Dress A Princess Can Be Proud Of"
FIGURINE: Sleeping Beauty's Dress
ITEM NUMBER: 41344
SIZE: 9.75"
DATE OF ISSUE: 6/99

PLUSSING: Glass Dome/Wooden Base: To keep it safe from evil spells. **Scissors:** Pewter. **Thread:** Wire. **Ribbon & Needle:** Metal. **Spools Of Thread:** 'Float' above dress on special wires. **Gown:** Opalescent finish makes it seem to glow.
PRODUCTION CHANGES: None.
PARTICULARS: Certificate of Authenticity. Incised Annual Production Mark.
STATUS: LIMITED EDITION: 5,000 Numbered Pieces.

YEAR	MARK	SRP	GBTru
☐ 1999	🎩	$545	**$545**

The Woodcutter's Cottage

TITLE: The Woodcutter's Cottage
SCULPTURE: The Woodcutter's Cottage
ITEM NUMBER: 41201
SIZE: 6.75"
DATE OF ISSUE: 7/95

PLUSSING: Props: Cast in Pewter and hand painted. **Creek:** Resin water.
PRODUCTION CHANGES: New logo and **backstamp** mid-1996. **Annual Production Mark** added mid-1996.
PARTICULARS: Enchanted Places. Certificate of Authenticity. Incised Annual Production Mark. Hand Engraved Serial Number. Registration Card redeemable for a deed "signed" by the setting's original "owner," transferring ownership. Sculpture comes with a wood display base with engraved brass nameplate.
STATUS: OPEN EDITION.

YEAR	MARK	SRP	GBTru
☐ 1995	No Mark	$170	**$170**
☐ 1996	⌒	170	**170**
☐ 1997	𓀀	170	**170**
☐ 1998	✝	170	**170**
☐ 1999	🎩	170	**170**

Sleeping Beauty

Briar Rose

TITLE: Briar Rose
MINIATURE: Briar Rose
ITEM NUMBER: 41214
SIZE: 1"
DATE OF ISSUE: 5/96

PLUSSING: Miniature: Bronze, hand painted.
PRODUCTION CHANGES: None.
PARTICULARS: Enchanted Places. Burgundy box, no picture on box, no Annual Production Mark.
STATUS: OPEN EDITION.

YEAR	MARK	SRP	GBTru
❏ 1996	No Mark	$50	**$50**

Sleeping Beauty's Castle

TITLE: Sleeping Beauty's Castle
SCULPTURE: Sleeping Beauty's Castle
ITEM NUMBER: 41263
SIZE: 9.5"
DATE OF ISSUE: 4/98

PLUSSING: None.
PRODUCTION CHANGES: None.
PARTICULARS: Enchanted Places. Certificate of Authenticity. Incised Annual Production Mark. Hand Engraved Serial Number. Registration Card redeemable for a deed "signed" by the setting's original "owner," transferring ownership. Sculpture comes with a wood display base with engraved brass nameplate.
STATUS: OPEN EDITION.

YEAR	MARK	SRP	GBTru
❏ 1998	⚒	$225	**$225**
❏ 1999	🕯	225	**225**

Sleeping Beauty's Castle

TITLE: Sleeping Beauty's Castle
ORNAMENT: Sleeping Beauty's Castle
ITEM NUMBER: 41391
SERIES: Enchanted Castles Ornament Series – 3rd of 6
SIZE: 3.25"
DATE OF ISSUE: 6/99

PLUSSING: Anniversary Backstamp: A special gold script message '*40th Anniversary*' is added to the backstamp of all ornaments crafted in 1999.
PRODUCTION CHANGES: None.
PARTICULARS: Enchanted Places. Certificate of Authenticity. Annual Production Mark.
STATUS: OPEN EDITION.

YEAR	MARK	SRP	GBTru
☐ 1999	Anniv. Mark	$45	$45

Late Addition!

Disneyana Convention
9/6-9/11/99

Limited Edition

"And Now You Shall Deal With Me"

Sleeping Beauty

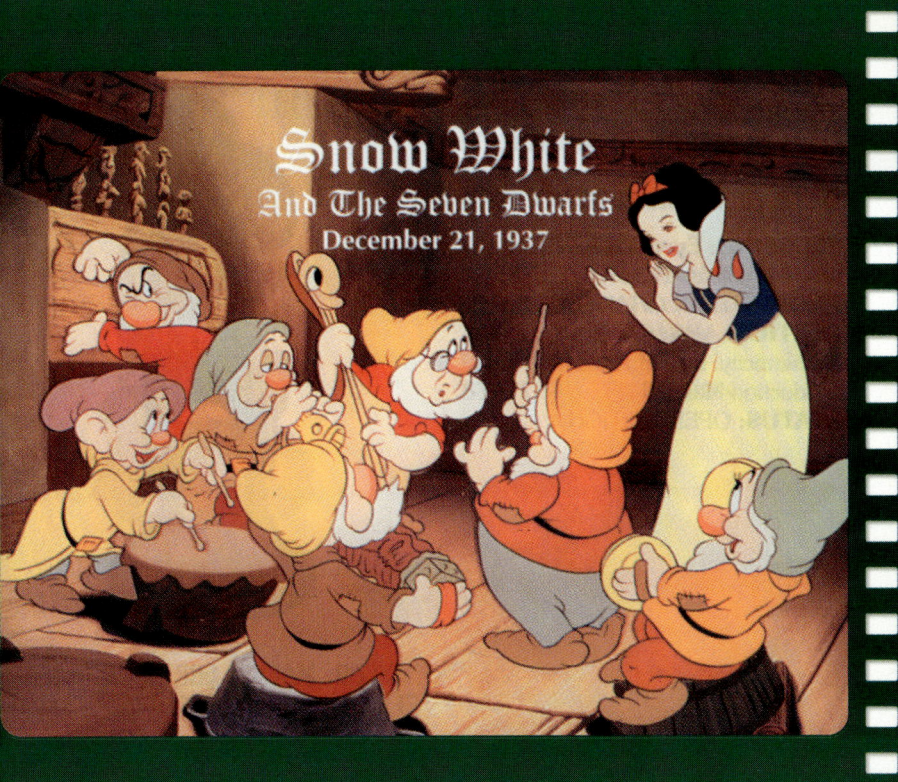

Snow White
And The Seven Dwarfs
December 21, 1937

Innovative, imaginative, creative.
"If you miss Disney's *Snow White And The Seven Dwarfs*, you'll be missing the ten best pictures of 1938." – Frank S. Nugent, NY Times.
Courageous, adventurous, daring.
"the greatest moving picture ever made." – Westbrook Peglar, New York World Telegram.
Pioneer, trailblazer, leader.
"a motion picture miracle." – Edwin Schallert, Los Angeles Times.

The quotations refer to the film. The adjectives and nouns to Walt Disney.

The legend of a Princess, her companions, and a jealous Queen provided the impetus that forever changed the art of animation. Faced with competition from both his peers and live-action movies, Disney realized the time had come to craft a full-length animation feature. To bring the characters to life, new techniques were created. Color became a subtle tool that underlined every character's personality. The Multiplane Camera added depth and perspective and opened the way for a range of special effects and a new department was created—Animation Effects.

Disney risked everything he had to finance the film. He enthusiastically encouraged every dream his teams of artists and animators created. Then, he thanked them, in writing, at the beginning of the film, for every viewer to see.

It is the details that made this film, and Disney, an enduring success.

SNOW WHITE AND THE SEVEN DWARFS QUIKREFERENCE

	TITLE	ITEM #	AVAILABLE
SCROLL:			
Scroll	*Snow White & The Seven Dwarfs Opening Title*	41083	11/94
OPEN EDITIONS:			
Snow White	"The Fairest One Of All"	41063	11/94
Happy	"Happy, That's Me!"	41064	6/95
Grumpy and Pipe Organ	"Humph!"	41065	8/95
Sleepy	"ZZZzzz"	41066	6/95
Bashful	"Aw Shucks!"	41069	6/95
Doc	Cheerful Leader	41071	6/95
Sneezy	"Ah-Choo!"	41073	3/95
Dopey	Dopey	41074	3/95
Snow White and Prince	"I'm Wishing For The One I Love"	41412	3/99
EVENT PIECES:			
Witch (The Queen)	"Take The Apple, Dearie"	41084	9/95 - 3/96
Evil Queen	"Bring Back Her Heart..."	41165	2/97 - 6/97
Dopey/Sneezy In Coat	Dancing Partners	41372	2/99 - 3/99
LIMITED EDITION:			
Snow White and Prince	A Kiss Brings Love Anew	41307	9/7 - 9/11/98

COMPLEMENTARY PIECES:

ENCHANTED PLACES

OPEN EDITIONS:			
Sculpture	Seven Dwarfs Cottage	41200	6/95
Sculpture	Seven Dwarfs Jewel Mine	41203	10/95
Miniature	Snow White	41212	2/96
Miniature	Dopey	41215	5/96
Miniature	Grumpy	41239	11/97
Sculpture	Snow White's Wishing Well	41248	9/97
Miniature	Doc	41271	5/98
Miniature	Happy	41272	7/98
Miniature	Bashful	41273	9/98
Miniature	Sneezy	41318	3/99
Miniature	Sleepy	41411	4/99

Snow White And The Seven Dwarfs Opening Title

TITLE: *Snow White And The Seven Dwarfs* Opening Title
SCROLL: Opening Title
ITEM NUMBER: 41083
SIZE: 1.6"
DATE OF ISSUE: 11/94

PLUSSING: None.
PRODUCTION CHANGES: None.
PARTICULARS: Certificate of Authenticity. Decal backstamp with WDCC logo and Annual Production Mark.
STATUS: OPEN EDITION.

YEAR	MARK	SRP	GBTru
☐ 1994		$29	$29
☐ 1995		29	29
☐ 1996		29	29
☐ 1997		29	29
☐ 1998		29	29
☐ 1999		29	29

"The Fairest One Of All"

TITLE: "The Fairest One Of All"
FIGURINE: Snow White
ITEM NUMBER: 41063
SIZE: 8.25"
DATE OF ISSUE: 11/94

PLUSSING: None.
PRODUCTION CHANGES: Dress Variations: 1) Plain yellow dress, and, 2) Folds in dress are accented in gray. **SRP Change:** $165 to $175 in 1998.
PARTICULARS: Certificate of Authenticity. Incised Annual Production Mark.
STATUS: OPEN EDITION.

YEAR	MARK	SRP	GBTru
☐ 1994		$165	$185
☐ 1995		165	175
☐ 1996		165	175
☐ 1997		165	175
☐ 1998		175	175
☐ 1999		175	175

"Happy, That's Me!"

TITLE: "Happy, That's Me!"
FIGURINE: Happy
ITEM NUMBER: 41064
SIZE: 5.5"
DATE OF ISSUE: 6/95

PLUSSING: Spigot: Spigot on keg is metal.
PRODUCTION CHANGES: None.
PARTICULARS: Certificate of Authenticity. Incised Annual Production Mark.
STATUS: OPEN EDITION.

YEAR	MARK	SRP	GBTru
☐ 1995		$125	**$125**
☐ 1996		125	**125**
☐ 1997		125	**125**
☐ 1998		125	**125**
☐ 1999		125	**125**

"Humph!"

TITLE: "Humph!"
FIGURINE: Grumpy and Pipe Organ
ITEM NUMBER: 41065
SIZE: Organ: 7.25", Grumpy: 4.5"
DATE OF ISSUE: 8/95

PLUSSING: 2 Piece Set: Organ : Made of resin, it is intricately carved with woodland creatures—rabbits support organ and race across front, squirrels fill each end. **Pipes:** Carved organ pipes resemble totems and feature frogs, owls, fish, rabbits and a baby bird in a nest. **Organ Stool:** Grumpy is seated on the bellows for the pipe organ.
PRODUCTION CHANGES: None.
PARTICULARS: Certificate of Authenticity. Incised Annual Production Mark.
STATUS: OPEN EDITION.

YEAR	MARK	SRP	GBTru
☐ 1995		$180	**$180**
☐ 1996		180	**180**
☐ 1997		180	**180**
☐ 1998		180	**180**
☐ 1999		180	**180**

Snow White And The Seven Dwarfs

"ZZZzzz"

TITLE: "ZZZzzz"
FIGURINE: Sleepy
ITEM NUMBER: 41066
SIZE: 3.25"
DATE OF ISSUE: 6/95

PLUSSING: Fly: Glass fly with crystal wings lands on Sleepy's ample nose as he plays a horn. Droopy eyelids emphasize his readiness to sleep.
PRODUCTION CHANGES: None.
PARTICULARS: Certificate of Authenticity. Incised Annual Production Mark.
STATUS: OPEN EDITION.

YEAR	MARK	SRP	GBTru
☐ 1995	∞	$95	**$95**
☐ 1996	◡	95	**95**
☐ 1997	呆	95	**95**
☐ 1998	⊥	95	**95**
☐ 1999	♟	95	**95**

"Aw Shucks!"

TITLE: "Aw Shucks!"
FIGURINE: Bashful
ITEM NUMBER: 41069
SIZE: 5"
DATE OF ISSUE: 6/95

PLUSSING: Buttons: Sparkling gold buttons and buckles.
PRODUCTION CHANGES: SRP Change: $85 to $90 in 1998.
PARTICULARS: Certificate of Authenticity. Incised Annual Production Mark.
STATUS: OPEN EDITION.

YEAR	MARK	SRP	GBTru
☐ 1995	∞	$85	**$90**
☐ 1996	◡	85	**90**
☐ 1997	呆	85	**90**
☐ 1998	⊥	90	**90**
☐ 1999	♟	90	**90**

Snow White And The Seven Dwarfs

Cheerful Leader

TITLE: Cheerful Leader
FIGURINE: Doc
ITEM NUMBER: 41071
SIZE: 5.25"
DATE OF ISSUE: 6/95

PLUSSING: Glasses: Doc wears miniature wire-rimmed glasses. **Musical Instrument:** "Swanette," carved in the shape of a swan with metal strings. **Sign Language:** Right hand signs 'Love.'
PRODUCTION CHANGES: SRP Change: $95 to $100 in 1998.
PARTICULARS: Certificate of Authenticity. Incised Annual Production Mark.
STATUS: OPEN EDITION.

YEAR	MARK	SRP	GBTru
1995		$95	**$100**
1996		95	**100**
1997		95	**100**
1998		100	**100**
1999		100	**100**

"Ah-Choo!"

TITLE: "Ah-Choo!"
FIGURINE: Sneezy
ITEM NUMBER: 41073
SIZE: 4.5"
DATE OF ISSUE: 3/95

PLUSSING: Buckle: The belt buckle on Sneezy's brown jacket is finished like sparkling gold.
PRODUCTION CHANGES: SRP Change: $90 to $95 in 1998.
PARTICULARS: Certificate of Authenticity. Incised Annual Production Mark.
STATUS: OPEN EDITION.

YEAR	MARK	SRP	GBTru
1995		$90	**$95**
1996		90	**95**
1997		90	**95**
1998		95	**95**
1999		95	**95**

Snow White And The Seven Dwarfs

Dopey

TITLE: Dopey
FIGURINE: Dopey
ITEM NUMBER: 41074
SIZE: 5"
DATE OF ISSUE: 3/95

PLUSSING: Cymbal & Striker: Dopey holds a porcelain striking stick in one hand and an antique-looking brushed gold cymbal by a leather cord in the other. **Buckles & Buttons:** The buckles and buttons on Dopey's green jacket are sparkling gold. **Ears:** Ears are oversized, adding to his silly look.
PRODUCTION CHANGES: SRP Change: $95 to $105 in 1998.
PARTICULARS: Certificate of Authenticity. Incised Annual Production Mark.
STATUS: OPEN EDITION.

YEAR	MARK	SRP	GBTru
❏ 1995	∽	$95	$105
❏ 1996	◡	95	105
❏ 1997	⚚	95	105
❏ 1998	⏉	105	105
❏ 1999	⏃	105	105

"I'm Wishing For The One I Love"

TITLE: "I'm Wishing For The One I Love"
FIGURINE: Snow White and Prince
ITEM NUMBER: 41412
SIZE: Snow White: 8.5", Prince: 9.25"
DATE OF ISSUE: 3/99

PLUSSING: Prince's Dagger: Made of pewter.
PRODUCTION CHANGES: None.
PARTICULARS: Two-figure set. Certificate of Authenticity. Incised Annual Production Mark.
STATUS: OPEN EDITION.

YEAR	MARK	SRP	GBTru
❏ 1999	⏃	$295	$295

Snow White And The Seven Dwarfs

"Take The Apple, Dearie"

TITLE: "Take The Apple, Dearie"
FIGURINE: Witch (The Queen)
ITEM NUMBER: 41084
SIZE: 7"
DATE OF ISSUE: 9/95

PLUSSING: Fingers: Witch's long gnarled fingers are sculpted in metal. **Wart:** Nose painted to highlight wart. **Glazing:** New glazing technique gives clothes texture of real fabric.
PRODUCTION CHANGES: None.
PARTICULARS: Certificate of Authenticity. Incised Annual Production Mark. This piece received the **1996 NALED Award Of Excellence.**
STATUS: EDITION CLOSED. Available exclusively at selected authorized retailers Special Events 9/1/95 to 3/31/96.

YEAR	MARK	SRP	GBTru
☐ 1995	∽	$130	**$350**
☐ 1996	∽	130	**325**

"Bring Back Her Heart…"

TITLE: "Bring Back Her Heart…"
FIGURINE: Evil Queen
ITEM NUMBER: 41165
SIZE: 9"
DATE OF ISSUE: 2/97

PLUSSING: None.
PRODUCTION CHANGES: None.
PARTICULARS: Certificate of Authenticity. Incised Annual Production Mark. A poster was a bonus with purchase. Poster has the ☥ Mark.
STATUS: EDITION CLOSED. 1997 Special Sculpture Event Piece available 2/97 through 6/97.

YEAR	MARK	SRP	GBTru
☐ 1996	∽	$150	**$185**
☐ 1997	☥	150	**175**

Snow White And The Seven Dwarfs

Dancing Partners

TITLE: Dancing Partners
FIGURINE: Dopey/Sneezy in Coat
ITEM NUMBER: 41372
SIZE: 8.5"
DATE OF ISSUE: 2/99

PLUSSING: Dopey's Coat Buttons & Sleeve Trim: Gold metallic paint. **Sneezy's Belt Buckle & Shirt Buttons:** Gold metallic paint.
PRODUCTION CHANGES: None.
PARTICULARS: Certificate of Authenticity. Incised Annual Production Mark. Sterling silver apple charm is gift with purchase.
STATUS: 1999 Spring Event Piece available at Events 2/20/99 to 3/7/99 at select retailers.

YEAR	MARK	SRP	GBTru
☐ 1998		$150	**$150**
☐ 1999		150	**150**

A Kiss Brings Love Anew

TITLE: A Kiss Brings Love Anew
FIGURINE: Snow White and Prince
ITEM NUMBER: 41307
SIZE: 11" long x 10" wide x 9.25" tall
DATE OF ISSUE: 9/98

PLUSSING: Flowers: Handmade flowers around pillow and base of bier. **Special Backstamp:** Includes the 1998 Disneyana Convention logo.
PRODUCTION CHANGES: None.
PARTICULARS: As a special Collectors Society Member benefit, 75 Artist Proof sculptures were available for purchase via a special sweepstakes drawing by mail. One entry per person with purchase to be completed by 12/31/98. GBTru$ for Artist Proof is $1500. Certificate of Authenticity. Incised Annual Production Mark.
STATUS: LIMITED EDITION: 1,650 Hand Numbered Pieces plus 75 Artist Proofs. Disneyana Convention Event Piece, 9/7 to 9/11/98, Orlando, Florida.

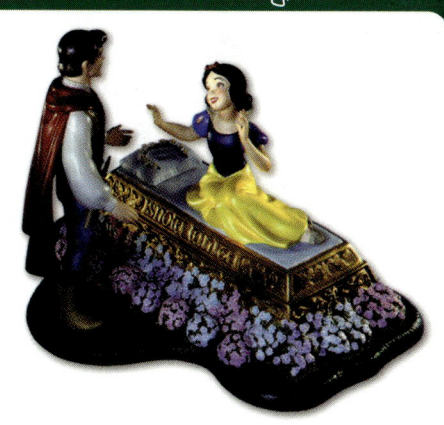

YEAR	MARK	SRP	GBTru
☐ 1998		$750	**$1440**

Snow White And The Seven Dwarfs

The Seven Dwarfs' Cottage

TITLE: The Seven Dwarfs' Cottage
SCULPTURE: The Seven Dwarfs' Cottage
ITEM NUMBER: 41200
SIZE: 7"
DATE OF ISSUE: 6/95

PLUSSING: Props: Picks and shovels, bar of soap cast in pewter and hand painted. **Water:** Clear resin.
PRODUCTION CHANGES: Shovel: Made to fit deeper in the ground. **New logo** and **backstamp** mid-1996. **Annual Production Mark** added mid-1996.
PARTICULARS: Enchanted Places. Certificate of Authenticity. Incised Annual Production Mark. Hand Engraved Serial Number. Registration Card redeemable for a deed "signed" by the setting's original "owner," transferring ownership.

Sculpture comes with a wood display base with engraved brass nameplate.
STATUS: OPEN EDITION.

YEAR	MARK	SRP	GBTru
☐ 1995		$180	**$180**
☐ 1996		180	**180**
☐ 1997		180	**180**
☐ 1998		180	**180**
☐ 1999		180	**180**

The Seven Dwarfs' Jewel Mine

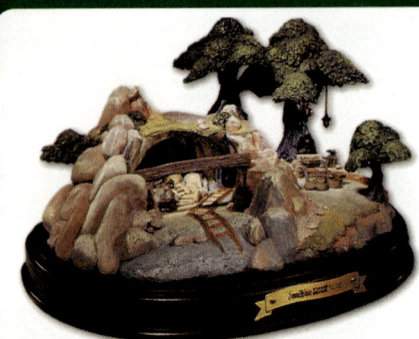

TITLE: The Seven Dwarfs' Jewel Mine
SCULPTURE: The Seven Dwarfs' Jewel Mine
ITEM NUMBER: 41203
SIZE: 4"
DATE OF ISSUE: 10/95

PLUSSING: Props: Cast in pewter and hand painted. **Jewels:** 53 Swarovski crystals: 6 emeralds, 9 sapphires, 6 rubies, 32 clear. **Key:** Metal, actually turns. **Lantern:** Hangs from tree by a wire.
PRODUCTION CHANGES: New logo and **backstamp** mid-1996. **Annual Production Mark** added mid-1996.
PARTICULARS: Enchanted Places. Certificate of Authenticity. Incised Annual Production Mark. Hand Engraved Serial Number. Registration Card redeemable for a deed "signed" by the setting's original "owner," transferring ownership. Sculpture comes with a wood display base with engraved brass nameplate.
STATUS: OPEN EDITION.

YEAR	MARK	SRP	GBTru
☐ 1995		$190	**$190**
☐ 1996		190	**190**
☐ 1997		190	**190**
☐ 1998		190	**190**
☐ 1999		190	**190**

Snow White

TITLE: Snow White
MINIATURE: Snow White
ITEM NUMBER: 41212
SIZE: 1"
DATE OF ISSUE: 2/96

PLUSSING: Miniature: Bronze, hand painted.
PRODUCTION CHANGES: None.
PARTICULARS: Enchanted Places. Burgundy box, no picture on box, no Annual Production Mark.
STATUS: OPEN EDITION.

YEAR	MARK	SRP	GBTru
❏ 1996	No Mark	$50	**$50**

Dopey

TITLE: Dopey
MINIATURE: Dopey
ITEM NUMBER: 41215
SIZE: 1"
DATE OF ISSUE: 5/96

PLUSSING: Miniature: Bronze, hand painted.
PRODUCTION CHANGES: None.
PARTICULARS: Enchanted Places. Burgundy box, no picture on box, no Annual Production Mark.
STATUS: OPEN EDITION.

YEAR	MARK	SRP	GBTru
❏ 1996	No Mark	$50	**$50**

Snow White And The Seven Dwarfs

Grumpy

TITLE: Grumpy
MINIATURE: Grumpy
ITEM NUMBER: 41239
SIZE: 1"
DATE OF ISSUE: 11/97

PLUSSING: Miniature: Bronze, hand painted.
PRODUCTION CHANGES: None.
PARTICULARS: Enchanted Places. Green box, picture on box, sticker Annual Production Mark on box and on base of miniature.
STATUS: OPEN EDITION.

YEAR	MARK	SRP	GBTru
☐ 1998	🍵	$50	**$50**
☐ 1999	🔔	50	**50**

Snow White's Wishing Well

TITLE: Snow White's Wishing Well
SCULPTURE: Snow White's Wishing Well
ITEM NUMBER: 41248
SIZE: 7"
DATE OF ISSUE: 9/97

PLUSSING: Water: Clear resin glistens like water. **Rope:** Real rope is threaded through metal pulley pole. **Bucket:** Metal handle. **Doves:** Individually added to sculpture.
PRODUCTION CHANGES: None.
PARTICULARS: Enchanted Places. Certificate of Authenticity. Incised Annual Production Mark. Hand Engraved Serial Number. Sculpture comes with a wood display base with engraved brass nameplate.
STATUS: OPEN EDITION.

YEAR	MARK	SRP	GBTru
☐ 1997	🧍	$160	**$160**
☐ 1998	🍵	160	**160**
☐ 1999	🔔	160	**160**

Snow White And The Seven Dwarfs

Doc

TITLE: Doc
MINIATURE: Doc
ITEM NUMBER: 41271
SIZE: 1"
DATE OF ISSUE: 5/98

PLUSSING: Miniature: Bronze, hand painted.
PRODUCTION CHANGES: None.
PARTICULARS: Enchanted Places. Green box, picture on box, sticker Annual Production Mark on box and on base of miniature.
STATUS: OPEN EDITION.

YEAR	MARK	SRP	GBTru
❐ 1998	🎩	$50	**$50**
❐ 1999	🔔	50	**50**

Happy

TITLE: Happy
MINIATURE: Happy
ITEM NUMBER: 41272
SIZE: 1"
DATE OF ISSUE: 7/98

PLUSSING: Miniature: Bronze, hand painted.
PRODUCTION CHANGES: None.
PARTICULARS: Enchanted Places. Green box, picture on box, sticker Annual Production Mark on box and on base of miniature.
STATUS: OPEN EDITION.

YEAR	MARK	SRP	GBTru
❐ 1998	🎩	$50	**$50**
❐ 1999	🔔	50	**50**

Snow White And The Seven Dwarfs

Bashful

TITLE: Bashful
MINIATURE: Bashful
ITEM NUMBER: 41273
SIZE: 1"
DATE OF ISSUE: 9/98

PLUSSING: Miniature: Bronze, hand painted.
PRODUCTION CHANGES: None.
PARTICULARS: Enchanted Places. Green box, picture on box, sticker Annual Production Mark on box and on base of miniature.
STATUS: OPEN EDITION.

YEAR	MARK	SRP	GBTru
☐ 1998		$50	**$50**
☐ 1999		50	**50**

Sneezy

TITLE: Sneezy
MINIATURE: Sneezy
ITEM NUMBER: 41318
SIZE: 1"
DATE OF ISSUE: 3/99

PLUSSING: Miniature: Bronze, hand painted.
PRODUCTION CHANGES: None.
PARTICULARS: Enchanted Places. Green box, picture on box, sticker Annual Production Mark on box and on base of miniature.
STATUS: OPEN EDITION.

YEAR	MARK	SRP	GBTru
☐ 1999		$50	**$50**

Snow White And The Seven Dwarfs

Sleepy

TITLE: Sleepy
MINIATURE: Sleepy
ITEM NUMBER: 41411
SIZE: 1"
DATE OF ISSUE: 4/99

PLUSSING: Miniature: Bronze, hand painted.
PRODUCTION CHANGES: None.
PARTICULARS: Enchanted Places. Green box, picture on box, sticker Annual Production Mark on box and on base of miniature.
STATUS: OPEN EDITION.

YEAR	MARK	SRP	GBTru
☐ 1999	⌂	$50	**$50**

Notes: _____

Snow White And The Seven Dwarfs

SONG OF THE SOUTH
November 2, 1946

Song Of The South, released in 1946, was Walt Disney's tuneful adaptation of the tales of Uncle Remus. This collection of authentic African-American folk stories, featured three characters forever plotting against each other. Brer Fox, Brer Rabbit, and Brer Bear reflected human weaknesses in their animated personalities. Brer Rabbit is foolhardy with a gigantic ego, but he outruns, outthinks, and outwits Brer Fox with cleverness and trickery. The crafty Brer Fox dreams of ways to capture his enemy Brer Rabbit, but is continually foiled and manipulated by the resourceful rabbit. Brer Bear is big, clumsy, slow-witted, slow–moving and is easily distracted by everyone and everything.

The film combines animation and live action. The wonderful fables Uncle Remus tells to the young boy Johnny, and his friend, Ginny, are cleverly used to illustrate morals applicable to the problems facing the boy.

A major highlight of the film, the infectious "Zip-A-Dee-Doo-Dah," won an Academy Award in 1946.

SONG OF THE SOUTH QUIKREFERENCE

	TITLE	ITEM #	AVAILABLE
RETIRED EDITIONS:			
Brer Fox	"I Gotcha, Brer Rabbit!"	41101	6/96 - 2/97
Brer Bear	"Duh!"	41102	6/96 - 2/97
Brer Rabbit	"Born And Bred In A Briar Patch"	41103	6/96 - 2/97
Scroll	*Song Of The South* Opening Title	41104	6/96 - 2/97

"I Gotcha, Brer Rabbit!"

TITLE: "I Gotcha, Brer Rabbit!"
FIGURINE: Brer Fox
ITEM NUMBER: 41101
SIZE: 4"
DATE OF ISSUE: 6/96

PLUSSING: Paw: Right paw is made of bronze. **Anniversary Backstamp:** A special gold script message '*50th Anniversary*' appears on the backstamp of sculptures crafted in 1996.
PRODUCTION CHANGES: None.
PARTICULARS: Certificate of Authenticity. Incised Annual Production Mark.
STATUS: RETIRED 2/97.

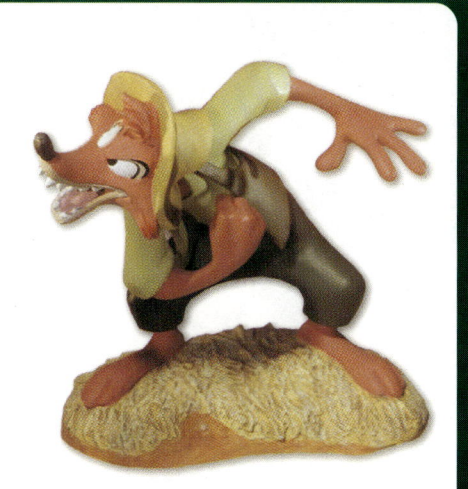

YEAR	MARK	SRP	GBTru
❏ 1996	ᴗ Anniv. Mark	$120	**$130**
❏ 1997	⚱	120	**130**

Song Of The South   207

"Duh!"

TITLE: "Duh!"
FIGURINE: Brer Bear
ITEM NUMBER: 41102
SIZE: 7.5"
DATE OF ISSUE: 6/96

PLUSSING: Anniversary Backstamp: A special gold script message *'50th Anniversary'* was added to the backstamp of sculptures crafted in 1996.
PRODUCTION CHANGES: None.
PARTICULARS: Certificate of Authenticity. Incised Annual Production Mark.
STATUS: RETIRED 2/97.

YEAR	MARK	SRP	GBTru
☐ 1996	Anniv. Mark	$175	**$190**
☐ 1997	⚒	175	190

"Born And Bred In A Briar Patch"

TITLE: "Born And Bred In A Briar Patch"
FIGURINE: Brer Rabbit
ITEM NUMBER: 41103
SIZE: 4.75"
DATE OF ISSUE: 6/96

PLUSSING: Briar Patch: Thorny vines are made of metal. **Anniversary Backstamp:** A special gold script message *'50th Anniversary'* was added to the backstamp of sculptures crafted in 1996.
PRODUCTION CHANGES: None.
PARTICULARS: Artist Proof: Item #31103. Certificate of Authenticity. Incised Annual Production Mark.
STATUS: RETIRED 2/97.

YEAR	MARK	SRP	GBTru
☐ 1996	Anniv. Mark	$150	**$190**
☐ 1997	⚒	150	190

Song Of The South

Song Of The South Opening Title

TITLE: *Song Of The South* Opening Title
SCROLL: Opening Title
ITEM NUMBER: 41104
SIZE: 1.6"
DATE OF ISSUE: 6/96

PLUSSING: None.
PRODUCTION CHANGES: None.
PARTICULARS: Certificate of Authenticity. Decal backstamp with WDCC logo and Annual Production Mark.
STATUS: RETIRED 2/97.

YEAR	MARK	SRP	GBTru
☐ 1996	〜	$29	**$35**
☐ 1997	𝆖	29	**29**

Notes:

STEAMBOAT WILLIE
November 18, 1928

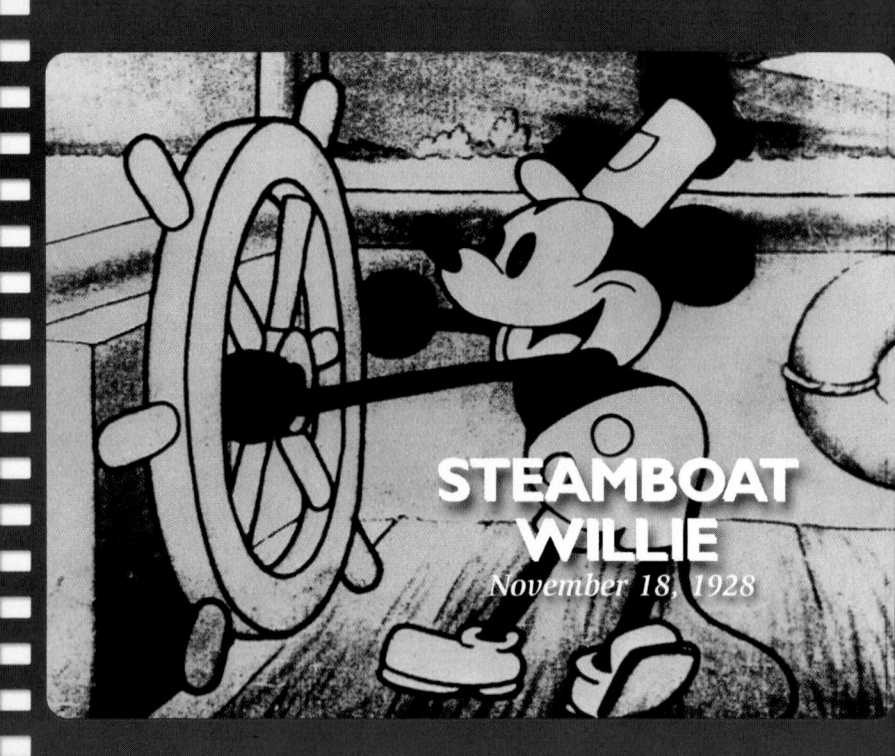

Mickey is the first mate in *Steamboat Willie*. He's got more on his mind than just hard work. Mickey whistles and tap dances through a musical romp with the noisy help of his washboard and the pots and pans hanging in the ship's galley. His boss, Captain Peg-Leg Pete is unimpressed with all the noise but the good fun captures the attention of a certain sweetheart named Minnie. Thus, the romance begins.

STEAMBOAT WILLIE QUIKREFERENCE

	TITLE	ITEM#	AVAILABLE
EVENT PIECE:			
Flat Ornament	Mickey Mouse	41424	10/31 - 12/12/98

COMPLEMENTARY PIECES:

ENCHANTED PLACES

ANNUALS:			
Background	Steamboat	41264	3/98 -12/98
Miniature	Mickey Mouse	41265	3/98 -12/98

WALT DISNEY COLLECTORS SOCIETY

5-YEAR ANNIVERSARY SCULPTURES: (see page 282)

Charter	Mickey's Debut	41136	1997
Non-Charter	Mickey's Debut	41255	1998

Mickey Mouse

TITLE: Mickey Mouse
ORNAMENT: Mickey Mouse
ITEM NUMBER: 41424
SIZE: 4" diameter
DATE OF ISSUE: 10/98

PLUSSING: Ship's Wheel: Flat porcelain wheel plussed with gold paint accents and a black and white decal of Mickey as Steamboat Willie in the center.
PRODUCTION CHANGES: None.
PARTICULARS: Certificate of Authenticity. Created in honor of 75th Anniversary of Walt Disney Company. Reads "75 years of Love and Laughter" on the back. Disney values the piece at $25.
STATUS: EDITION CLOSED. Fall 1998 WDCC Promotional Piece was available from 10/31 to 12/12/98 with purchase of any WDCC product, excluding Event merchandise, only at authorized Disney Stores.

YEAR	MARK	SRP	GBTru
❏ 1998	No Mark	$5.00	**$25**

Steamboat Willie 211

Steamboat

TITLE: Steamboat
SCULPTURE: Steamboat
ITEM NUMBER: 41264
SIZE: 4.5"
DATE OF ISSUE: 3/98

PLUSSING: Pots & Pans: Made of pewter. **Rope:** Real rope on whistles and pulley. **Pulley & Hook:** Pewter pulley, metal hook. **Flag:** Metal flag on bow. **Paint:** Black and white colors reminiscent of early Disney animation. **Birthday Backstamp:** A special teal block print message *'Mickey's 70th Birthday'* was added to the backstamp of sculptures crafted in 1998.
PRODUCTION CHANGES: None.
PARTICULARS: Enchanted Places. Certificate of Authenticity. Incised Annual Production Mark. Hand Engraved Serial Number. Registration Card redeemable for a deed "signed" by the setting's original "owner," transferring ownership. Sculpture comes with a wood display base with engraved brass nameplate.
STATUS: 1998 ANNUAL.

YEAR	MARK	SRP	GBTru
☐ 1998	⬆	$160	**$160**

Mickey Mouse

TITLE: Mickey Mouse
MINIATURE: Mickey Mouse
ITEM NUMBER: 41265
SIZE: 1"
DATE OF ISSUE: 3/98

PLUSSING: Miniature: Bronze, hand painted in black, white, and shades of gray to replicate early animation art.
PRODUCTION CHANGES: None.
PARTICULARS: Enchanted Places. Green box, picture on box, sticker Annual Production Mark on box and on base of miniature.
STATUS: 1998 ANNUAL.

YEAR	MARK	SRP	GBTru
☐ 1998	⬆	$50	**$50**

Steamboat Willie

SYMPHONY HOUR
1942

Symphony Hour is a hit musical program. The orchestra, comprised of favorite Disney cartoon characters, has been called the Disney Stock Company. The Company not only boosted Mickey Mouse's star to shine brighter, but they themselves became audience favorites in their own right, appearing many times, in many films.

This "instrumental" film was a major step for Disney. It made the transition from black-and-white to color, and was a showcase for almost the entire Disney cast. The feature begins at an orchestra rehearsal, prior to the evening's concert performance. Goofy accidentally squashes all the instruments flat as pancakes. The musicians then have to cope with this dilemma because the show must go on! Each twist of the plot highlighted hilarious obstacles and ongoing absurdities.

The animators created the Great Ear Experiment in this feature. Mickey Mouse's Ears were made three dimensional to see if it would enhance his character and appearance. When the vote came in it was decided it was a failure. The famous Mouse ears went back to being flat and have remained flat ever since.

Mickey Mouse, Donald Duck and Goofy emerged as featured players and remained so in their ongoing successful film careers. Horace, Clarabelle and

Clara Cluck became and remained supporting players whenever they appeared in films, and showed themselves to be outstanding team players.

SYMPHONY HOUR QUIKREFERENCE

	TITLE	ITEM #	AVAILABLE
LIMITED EDITION:			
Pete	Sylvester Macaroni	41106	8/96
RETIRED EDITIONS:			
Goofy	Goofy's Grace Notes	41026	5/93 - 9/97
Clarabelle Cow	Clarabelle's Crescendo	41027	3/93 - 9/97
Horace Horsecollar	Horace's High Notes	41028	3/93 - 9/97
Mickey Mouse	Maestro Michel Mouse	41029	3/93 - 9/97
Scroll	*Symphony Hour* Opening Title	41031	3/93 - 9/97
Clara Cluck	Bravo Bravissimo	41061	1/95 - 9/97
Donald Duck	Donald's Drum Beat	41105	4/96 - 9/97

Sylvester Macaroni

TITLE: Sylvester Macaroni
FIGURINE: Pete
ITEM NUMBER: 41106
SIZE: 5"
DATE OF ISSUE: 8/96

PLUSSING: Cufflinks & Shirt Studs: Cufflinks and shirt studs are crystal.
PRODUCTION CHANGES: None.
PARTICULARS: Hand Numbered Certificate of Authenticity. Incised Annual Production Mark. Artist Proof is Item Number 31106, they are marked "A.P." and are not numbered.
STATUS: LIMITED EDITION: 12,500 Hand Numbered Pieces.

YEAR	MARK	SRP	GBTru
☐ 1996	~	$395	**$395**

Symphony Hour

Goofy's Grace Notes

TITLE: Goofy's Grace Notes
FIGURINE: Goofy
ITEM NUMBER: 41026
SIZE: 6.8"
DATE OF ISSUE: 5/93

PLUSSING: Contrabassoon: Made of cast metal, 24 karat gold-plated. **Anniversary Backstamp:** A special gold script message *'50th Anniversary'* was added to the backstamp of sculptures crafted in 1992. **PRODUCTION CHANGES: Packaging:** Revised to provide greater protection. **Ears:** ✣ production ears were porcelain with wire running through them–most broke in shipping; revised to be all metal ears. **SRP Change:** Effective 3/15/94 to $235.00. **PARTICULARS:** Certificate of Authenticity. Incised Annual Production Mark. The instrument that Goofy plays is a contrabassoon, a woodwind instrument; however, during the plussing process, enthusiastic Disney artists accidentally plated the entire horn.
STATUS: RETIRED 9/97.

YEAR	MARK	SRP	GBTru
❏ 1992	✣ Anniv. Mark	$198	**$2600**
❏ 1993	𝄞	198	**235**
❏ 1994	♁	235	**235**
❏ 1995	⌇	235	**235**
❏ 1996	◡	235	**235**
❏ 1997	♀	235	**235**

Clarabelle's Crescendo

TITLE: Clarabelle's Crescendo
FIGURINE: Clarabelle Cow
ITEM NUMBER: 41027
SIZE: 6.8"
DATE OF ISSUE: 3/93

PLUSSING: Violin Bow: A painted, separate metal piece. **Anniversary Backstamp:** A special gold script message *'50th Anniversary'* was added to the backstamp of sculptures crafted in 1992.
PRODUCTION CHANGES: None.
PARTICULARS: Certificate of Authenticity. Incised Annual Production Mark.
STATUS: RETIRED 9/97.

YEAR	MARK	SRP	GBTru
❏ 1992	✣ Anniv. Mark	$198	**$245**
❏ 1993	𝄞	198	**198**
❏ 1994	♁	198	**198**
❏ 1995	⌇	198	**198**
❏ 1996	◡	198	**198**
❏ 1997	♀	198	**198**

Horace's High Notes

TITLE: Horace's High Notes
FIGURINE: Horace Horsecollar
ITEM NUMBER: 41028
SIZE: 6.8"
DATE OF ISSUE: 3/93

PLUSSING: Trumpet: Plated with 24 karat gold. **Anniversary Backstamp:** A special gold script message *'50th Anniversary'* was added to backstamp of sculptures crafted in 1992.
PRODUCTION CHANGES: Color Variations: **Shoes:** Painted black or dark brown. **Jacket Lapels:** Painted black or blue. **Coat Button:** Painted bright lime green or blue.
PARTICULARS: Certificate of Authenticity. Incised Annual Production Mark.
STATUS: RETIRED 9/97.

YEAR	MARK	SRP	GBTru
☐ 1992	Anniv. Mark	$198	**$245**
☐ 1993		198	**215**
☐ 1994		198	**198**
☐ 1995		198	**198**
☐ 1996		198	**198**
☐ 1997		198	**198**

"Maestro Michel Mouse"

TITLE: "Maestro Michel Mouse"
FIGURINE: Mickey Mouse
ITEM NUMBER: 41029
SIZE: 7.38"
DATE OF ISSUE: 3/93

PLUSSING: Anniversary Backstamp: A special gold script message *'50th Anniversary'* was added to the backstamp of sculptures crafted in 1992.
PRODUCTION CHANGES: None.
PARTICULARS: Certificate of Authenticity. Incised Annual Production Mark.
STATUS: RETIRED 9/97.

YEAR	MARK	SRP	GBTru
☐ 1992	Anniv. Mark	$185	**$230**
☐ 1993		185	**185**
☐ 1994		185	**185**
☐ 1995		185	**185**
☐ 1996		185	**185**
☐ 1997		185	**185**

Symphony Hour

Symphony Hour Opening Title

TITLE: *Symphony Hour* Opening Title
SCROLL: Opening Title
ITEM NUMBER: 41031
SIZE: 1.6"
DATE OF ISSUE: 3/93

PLUSSING: None.
PRODUCTION CHANGES: None.
PARTICULARS: Certificate of Authenticity. Decal backstamp with WDCC logo and Annual Production Mark.
STATUS: RETIRED 9/97.

YEAR	MARK	SRP	GBTru
☐ 1993		$29	**$29**
☐ 1994		29	**29**
☐ 1995		29	**29**
☐ 1996		29	**29**
☐ 1997		29	**29**

Bravo Bravissimo

TITLE: Bravo Bravissimo
FIGURINE: Clara Cluck
ITEM NUMBER: 41061
SIZE: 6"
DATE OF ISSUE: 1/95

PLUSSING: Cello: Painted two shades of brown. **Hat:** Detailed in two shades of blue. **Bass Cello Bow:** Metal, with keys enhanced with gold, as is metal support. Cello is sculpted as a separate add-on piece.
PRODUCTION CHANGES: None.
PARTICULARS: Certificate of Authenticity. Incised Annual Production Mark.
STATUS: RETIRED 9/97.

YEAR	MARK	SRP	GBTru
☐ 1994		$185	**$185**
☐ 1995		185	**185**
☐ 1996		185	**185**
☐ 1997		185	**185**

Donald's Drum Beat

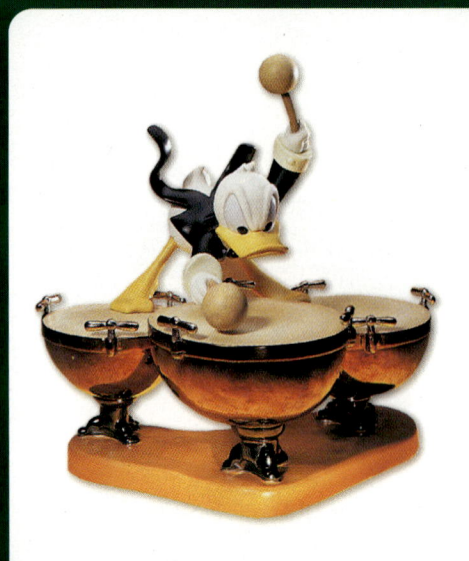

TITLE: Donald's Drum Beat
FIGURINE: Donald Duck
ITEM NUMBER: 41105
SIZE: 8.25"
DATE OF ISSUE: 4/96

PLUSSING: Drums: Drums are painted with a copper and steel metallic paint. **Drum Tuners:** Tuners are pewter.
PRODUCTION CHANGES: None.
PARTICULARS: Certificate of Authenticity. Incised Annual Production Mark.
STATUS: RETIRED 9/97.

YEAR	MARK	SRP	GBTru
☐ 1996	◡	$225	**$350**
☐ 1997	♀	225	**325**

Notes: _____

_____
_____
_____
_____
_____
_____
_____
_____
_____
_____
_____

Symphony Hour

Disney's Tarzan
June 18, 1999

Walt Disney Pictures' animated adventure *Tarzan* is an innovative and entertaining exploration of the classic tale by Edgar Rice Burroughs, with music by award-winning singer/songwriter Phil Collins. *Tarzan* is an adventure that traces the story of a human baby who is orphaned in the African jungle and lovingly raised by a family of apes. Tarzan's peaceful and sheltered world is turned upside down by the arrival of a human expedition and the revelation that he is one of them. As he struggles to decide which "family" he belongs with, his dilemma is further complicated by his feelings for a beautiful young woman named Jane and the discovery that a trusted member of his new human "family" is plotting to harm the apes.

TARZAN QUIKREFERENCE

	TITLE	ITEM #	AVAILABLE
SCROLL:			
Scroll	*Tarzan* Opening Title	41426	7/99
ANNUALS:			
Tarzan	Tarzan Of The Jungle	41427	7/99
Jane	Miss Jane Porter	41428	7/99
Terk	Jungle Rhythm	41429	7/99

Tarzan Opening Title

Photo not available at press time.

TITLE: *Tarzan* Opening Title
SCROLL: Opening Title
ITEM NUMBER: 41426
SIZE: 1.6"
DATE OF ISSUE: 7/99

PLUSSING: None.
PRODUCTION CHANGES: None.
PARTICULARS: Certificate of Authenticity. Decal backstamp with WDCC logo and Annual Production Mark.
STATUS: OPEN EDITION.

YEAR	MARK	SRP	GBTru
☐ 1999	🎩	$29	**$29**

Tarzan

Tarzan Of The Jungle

TITLE: Tarzan Of The Jungle
FIGURINE: Tarzan
ITEM NUMBER: 41427
SIZE: 4.5"
DATE OF ISSUE: 7/99

PLUSSING: None.
PRODUCTION CHANGES: None.
PARTICULARS: Certificate of Authenticity. Incised Annual Production Mark.
STATUS: 1999 ANNUAL.

YEAR	MARK	SRP	GBTru
☐ 1999	🎩	$165	**$165**

Miss Jane Porter

TITLE: Miss Jane Porter
FIGURINE: Jane
ITEM NUMBER: 41428
SIZE: 8.75"
DATE OF ISSUE: 7/99

PLUSSING: Ladle: Jane holds a ladle made of brass and painted silver.
PRODUCTION CHANGES: None.
PARTICULARS: Certificate of Authenticity. Incised Annual Production Mark.
STATUS: 1999 ANNUAL.

YEAR	MARK	SRP	GBTru
☐ 1999	🎩	$150	**$150**

Tarzan 221

Jungle Rhythm

TITLE: Jungle Rhythm
FIGURINE: Terk
ITEM NUMBER: 41429
SIZE: 10.25"
DATE OF ISSUE: 7/99

PLUSSING: Pots & Pans: Some are made of metal and hang from strings. **Bamboo:** Metal. **Barrel:** Silver Paint.
PRODUCTION CHANGES: None.
PARTICULARS: Certificate of Authenticity. Incised Annual Production Mark.
STATUS: 1999 ANNUAL.

YEAR	MARK	SRP	GBTru
☐ 1999		$225	**$225**

Notes: _____

222 Tarzan

The Three Caballeros

February 3, 1945

The Three Caballeros arrived at movie theaters in 1945, like a fast paced travelogue of South America. Everyone's favorite fowl, Donald Duck, is our host, and for once he plays the straight man. Donald is reunited with a co-star from *Saludos Amigos*, José Carioca, a brightly colored Brazilian parrot. José is a combination of a popular folklore figure and a travel guide Disney animators had while on a tour of Rio De Janeiro. The third member of the team is Panchito who evolved to be a combination of a wild gaucho and a hyperactive Mexican rooster.

The research for this film began during World War II, when Walt Disney was invited by the coordinator of Inter-American Affairs to take a goodwill tour of South America. The objective was to encourage friendlier relations with our neighbors to the South. Walt took artists and animators on his tour and the research notes they brought back became the framework for two films. The music with its Latin pulsating rhythms and the bright colors were captured on film by the three unforgettable birds chosen to be the stars. This was Donald's first feature film and Disney's early attempt to mix animation and live action.

THE THREE CABALLEROS QUIKREFERENCE

	TITLE	ITEM #	AVAILABLE
RETIRED EDITIONS:			
Scroll	*The Three Caballeros* Opening Title	41070	8/95 - 4/96
Donald Duck	Amigo Donald	41076	8/95 - 4/96
Jose Carioca (Parrot)	Amigo José	41077	8/95 - 4/96
Panchito (Rooster)	Amigo Panchito	41078	8/95 - 4/96

The Three Caballeros Opening Title

TITLE: *The Three Caballeros* Opening Title
SCROLL: Opening Title
ITEM NUMBER: 41070
SIZE: 1.6"
DATE OF ISSUE: 8/95

PLUSSING: None.
PRODUCTION CHANGES: None.
PARTICULARS: Certificate of Authenticity. Backstamp decal with WDCC logo and Annual Production Mark.
STATUS: RETIRED 4/96.

YEAR	MARK	SRP	GBTru
☐ 1995		$29	**$29**
☐ 1996		29	**29**

Three Caballeros, The

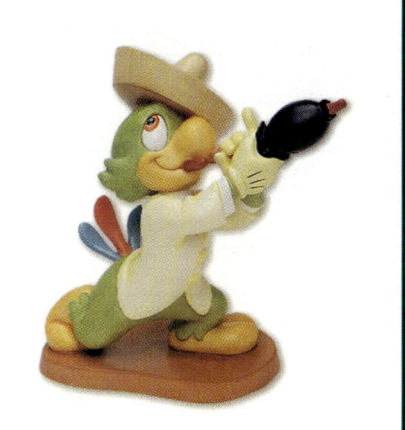

Amigo Donald

TITLE: Amigo Donald
FIGURINE: Donald Duck
ITEM NUMBER: 41076
SIZE: 7"
DATE OF ISSUE: 8/95

PLUSSING: Feathers & Clothes: Special paint formulation on feathers and clothes to highlight vibrant colors. **Anniversary Backstamp:** A special message '*50th Anniversary*' was added to the backstamp of sculptures crafted in 1995.
PRODUCTION CHANGES: None.
PARTICULARS: Certificate of Authenticity. Incised Annual Production Mark.
STATUS: RETIRED 4/96.

YEAR	MARK	SRP	GBTru
☐ 1995	Anniv. Mark	$180	**$180**
☐ 1996		180	**180**

Amigo José

TITLE: Amigo José
FIGURINE: José Carioca
ITEM NUMBER: 41077
SIZE: 7"
DATE OF ISSUE: 8/95

PLUSSING: Feathers & Clothes: Special paint formulation on feathers and clothes to highlight vibrant colors. **Anniversary Backstamp:** A special message '*50th Anniversary*' was added to the backstamp of sculptures crafted in 1995.
PRODUCTION CHANGES: None.
PARTICULARS: Certificate of Authenticity. Incised Annual Production Mark.
STATUS: RETIRED 4/96.

YEAR	MARK	SRP	GBTru
☐ 1995	Anniv. Mark	$180	**$180**
☐ 1996		180	**180**

Three Caballeros, The

Amigo Panchito

TITLE: Amigo Panchito
FIGURINE: Panchito
ITEM NUMBER: 41078
SIZE: 7"
DATE OF ISSUE: 8/95

PLUSSING: Spurs: Has metal spurs that can whirl. **Feathers & Clothes:** Special paint formulation on feathers and clothes to highlight vibrant colors. **Anniversary Backstamp:** A special message '*50th Anniversary*' was added to the backstamp of sculptures crafted in 1995.
PRODUCTION CHANGES: None.
PARTICULARS: Certificate of Authenticity. Incised Annual Production Mark.
STATUS: RETIRED 4/96.

YEAR	MARK	SRP	GBTru
☐ 1995	Anniv. Mark	$180	**$180**
☐ 1996		180	**180**

Three Caballeros, The

THREE LITTLE PIGS
May 27, 1933

The *Three Little Pigs* was part of a 1933 *Silly Symphony* cartoon. It marked a milestone in animation development with imaginative use of color, costuming, movement, sound effects and a great attention to detail.

The Fifer and Fiddler Pigs are carefree musical mates who only want to sing, dance and play. Practical Pig warns that "work and play don't mix" and saves the others from the villainous Big Bad Wolf. The Wolf, of course, schemes to capture the delicious pig trio and add them to his dinner pot.

Music added to the success of the cartoon and the melody "Who's Afraid of the Big Bad Wolf" became so popular that it was also used in a Marx Brothers comedy *Duck Soup*, as well as the Academy Award winning classic *It Happened One Night*.

Sound effects allowed you to hear the huffing and puffing roar of wind as the Wolf blew down the straw house. The audience also heard the sloshing and squishing sound of bricks and mortar as the Practical Pig built his very safe and sturdy house.

The cartoon short was so popular that three sequels were produced: *The Big Bad Wolf* – 1934; *Three Little Wolves* – 1936; and *The Practical Pig* – 1939. All four characters also appeared in the Disney Studios film *Who Framed Roger Rabbit?* produced in 1988. In fact, this cartoon was the most successful one-reel animated short in film history.

THREE LITTLE PIGS QUIKREFERENCE

	TITLE	ITEM #	AVAILABLE
LIMITED EDITION:			
Big Bad Wolf	"Who's Afraid Of The Big Bad Wolf?"	41039	7/93 - 6/94
RETIRED EDITIONS:			
Practical Pig	"Work And Play Don't Mix"	41036	7/93 - 9/98
Fifer Pig	"I Toot My Flute, I Don't Give A Hoot"	41037	7/93 - 9/98
Fiddler Pig	"Hey Diddle Diddle, I Play On My Fiddle"	41038	7/93 - 9/98
Scroll	*Three Little Pigs* Opening Title	41046	7/93 - 9/98
Big Bad Wolf	"I'm A Poor Little Sheep..."	41094	8/96 - 9/98

COMPLEMENTARY PIECES:

ENCHANTED PLACES

RETIRED EDITIONS:			
Sculpture	Fiddler Pig's Stick House	41204	2/96 - 9/98
Sculpture	Fifer Pig's Straw House	41205	2/96 - 9/98
Sculpture	Practical Pig's Brick House	41206	2/96 - 9/98
Miniature	Practical Pig	41216	6/96 - 9/98
Miniature	Fifer Pig	41223	6/96 - 9/98
Miniature	Fiddler Pig	41224	6/96 - 9/98

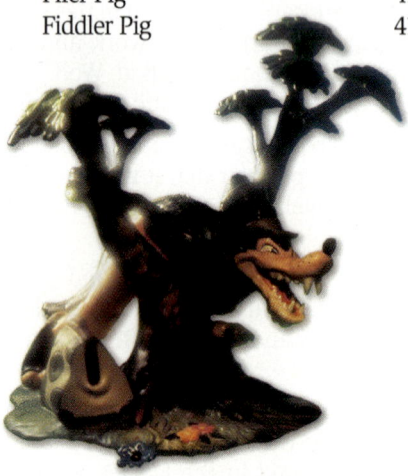

See description page 229.

"Who's Afraid Of The Big Bad Wolf?"

TITLE: "Who's Afraid Of The Big Bad Wolf?"
FIGURINE: Big Bad Wolf
ITEM NUMBER: 41039
SIZE: 8.25"
DATE OF ISSUE: 7/93

PLUSSING: Snarl: A special acrylic clear glaze coating enhances Wolf's devious expression and forms a pool of drool on the ground. **Anniversary Backstamp:** A special gold script message '*60th Anniversary*' was added to backstamp of sculptures crafted in 1993. **Of Special Note:** *Higher numbers were crafted first.*
PRODUCTION CHANGES: Teeth: Enlarged to intensify snarl. Drool changed from milky and bubbly to clear. **Grass:** Out-of-scale grass texture made subtler. **Left Suspender Strap:** Detail increased. **Base:** Increased in size and bottom flattened for backstamp application ease. **Four Distinct Versions:** *Version 1:* Short, straight teeth & hollow core base that looks like *Friend Owl* base. *Version 2:* Short, straight teeth & flat bottom base with reinforcement bar across bottom to prevent shrinkage. *Version 3:* Short, curved teeth. *Version 4:* Long, curved teeth.
PARTICULARS: Hand Numbered Certificate of Authenticity. Incised Annual Production Mark.
STATUS: LIMITED EDITION: 7,500 Hand Numbered Pieces. EDITION CLOSED 6/94.

YEAR	MARK	SRP	GBTru
❏ 1993	𝄞 Anniv. Mark, *Version 1*	$295	**$900**
❏ 1993	𝄞 Anniv. Mark, *Version 2*	295	**800**
❏ 1993	𝄞 Anniv. Mark, *Versions 3 & 4*	295	**600**

"Work And Play Don't Mix"

TITLE: "Work And Play Don't Mix"
FIGURINE: Practical Pig
ITEM NUMBER: 41036
SIZE: 4.5"
DATE OF ISSUE: 7/93

PLUSSING: Trowel: Crafted of real metal. **Anniversary Backstamp:** A special gold script message '*60th Anniversary*' was added to backstamp of sculptures crafted in 1993.
PRODUCTION CHANGES: 𝄞 crafted in Taiwan. Later pieces made in Thailand appear rosier than those made in Taiwan. Note: it's tough to mix other Annual Production Marks with the 𝄞 and have flesh tones match. **SRP Change:** $75 to $85 in 1998.
PARTICULARS: Certificate of Authenticity. Incised Annual Production Mark.

STATUS: RETIRED 9/98.

YEAR	MARK	SRP	GBTru
❏ 1993	𝄞 Anniv. Mark	$75	**$85**
❏ 1994	☥	75	**85**
❏ 1995	∽	75	**85**
❏ 1996	◡	75	**85**
❏ 1997	☥	75	**85**
❏ 1998	⍑	85	**85**

Three Little Pigs

"I Toot My Flute, I Don't Give A Hoot"

TITLE: "I Toot My Flute, I Don't Give A Hoot"
FIGURINE: Fifer Pig
ITEM NUMBER: 41037
SIZE: 4.5"
DATE OF ISSUE: 7/93

PLUSSING: Flute: Crafted of brass, hand painted to look like wood, it is an exact miniature replica with finger holes in the proper positions. **Anniversary Backstamp:** A special gold script message '*60th Anniversary*' was added to backstamp of sculptures crafted in 1993.
PRODUCTION CHANGES: 𝄞 crafted in Taiwan. Later pieces made in Thailand appear rosier than those made in Taiwan. Note: it's tough to mix other Annual Production Marks with the 𝄞 and have flesh tones match. **SRP Change:** $75 to $85 in 1998.
PARTICULARS: Certificate of Authenticity. Incised Annual Production Mark.
STATUS: RETIRED 9/98.

YEAR	MARK	SRP	GBTru
☐ 1993	𝄞	$75	**$85**
	Anniv. Mark		
☐ 1994	🌹	75	**85**
☐ 1995	∽	75	**85**
☐ 1996	⌒	75	**85**
☐ 1997	웃	75	**85**
☐ 1998	✝	85	**85**

"Hey Diddle, Diddle, I Play On My Fiddle"

TITLE: "Hey Diddle, Diddle, I Play On My Fiddle"
FIGURINE: Fiddler Pig
ITEM NUMBER: 41038
SIZE: 4.5"
DATE OF ISSUE: 7/93

PLUSSING: Fiddle Bow: Crafted of metal. **Anniversary Backstamp:** A special gold script message '*60th Anniversary*' was added to backstamp of sculptures crafted in 1993.
PRODUCTION CHANGES: 𝄞 crafted in Taiwan. Later pieces made in Thailand appear rosier than those made in Taiwan. Note: it's tough to mix other Annual Production Marks with the 𝄞 and have flesh tones match. **SRP Change:** $75 to $85 in 1998.
PARTICULARS: Certificate of Authenticity. Incised Annual Production Mark.
STATUS: RETIRED 9/98.

YEAR	MARK	SRP	GBTru
☐ 1993	𝄞	$75	**$85**
	Anniv. Mark		
☐ 1994	🌹	75	**85**
☐ 1995	∽	75	**85**
☐ 1996	⌒	75	**85**
☐ 1997	웃	75	**85**
☐ 1998	✝	85	**85**

Three Little Pigs

Three Little Pigs Opening Title

TITLE: *Three Little Pigs* Opening Title
SCROLL: Opening Title
ITEM NUMBER: 41046
SIZE: 1.6"
DATE OF ISSUE: 7/93

PLUSSING: None.
PRODUCTION CHANGES: None.
PARTICULARS: Certificate of Authenticity. Decal backstamp with WDCC logo and Annual Production Mark.
STATUS: RETIRED 9/98.

YEAR	MARK	SRP	GBTru
☐ 1993		$29	**$29**
☐ 1994		29	29
☐ 1995		29	29
☐ 1996		29	29
☐ 1997		29	29
☐ 1998		29	29

"I'm A Poor Little Sheep..."

TITLE: "I'm A Poor Little Sheep..."
FIGURINE: Big Bad Wolf
ITEM NUMBER: 41094
SIZE: 6"
DATE OF ISSUE: 8/96

PLUSSING: None.
PRODUCTION CHANGES: None.
PARTICULARS: Certificate of Authenticity. Incised Annual Production Mark.
STATUS: RETIRED 9/98.

YEAR	MARK	SRP	GBTru
☐ 1996		$225	**$225**
☐ 1997		225	225
☐ 1998		225	225

Fiddler Pig's Stick House

Sculpture comes with a wood display base with engraved brass nameplate.
STATUS: RETIRED 9/98.

YEAR	MARK	SRP	GBTru
❏ 1996	No Mark	$85	**$85**
❏ 1996	〜	85	**85**
❏ 1997	早	85	**85**
❏ 1998	㐅	85	**85**

TITLE: Fiddler Pig's Stick House
SCULPTURE: Fiddler Pig's Stick House
ITEM NUMBER: 41204
SIZE: 2"
DATE OF ISSUE: 2/96

PLUSSING: Props: Pewter pickax, horseshoe over door, sunflowers. Loose sticks are scattered all over. Props are hand painted.
PRODUCTION CHANGES: New logo and **backstamp** mid-1996. **Annual Production Mark** added mid-1996.
PARTICULARS: Enchanted Places. Certificate of Authenticity. Incised Annual Production Mark. Hand Engraved Serial Number. Registration Card redeemable for a deed "signed" by the setting's original "owner," transferring ownership.

Fifer Pig's Straw House

transferring ownership. Sculpture comes with a wood display base with engraved brass nameplate. Some bases had Fiddler Pig's Stick House nameplate in error.
STATUS: RETIRED 9/98.

YEAR	MARK	SRP	GBTru
❏ 1996	No Mark	$85	**$85**
❏ 1996	〜	85	**85**
❏ 1997	早	85	**85**
❏ 1998	㐅	85	**85**

TITLE: Fifer Pig's Straw House
SCULPTURE: Fifer Pig's Straw House
ITEM NUMBER: 41205
SIZE: 2.5"
DATE OF ISSUE: 2/96

PLUSSING: Props: Door knocker and weather vane are hand-painted pewter. **Flowers:** Sunflowers are poly-resin. **Water:** Water in pail is clear resin.
PRODUCTION CHANGES: New logo and **backstamp** mid-1996. **Annual Production Mark** added mid-1996.
PARTICULARS: Enchanted Places. Certificate of Authenticity. Incised Annual Production Mark. Hand Engraved Serial Number. Registration Card redeemable for a deed "signed" by the setting's original "owner,"

Three Little Pigs

Practical Pig's Brick House

TITLE: Practical Pig's Brick House
SCULPTURE: Practical Pig's Brick House
ITEM NUMBER: 41206
SIZE: 3.75"
DATE OF ISSUE: 2/96

PLUSSING: Props: Fence, shovel, paint bucket, tub, sprinkler and flowerpots are pewter. **Flowers:** Sunflowers are poly-resin. **Cement:** Individually cast sacks of wolf-proof cement. All props are hand painted.
PRODUCTION CHANGES: New logo and **backstamp** mid-1996. **Annual Production Mark** added mid-1996.
PARTICULARS: Enchanted Places. Certificate of Authenticity. Incised Annual Production Mark. Hand Engraved Serial Number. Registration Card redeemable for a deed "signed" by the setting's original "owner," transferring ownership. Sculpture comes with a wood display base with engraved brass nameplate.
STATUS: RETIRED 9/98.

YEAR	MARK	SRP	GBTru
❐ 1996	No Mark	$115	**$115**
❐ 1996	〜	115	**115**
❐ 1997	只	115	**115**
❐ 1998	⟟	115	**115**

Practical Pig

TITLE: Practical Pig
MINIATURE: Practical Pig
ITEM NUMBER: 41216
SIZE: 1"
DATE OF ISSUE: 6/96

PLUSSING: Miniature: Bronze, hand painted.
PRODUCTION CHANGES: None.
PARTICULARS: Enchanted Places. Burgundy box, no picture on box, no Annual Production Mark.
STATUS: RETIRED 9/98.

YEAR	MARK	SRP	GBTru
❐ 1996	No Mark	$50	**$50**

Three Little Pigs

Fifer Pig

TITLE: Fifer Pig
MINIATURE: Fifer Pig
ITEM NUMBER: 41223
SIZE: 1"
DATE OF ISSUE: 6/96

PLUSSING: Miniature: Bronze, hand painted.
PRODUCTION CHANGES: None.
PARTICULARS: Enchanted Places. Burgundy box, no picture on box, no Annual Production Mark.
STATUS: RETIRED 9/98.

YEAR	MARK	SRP	GBTru
❑ 1996	No Mark	$50	**$50**

Fiddler Pig

TITLE: Fiddler Pig
MINIATURE: Fiddler Pig
ITEM NUMBER: 41224
SIZE: 1"
DATE OF ISSUE: 6/96

PLUSSING: Miniature: Bronze, hand painted.
PRODUCTION CHANGES: None.
PARTICULARS: Enchanted Places. Burgundy box, no picture on box, no Annual Production Mark.
STATUS: RETIRED 9/98.

YEAR	MARK	SRP	GBTru
❑ 1996	No Mark	$50	**$50**

Three Little Pigs

'TOUCHDOWN MICKEY'
1932

Mickey, though tiny compare to his sizable opponents, does fancy footwork to gain yard after yard. He gets the winning touchdown and everyone cheers.

Touchdown Mickey

TOUCHDOWN MICKEY QUIKREFERENCE

	TITLE	ITEM #	AVAILABLE
OPEN EDITION:			
Mickey Mouse	"Rah, Rah, Mickey!"	41252	9/98

"Rah, Rah, Mickey!"

TITLE: "Rah, Rah, Mickey!"
FIGURINE: Mickey Mouse
ITEM NUMBER: 41252
SIZE: 5.75"
DATE OF ISSUE: 9/98

PLUSSING: Paint: Black and white tones to honor early Disney animation. **Birthday Backstamp:** A special teal block print message *'Mickey's 70th Birthday'* was added to the backstamp of sculptures crafted in 1998.
PRODUCTION CHANGES: None.
PARTICULARS: Certificate of Authenticity. Incised Annual Production Mark.
STATUS: OPEN EDITION.

YEAR	MARK	SRP	GBTru
☐ 1998	⊤	$150	**$150**
☐ 1999	🕯	150	**150**

TOY STORY
November 22, 1995

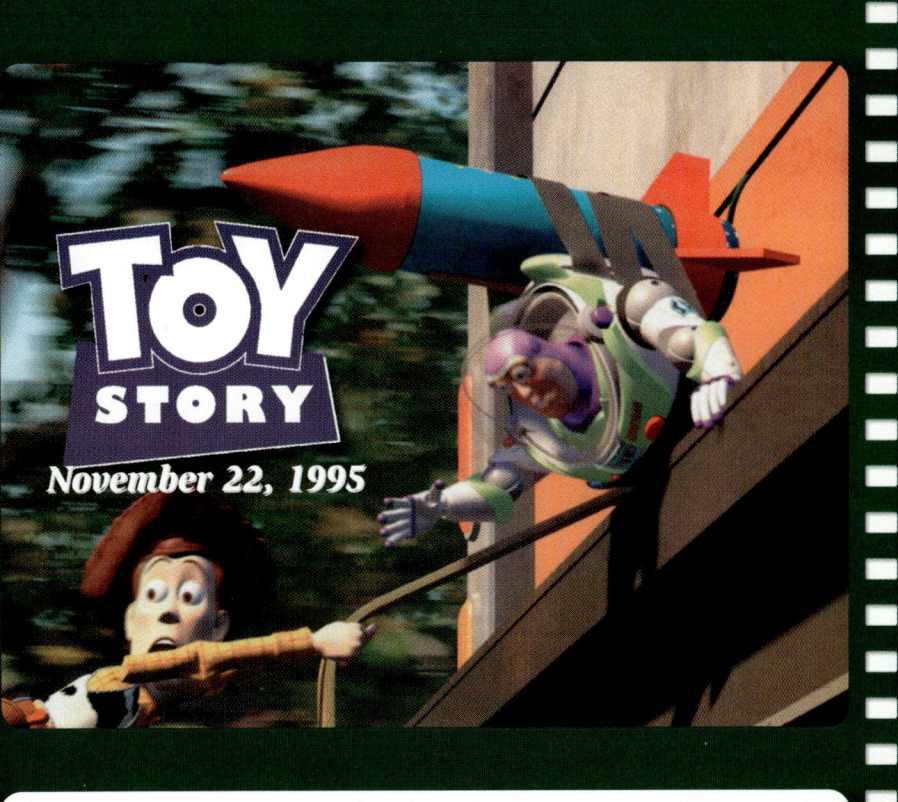

John Lasseter worked as a Disney animator for five years before becoming intrigued with computer graphics. In 1984 he joined Pixar, a computer graphics studio in San Francisco. Following Disney's early years example, Pixar experimented with short films perfecting their craft. When they decided to launch a full-length feature, Disney agreed to sponsor the project. In this medium the artist works with a computer to design and animate the characters. The emphasis is the illusion of life, not just movement. Computer animation is as creative and artistic as that of traditional animation. The computer creates a virtual, three-dimensional onscreen environment.

Suddenly a new space-age traveler appears in six-year-old Andy's room as a brand new toy. It looks like things will never be the same. Buzz Lightyear is a dazzling spectacle of gizmos and gadgets. Sheriff Woody, a pull-string talking cowboy, has always been Andy's favorite toy. All the toys, including Buzz and Woody, view their purpose of providing pleasure for Andy as a job.

Toy Story was a hit with critics and audiences. On March 25, 1996, the Motion Picture Academy presented John Lasseter with a Special Achievement Oscar for "the development and inspired application of techniques that have made possible the first feature-length computer-animated film."

TOY STORY QUIKREFERENCE

	TITLE	ITEM #	AVAILABLE
SCROLL:			
Scroll	*Toy Story* Opening Title	41306	9/98
OPEN EDITIONS:			
Buzz	"To Infinity And Beyond!"	41304	9/98
Woody	"I'm Still Andy's Favorite Toy."	41305	9/98
Bo Peep	"I Found My Moving Buddy."	41320	10/98
Hamm	"It's Showtime."	41321	10/98
LIMITED EDITION:			
Rex	"I'm So Glad You're Not A Dinosaur"	41334	1/99

Toy Story Opening Title

TITLE: *Toy Story* Opening Title
SCROLL: Opening Title
ITEM NUMBER: 41306
SIZE: 1.6"
DATE OF ISSUE: 9/98

PLUSSING: None.
PRODUCTION CHANGES: None.
PARTICULARS: First feature-length film created entirely with computer animation. Certificate of Authenticity. Decal backstamp with WDCC logo and Annual Production Mark.
STATUS: OPEN EDITION.

YEAR	MARK	SRP	GBTru
☐ 1998	T	$29	**$29**
☐ 1999	A	29	**29**

Toy Story

"To Infinity And Beyond!"

TITLE: "To Infinity And Beyond!"
FIGURINE: Buzz
ITEM NUMBER: 41304
SIZE: 6.5"
DATE OF ISSUE: 9/98

PLUSSING: Space Helmet: Real glass dome.
PRODUCTION CHANGES: None.
PARTICULARS: Bases for all pieces are fashioned like Andy's bed quilt. Certificate of Authenticity. Incised Annual Production Mark.
STATUS: OPEN EDITION.

YEAR	MARK	SRP	GBTru
❏ 1998	⊤	$165	**$165**
❏ 1999	◬	165	**165**

"I'm Still Andy's Favorite Toy."

TITLE: "I'm Still Andy's Favorite Toy."
FIGURINE: Woody
ITEM NUMBER: 41305
SIZE: 7.5"
DATE OF ISSUE: 9/98

PLUSSING: Legs: Cast in bronze. **Outfit Accessories: Badge, Holster & Knot On Scarf:** Pewter. **Spurs:** Made of brass and can actually whirl. **Pull Cord Ring:** Brass.
PRODUCTION CHANGES: None.
PARTICULARS: Certificate of Authenticity. Incised Annual Production Mark.
STATUS: OPEN EDITION.

YEAR	MARK	SRP	GBTru
❏ 1998	⊤	$155	**$155**
❏ 1999	◬	155	**155**

Toy Story

"I Found My Moving Buddy."

TITLE: "I Found My Moving Buddy."
FIGURINE: Bo Peep
ITEM NUMBER: 41320
SIZE: 7"
DATE OF ISSUE: 10/98

PLUSSING: Staff: Real metal.
PRODUCTION CHANGES: None.
PARTICULARS: Certificate of Authenticity. Incised Annual Production Mark.
STATUS: OPEN EDITION.

YEAR	MARK	SRP	GBTru
❐ 1998	⊤	$150	**$150**
❐ 1999	◮	150	**150**

"It's Showtime."

TITLE: "It's Showtime."
FIGURINE: Hamm
ITEM NUMBER: 41321
SIZE: 3.25"
DATE OF ISSUE: 10/98

PLUSSING: None.
PRODUCTION CHANGES: None.
PARTICULARS: Certificate of Authenticity. Incised Annual Production Mark.
STATUS: OPEN EDITION.

YEAR	MARK	SRP	GBTru
❐ 1998	⊤	$90	**$90**
❐ 1999	◮	90	**90**

Toy Story

"I'm So Glad You're Not A Dinosaur"

TITLE: "I'm So Glad You're Not A Dinosaur"
FIGURINE: Rex, the Nervous Dinosaur
ITEM NUMBER: 41334
SIZE: 4.5"
DATE OF ISSUE: 1/99

PLUSSING: None.
PRODUCTION CHANGES: None.
PARTICULARS: Certificate of Authenticity. Incised Annual Production Mark.
STATUS: LIMITED EDITION: 4,000 Pieces.

YEAR	MARK	SRP	GBTru
❏ 1998	⚒	$140	**$140**
❏ 1999	🎩	140	**140**

Notes: _____

_____
_____
_____
_____
_____
_____
_____
_____
_____
_____
_____

Toy Story

Who Framed Roger Rabbit?
June 22, 1988

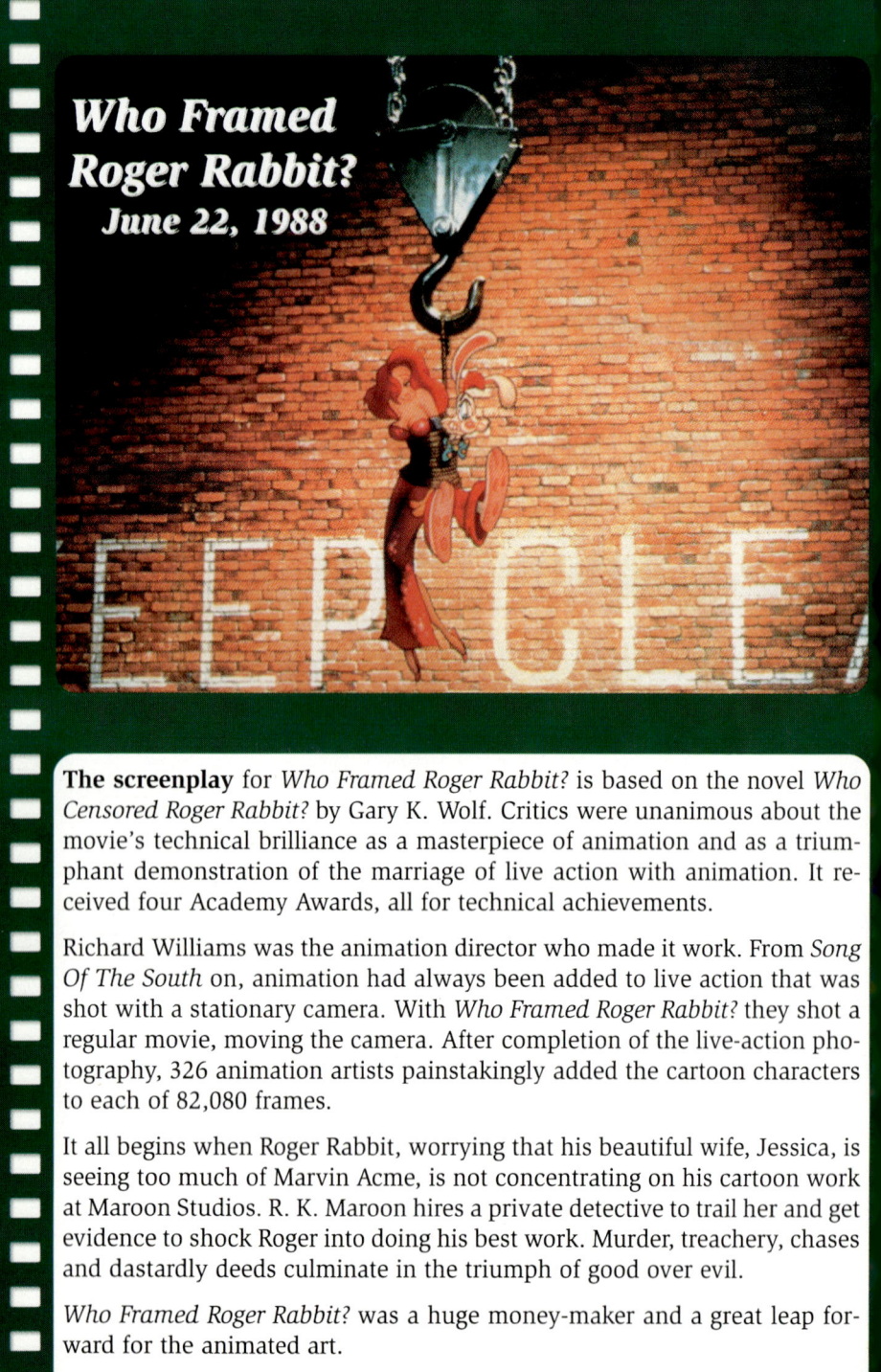

The screenplay for *Who Framed Roger Rabbit?* is based on the novel *Who Censored Roger Rabbit?* by Gary K. Wolf. Critics were unanimous about the movie's technical brilliance as a masterpiece of animation and as a triumphant demonstration of the marriage of live action with animation. It received four Academy Awards, all for technical achievements.

Richard Williams was the animation director who made it work. From *Song Of The South* on, animation had always been added to live action that was shot with a stationary camera. With *Who Framed Roger Rabbit?* they shot a regular movie, moving the camera. After completion of the live-action photography, 326 animation artists painstakingly added the cartoon characters to each of 82,080 frames.

It all begins when Roger Rabbit, worrying that his beautiful wife, Jessica, is seeing too much of Marvin Acme, is not concentrating on his cartoon work at Maroon Studios. R. K. Maroon hires a private detective to trail her and get evidence to shock Roger into doing his best work. Murder, treachery, chases and dastardly deeds culminate in the triumph of good over evil.

Who Framed Roger Rabbit? was a huge money-maker and a great leap forward for the animated art.

WHO FRAMED ROGER RABBIT? QUIKREFERENCE

	TITLE	ITEM #	AVAILABLE
LIMITED EDITION:			
Roger Rabbit and Jessica	"Dear Jessica, How Do I Love Thee?"	41322	11/98

"Dear Jessica, How Do I Love Thee?"

TITLE: "Dear Jessica, How Do I Love Thee?"
FIGURINE: Roger Rabbit and Jessica
ITEM NUMBER: 41322
SIZE: 7.5"
DATE OF ISSUE: 11/98

PLUSSING: Jessica's Shoes: Spike heels are pewter. **Jessica's Gown:** Glitter paint to resemble sequins. **Anniversary Backstamp:** A special gold script message '10th Anniversary' was added to the backstamp of sculptures crafted in 1998.
PRODUCTION CHANGES: None.
PARTICULARS: Certificate of Authenticity. Incised Annual Production Mark.
STATUS: LIMITED EDITION: 7,500 Hand Numbered Pieces.

YEAR	MARK	SRP	GBTru
☐ 1998	⊤	$295	**$295**
	Anniv. Mark		

Who Framed Roger Rabbit? 243

Winnie the Pooh and the honey tree

February 4, 1966

Deep in the Hundred Acre Wood a cuddly old bear lives in a quaint little tree house, under the name of Sanders. Don't be fooled, it's Winnie The Pooh. Here in the woods, Winnie has the time to dream of long explorations, heffalumps and honey. Here in the woods he shares adventures with his special friends and of course, with his biggest human friend, Christopher Robin. Walt Disney was charmed by Pooh's pursuits. He was captivated when he discovered his daughter, Diane, enjoying A. A. Milne's lovable stories.

WINNIE THE POOH AND THE HONEY TREE QUIKREFERENCE

	TITLE	ITEM #	AVAILABLE
EVENT PIECE:			
Winnie the Pooh Ornament	"Up To The Honey Tree"	41176	6/7 & 6/8/97

COMPLEMENTARY PIECES:

ENCHANTED PLACES

OPEN EDITIONS:			
Sculpture	Pooh Bear's House	41231	4/97
Miniature	Winnie The Pooh	41238	4/97
Miniature	Tigger	41274	6/98
Miniature	Eeyore	41319	1/99
Miniature	Piglet	41337	4/99

WALT DISNEY COLLECTORS SOCIETY

MEMBERSHIP GIFT SCULPTURE: (see page 266)
Winnie the Pooh	"Time For Something Sweet"	41091	1996

MEMBERS-ONLY ORNAMENT: (see page 275)
Winnie the Pooh	"Time For Something Sweet"	41096	1/96 - 3/97

"Up To The Honey Tree"

TITLE: "Up To The Honey Tree"
ORNAMENT: Winnie The Pooh
ITEM NUMBER: 41176
SIZE: 5.75"
DATE OF ISSUE: 6/97

PLUSSING: Balloon String: Metal.
PRODUCTION CHANGES: None.
PARTICULARS: Ornament can also be displayed as a freestanding figurine. Certificate of Authenticity. Annual Production Mark.
STATUS: EDITION CLOSED. 1997 Spring Open House Event Piece available 6/7/97 and 6/8/97.

YEAR	MARK	SRP	GBTru
☐ 1997	🯄	$59	**$59**

Pooh Bear's House

TITLE: Pooh Bear's House
SCULPTURE: Pooh Bear's House
ITEM NUMBER: 41231
SIZE: 7.15"
DATE OF ISSUE: 4/97

PLUSSING: Flowers: Honeysuckle and flowers plus other details are pewter. **Mirror:** Painted with special reflective paint.
PRODUCTION CHANGES: None.
PARTICULARS: Enchanted Places. Certificate of Authenticity. Incised Annual Production Mark. Hand Engraved Serial Number. Sculpture comes with a wood display base with engraved brass nameplate.
STATUS: OPEN EDITION.

YEAR	MARK	SRP	GBTru
☐ 1997	🯄	$150	**$150**
☐ 1998	🯅	150	**150**
☐ 1999	🯆	150	**150**

Winnie The Pooh And The Honey Tree

Winnie The Pooh

TITLE: Winnie The Pooh
MINIATURE: Winnie The Pooh
ITEM NUMBER: 41238
SIZE: 1"
DATE OF ISSUE: 4/97

PLUSSING: Miniature: Bronze, hand painted.
PRODUCTION CHANGES: None.
PARTICULARS: Enchanted Places. Green box, picture on box, sticker Annual Production Mark on box and on base of miniature. NALED (National Association Of Limited Edition Dealers) Miniature Of The Year Award.
STATUS: OPEN EDITION.

YEAR	MARK	SRP	GBTru
❏ 1997	♀	$50	**$50**
❏ 1998	↑	50	**50**
❏ 1999	♟	50	**50**

Tigger

TITLE: Tigger
MINIATURE: Tigger
ITEM NUMBER: 41274
SIZE: 1"
DATE OF ISSUE: 6/98

PLUSSING: Miniature: Bronze, hand painted.
PRODUCTION CHANGES: None.
PARTICULARS: Enchanted Places. Green box, picture on box, sticker Annual Production Mark on box and on base of miniature.
STATUS: OPEN EDITION.

YEAR	MARK	SRP	GBTru
❏ 1998	↑	$50	**$50**
❏ 1999	♟	50	**50**

Winnie The Pooh And The Honey Tree

Eeyore

TITLE: Eeyore
MINIATURE: Eeyore
ITEM NUMBER: 41319
SIZE: 1"
DATE OF ISSUE: 1/99

PLUSSING: Miniature: Bronze, hand painted.
PRODUCTION CHANGES: None.
PARTICULARS: Enchanted Places. Green box, picture on box, sticker Annual Production Mark on box and on base of miniature.
STATUS: OPEN EDITION.

YEAR	MARK	SRP	GBTru
☐ 1998	⊤	$50	**$50**
☐ 1999	♟	50	**50**

Piglet

TITLE: Piglet
MINIATURE: Piglet
ITEM NUMBER: 41337
SIZE: 1"
DATE OF ISSUE: 4/99

PLUSSING: Miniature: Bronze, hand painted.
PRODUCTION CHANGES: None.
PARTICULARS: Enchanted Places. Green box, picture on box, sticker Annual Production Mark on box and on base of miniature.
STATUS: OPEN EDITION.

YEAR	MARK	SRP	GBTru
☐ 1999	♟	$50	**$50**

Winnie The Pooh And The Honey Tree

The Wise Little Hen
June 9, 1934

In his first film, Donald is anxious to dodge anything as exhausting as work and feigns a bellyache when the Wise Little Hen asks him to help plant the corn. Then, on baking day she asks him to help her again, but this time it is to help her eat the delights she has baked. Of course he does, but the bowl she passes to him does not contain some rich delicacy, instead it contains a bottle of castor oil!

THE WISE LITTLE HEN QUIKREFERENCE

	TITLE	ITEM #	AVAILABLE
LIMITED EDITION:			
Donald Duck	Donald's Debut	41175	7/97

Donald's Debut

TITLE: Donald's Debut
FIGURINE: Donald Duck
ITEM NUMBER: 41175
SIZE: 5.5"
DATE OF ISSUE: 7/97

PLUSSING: Backstamp: Special Gold Circle Dealer backstamp.
PRODUCTION CHANGES: None.
PARTICULARS: Certificate of Authenticity. Incised Annual Production Mark. In 1997 there were approximately 50 Gold Circle Dealers.
STATUS: LIMITED EDITION: 7,500 Pieces. 1997 Gold Circle Exclusive – 1st Issue.

YEAR	MARK	SRP	GBTru
☐ 1997	？	$110	**$200**

Wise Little Hen, The

MICKEY
Through The Years
1928 - 1990

In 1998 Mickey celebrated ear-to-ear smiles on his 70th Birthday. Walt Disney always had a special bond with his favorite mouse for it is said that Mickey and Walt were connected by heart and soul. Through the years Mickey has become an international icon, a champion of laughter, a symbol of childlike fun the world over and continues to point the way to new adventures and to stand for all things Disney. The four commemorative sculptures introduce this new series. With them Disney fans can enjoy the evolution of Mickey.

MICKEY THROUGH THE YEARS QUIKREFERENCE

Created In Honor Of Mickey's 70th Birthday

	TITLE	ITEM #	AVAILABLE
OPEN EDITIONS:			
Plane Crazy, 1928	How To Fly	41268	4/98
The Band Concert, 1935	From The Top	41277	6/98
Fantasia, 1940	Summoning The Stars	41278	8/98
The Prince And The Pauper, 1990	Long Live The King	41279	9/98
ANNUAL:			
Display Base Set	Mickey Through The Years Base Set	41301	6/98 - 12/98

How To Fly

Production Mark. First Mickey Mouse cartoon ever produced, but the third to be released and then was re-released with sound added after the success of *Steamboat Willie*.

STATUS: OPEN EDITION.

YEAR	MARK	SRP	GBTru
❏ 1998	⊼	$100	$100
	BDay Backstamp		
❏ 1999	⌂	100	100

TITLE: How To Fly
FIGURINE: Mickey Mouse
ITEM NUMBER: 41268
SERIES: Mickey Through The Years Series: 1st Issue
FILM: *Plane Crazy*, 1928
In a tribute to Charles Lindbergh, Mickey stars as a first-time pilot who takes sweetheart Minnie on a hair-raising ride in a plane he built himself.
SIZE: 4.75"
DATE OF ISSUE: 4/98

PLUSSING: Birthday Backstamp: A special teal block print message 'Mickey's 70th Birthday' was added to the backstamp of sculptures crafted in 1998. **Tail:** Metal.
PRODUCTION CHANGES: None.
PARTICULARS: Certificate of Authenticity. Incised Annual

From The Top

TITLE: From The Top
FIGURINE: Mickey Mouse
ITEM NUMBER: 41277
SERIES: Mickey Through The Years Series: 2nd Issue
FILM: *The Band Concert*, 1935
Even a tornado can't break Mickey's concentration as he leads an outdoor concert band in the William Tell Overture.
SIZE: 5.5"
DATE OF ISSUE: 6/98

PLUSSING: Birthday Backstamp: A special teal block print message *'Mickey's 70th Birthday'* was added to the backstamp of sculptures crafted in 1998.
PRODUCTION CHANGES: Baton: Real metal.
PARTICULARS: Certificate of Authenticity. Incised Annual Production Mark. The first Mickey Mouse cartoon produced in color.
STATUS: OPEN EDITION.

YEAR	MARK	SRP	GBTru
☐ 1998	⚒	$100	**$100**
	BDay Backstamp		
☐ 1999	🎩	100	**100**

Summoning The Stars

TITLE: Summoning The Stars
FIGURINE: Mickey Mouse
ITEM NUMBER: 41278
SERIES: Mickey Through The Years Series: 3rd Issue
FILM: *Fantasia*, 1940
SIZE: 5.5"
DATE OF ISSUE: 8/98

PLUSSING: Birthday Backstamp: A special teal block print message *'Mickey's 70th Birthday'* was added to the backstamp of sculptures crafted in 1998.
PRODUCTION CHANGES: None.
PARTICULARS: When Yensid (Disney spelled backward), the Sorcerer, leaves his magic hat, Mickey can't resist trying it on to do a little helpful magic. However, he conjures up an army of brooms that he can't control. Certificate of Authenticity. Incised Annual Production Mark. The first film to show the modernized Mickey, the way we recognize him today.
STATUS: OPEN EDITION.

YEAR	MARK	SRP	GBTru
☐ 1998	⚒	$100	**$100**
	BDay Backstamp		
☐ 1999	🎩	100	**100**

Mickey Through The Years

Long Live The King

TITLE: Long Live The King
FIGURINE: Mickey Mouse
ITEM NUMBER: 41279
SERIES: Mickey Through The Years Series: 4th Issue
FILM: *The Prince And The Pauper*, 1990

Mickey stars in a dual role in this classic tale about look-alikes who swap places for a day. Problems arise when the evil Captain of the Guard plans a takeover.
SIZE: 4.25"
DATE OF ISSUE: 9/98

PLUSSING: Crown & Scepter: Gold accents on both. **Birthday Backstamp:** A special teal block print message *'Mickey's 70th Birthday'* was added to the backstamp of sculptures crafted in 1998.

PRODUCTION CHANGES: None.
PARTICULARS: Certificate of Authenticity. Incised Annual Production Mark. This is only the third time in over 35 years that Mickey has appeared in a new film.
STATUS: OPEN EDITION.

YEAR	MARK	SRP	GBTru
☐ 1998	⊥	$100	$100
	BDay Backstamp		
☐ 1999	⛵	100	100

Mickey Through The Years Base Set

TITLE: Mickey Through The Years Base Set
ACCESSORY BASE SET: Display Bases
ITEM NUMBER: 41301
DATE OF ISSUE: 6/98

PLUSSING: Birthday Backstamp: A special teal block print message *'Mickey's 70th Birthday'* was added to the backstamp of sculptures crafted in 1998.
PRODUCTION CHANGES: None.
PARTICULARS: Set of four bases with each base having a plaque with the individual film name. In sizes ranging from .75" to 2.5". No Certificate of Authenticity. No Annual Production Mark.
STATUS: 1998 ANNUAL.

YEAR	MARK	SRP	GBTru
☐ 1998	No Mark	$30	$30

Theme Park Attractions

Premiered at Disneyland on June 17, 1972 and retired November 1996, The Main Street Electrical Parade remains one of the most popular legacies in Disneyland history.

"The music started and you stretched to catch a glimpse of the first twinkling lights. Soon the night glowed with Disney's magic. Stretching over a quarter of a mile and featuring over half-a-million twinkling lights, The Main Street Electrical Parade was performed for over 6 million guests. A befuddled green turtle squinted through glasses as he spun along the route. Taking up the end of the parade was Pete's Dragon, Elliott. His purple wings towered above the gathered crowd as he blew smoke into the night air."

THEME PARK ATTRACTIONS QUIKREFERENCE

TITLE		ITEM #	AVAILABLE

MAIN STREET ELECTRICAL PARADE:

ENCHANTED PLACES

OPEN EDITIONS:

Train	Goofy's Train	41289	8/98
Drum	Mickey's Drum	41290	8/98
Bug	Lightning Bug	41291	8/98
Elliot	Pete's Dragon	41384	5/99
Turtle	Twinkling Turtle	41385	5/99

HAUNTED MANSION ATTRACTION:
EVENT PIECE:

Hitchhiking Ghosts	Beware of Hitchhiking Ghosts	41418	3/99

Goofy's Train

TITLE: Goofy's Train
FIGURINE: Goofy's Train
ITEM NUMBER: 41289
SIZE: 6.5"
DATE OF ISSUE: 8/98

PLUSSING: Sculpture Lights: Battery powered. **Paint Trim:** Gold paint highlights all details. **Flagpole:** Metal. **Material:** Clear resin mold, hand painted with areas undone for lights to shine through. **PRODUCTION CHANGES:** None. **PARTICULARS:** Enchanted Places. From 1972 through 1996, Disneyland featured a one-of-kind spectacle, The Main Street Electrical Parade, where guests would line Main Street and enjoy each float as it passed by. The commemorative sculpture comes with a wood base with an engraved brass plaque.

Certificate of Authenticity. Incised Annual Production Mark.
STATUS: OPEN EDITION.

YEAR	MARK	SRP	GBTru
☐ 1998	𐃯	$145	**$145**
☐ 1999	🪔	145	**145**

256 Theme Park Attractions

Mickey's Drum

TITLE: Mickey's Drum
FIGURINE: Mickey's Drum
ITEM NUMBER: 41290
SIZE: 7.5"
DATE OF ISSUE: 8/98

PLUSSING: Sculpture Lights: Battery powered. **Paint Trim:** Gold paint highlights all details. **Flagpole:** Metal. **Material:** Clear resin mold, hand painted with areas undone for lights to shine through.
PRODUCTION CHANGES: None.
PARTICULARS: Enchanted Places. From 1972 through 1996, Disneyland featured a one-of-kind spectacle, The Main Street Electrical Parade, where guests would line Main Street and enjoy each float as it passed by. The commemorative sculpture comes with a wood base with an engraved brass plaque.

Certificate of Authenticity. Incised Annual Production Mark.
STATUS: OPEN EDITION.

YEAR	MARK	SRP	GBTru
❏ 1998	⌂	$145	**$145**
❏ 1999	⌂	145	**145**

Lightning Bug

TITLE: Lightning Bug
FIGURINE: Lightning Bug
ITEM NUMBER: 41291
SIZE: 4.75"
DATE OF ISSUE: 8/98

PLUSSING: Sculpture Lights: Battery powered. **Paint Trim:** Gold paint highlights all details. **Material:** Clear resin mold, hand painted with areas undone for lights to shine through.
PRODUCTION CHANGES: None.
PARTICULARS: Enchanted Places. From 1972 through 1996, Disneyland featured a one-of-kind spectacle, The Main Street Electrical Parade, where guests would line Main Street and enjoy each float as it passed by. The commemorative sculpture comes with a wood base with an engraved brass plaque.

Certificate of Authenticity. Incised Annual Production Mark.
STATUS: OPEN EDITION.

YEAR	MARK	SRP	GBTru
❏ 1998	⌂	$85	**$85**
❏ 1999	⌂	85	**85**

Theme Park Attractions

Pete's Dragon

TITLE: Pete's Dragon
FIGURINE: Elliott
ITEM NUMBER: 41384
SIZE: 7"
DATE OF ISSUE: 5/99

PLUSSING: Sculpture Lights: Battery powered. **Paint Trim:** Gold paint highlights all details. **Material:** Clear resin mold, hand painted with areas undone for lights to shine through.
PRODUCTION CHANGES: None.
PARTICULARS: Enchanted Places. From 1972 through 1996, Disneyland featured a one-of-kind spectacle, The Main Street Electrical Parade, where guests would line Main Street and enjoy each float as it passed by. The commemorative sculpture comes with a wood base with an engraved brass plaque.

Certificate of Authenticity. Incised Annual Production Mark.
STATUS: OPEN EDITION.

YEAR	MARK	SRP	GBTru
☐ 1999	🎩	$165	**$165**

Twinkling Turtle

TITLE: Twinkling Turtle
FIGURINE: Turtle
ITEM NUMBER: 41385
SIZE: 4.5"
DATE OF ISSUE: 5/99

PLUSSING: Sculpture Lights: Battery powered. **Paint Trim:** Gold paint highlights all details. **Material:** Clear resin mold, hand painted with areas undone for lights to shine through.
PRODUCTION CHANGES: None.
PARTICULARS: Enchanted Places. From 1972 through 1996, Disneyland featured a one-of-kind spectacle, The Main Street Electrical Parade, where guests would line Main Street and enjoy each float as it passed by. The commemorative sculpture comes with a wood base with an engraved brass plaque.

Certificate of Authenticity. Incised Annual Production Mark.
STATUS: OPEN EDITION.

YEAR	MARK	SRP	GBTru
☐ 1999	🎩	$85	**$85**

TITLE: Beware Of Hitchhiking Ghosts
FIGURINE: Hitchhiking Ghosts
ITEM NUMBER: 41418
SIZE: Various
DATE OF ISSUE: 3/99

PLUSSING: Special Commemorative Backstamp: Commemorates First WDAC Convention. **3 Piece Set. Chain:** Metal.
PRODUCTION CHANGES: None.
PARTICULARS: Created to honor the Haunted Mansion Attraction. Certificate of Authenticity. Incised Annual Production Mark.
STATUS: LIMITED EDITION: 1,500 Hand Numbered Pieces. Available at First Collector's Convention for Walt Disney Art Classics, 3/19 to 3/21/99, Orlando, Florida.

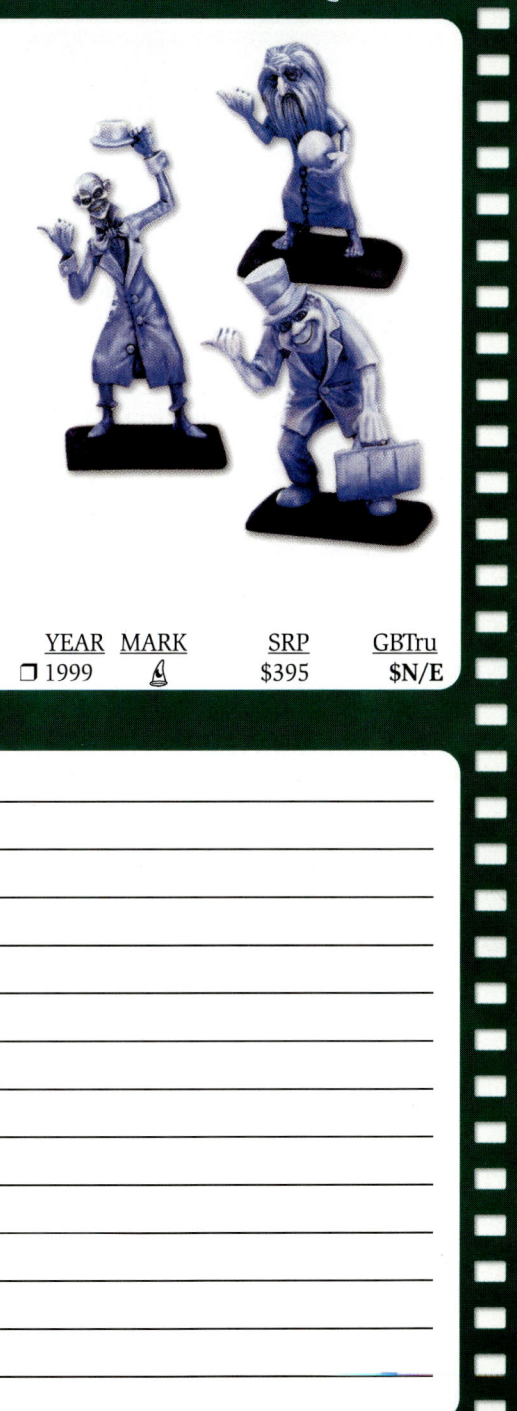

YEAR	MARK	SRP	GBTru
❒ 1999	🎩	$395	$N/E

Notes:

THE WALT DISNEY COLLECTORS SOCIETY

The Charter Year 1993
The Walt Disney Collectors Society was launched in January, 1993. It had taken only one short year for collectors to ask for a forum that would enhance their enjoyment of the sculptures that comprise the WDCC.

The Classics Collection responded by enlisting respected Disney archivist and writer, Paula Sigman, to lead a team in forming the Society. Everyone who signed up from January through December 31, 1993 would become a Charter Member. Membership was priced at $52 in the US and $54 in Canada. Benefits of membership included:

- A personalized, embossed plastic Membership Card.
- A cloisonne Charter Year Membership Pin.
- A folio box to hold Society memorabilia.
- The opportunity to acquire pieces crafted for Members only.
- A four-issue subscription to the full color magazine, *SKETCHES*.
- A gift sculpture of Jiminy Cricket, Society symbol and mascot.

The Second Year 1994
Membership benefits increased in 1994, with the addition of a hot-line newsletter produced by Society Manager, Paula Sigman. Conceived as a vehicle to keep collectors informed up-to-the-minute about production timetables, rumors and queries, the *NewsFlash* was an immediate success.

SKETCHES, the Society magazine, grew to 16 full-color pages from 12. The Society Membership Gift Sculpture and cloisonne pin featured that ever-grinning, pink and purple rascal, the Cheshire Cat from *Alice In Wonderland*. Members renewing early received a sketch of the animators' work in developing the Cheshire Cat sculpture. A paper portfolio was included in the renewal materials to hold welcome information and an order form for back issues of *SKETCHES*. Renewing members dues were $49 and new members paid $55. Canadian rates: $68 and $76, respectively.

SHARE THE MAGIC – The Society launched a Friendship Membership Drive in the Fall with the offer of a portfolio of *The Lion King* animation art prints to any member giving a membership as a gift. The drive lasted from September 15 to December 31, 1994.

The Third Year 1995

In addition to the benefits described in the first 2 years, a fine art print of the original animation drawing that inspired the WDCS Membership Gift Sculpture, Dumbo, was a special premium for members renewing at least one month before their expiration date. A Society Hotline 800-932-5749 or 800-WD-CLSIX was added. 1995 also saw the introduction of the Members-Only Ornaments.

The WDCS Folio @ $15, back issues of *SKETCHES* ($3.50 - $5.00), and *Making Of The WDCS Video* @ $12.50 were made available via direct response. The Society's Signature Boutique featuring Members-Only Society logo merchandise made its debut.

Fees remained the same.

The Fourth Year 1996

All benefits as previously described. Again this year, members renewing early received a 5 x 7 fine art print of the actual drawing that inspired 1996's Membership Gift Sculpture, Winnie the Pooh.

Fees were $49 US and $76 Canadian.

Beginning in 1996, the Annual Production Mark on Membership Sculptures was replaced by a simple year mark indicating the membership year for which the sculpture is intended.

The Fifth Year 1997

All benefits as previously described. Beginning in 1997, a special piece was offered to all members celebrating their 5th Anniversary with the Society. The piece features Mickey as Steamboat Willie and was available to Charter Members in 1997 since that was the Society's 5th Birthday. The sculpture featured a special Charter Member backstamp. The same piece, without the Charter Member backstamp, is offered to all members upon their fifth consecutive year with the Club.

Again this year, members renewing early received a fine art print of the actual drawing that inspired 1997's Membership Gift Sculpture, Magician Mickey.

The WDCS Folio Box is now available separately from the Society for $10.00.

Also included in kit–exclusive WDCS Coupon Book and Member Services Guide.

Fees were $49 US and $68 Canadian.

The Sixth Year 1998
All benefits as previously described. The 1998 Membership Gift Sculpture was Timon from *The Lion King* and this year the Membership Pin also featured Timon.

Fees were $49 US and $76 Canadian.

The Seventh Year 1999
In addition to the previously described benefits, members receive a copy of the 1999 WDCC Catalog.

The 1999 Membership Gift Sculpture is Lady from *Lady And The Tramp*, with the cloisonne Membership Pin also featuring Lady.

Fees are $50 US and $76 Canadian.

Annual Production Marks have been re-instated on Society pieces, the only exception being the Membership Gift Sculpture.

THE WALT DISNEY COLLECTORS SOCIETY QUIKREFERENCE

	TITLE	ITEM #	AVAILABLE
MEMBERSHIP GIFT SCULPTURES:			
CHARTER:			
Jiminy Cricket	"Cricket's The Name, Jiminy Cricket!"	41035	1993
MEMBERSHIP & RENEWAL:			
Cheshire Cat	" 'Twas Brillig"	41057	1994
Dumbo	"Simply Adorable"	41082	1995
Winnie The Pooh	"Time For Something Sweet"	41091	1996
Mickey Mouse	"On With The Show!"	41134	1997
Timon	"Luau!"	41197	1998
Lady	"A Perfectly Beautiful Little Lady"	41327	1999

ANIMATORS' CHOICE SCULPTURES:

Mickey Mouse	"I Let 'Em Have It!"	41048	1993
Donald Duck	Admiral Duck	41055	1994
Cruella De Vil	"Anita Daahling!"	41088	1995
Minnie Mouse	Princess Minnie	41095	1996
Goofy	"Oh, The World Owes Me A Livin'"	41138	1997
Pluto	Sticky Situation	41199	1998
Tinker Bell	"Tinker Bell Pauses To Reflect"	41366	1999

AMERICAN FOLK HEROES:

Pecos Bill and Widowmaker	Pecos Bill	41059	1994
Slue Foot Sue	Slue Foot Sue	41075	1995
Casey	Casey At The Bat	41107	1996

DISPLAY BASES FOR MEMBERSHIP SCULPTURES:

Display Base	Membership Gift	41052	9/94
Display Base	Members-Only	41053	9/94

MEMBERS-ONLY ORNAMENTS:

Dumbo	"Simply Adorable"	41081	1995
Winnie The Pooh	"Time For Something Sweet"	41096	1996
Mickey Mouse	"On With The Show!"	41135	1997
Timothy Mouse	Friendship Offering	41179	1998
Timon	"Luau!"	41262	1998
White Rabbit	"No Time To Say Hello - Goodbye!"	41373	1999

MEMBERS-ONLY SERICELS:

Mickey & Minnie	Storybook Sweethearts	12K-2BLT-010	1996
Goofy	Goofy Delivery	12K-2GOF-050	1997
Pluto	Sticky Situation	12K-2PLU-020	1998
White Rabbit	"I'm Late"	1035092	1999

DISNEY VILLAIN SERIES:

Maleficent	"The Mistress Of All Evil"	41177	1997
Jafar	"Oh Mighty Evil One"	41280	1998
Cruella De Vil	"It's That De Vil Woman!"	41405	1999

Walt Disney Collectors Society

FIVE-YEAR ANNIVERSARY SCULPTURES:

Mickey Mouse	Mickey's Debut (CHARTER)	41136	1997
Mickey Mouse	Mickey's Debut (NON-CHARTER)	41255	1998

MEMBERS-ONLY NUMBERED LIMITED EDITION SCULPTURE:

Autumn Fairy	The Touch Of An Autumn Fairy	41281	7/98

MEMBERS-ONLY SCENE COMPLETER SCULPTURE:

Pumbaa & Timon	Double Trouble	41416	5/99

"Cricket's The Name, Jiminy Cricket"

TITLE: "Cricket's The Name, Jiminy Cricket"
FIGURINE: Jiminy Cricket
ITEM NUMBER: 41035
FILM: *Pinocchio*, 1940
SIZE: 4"
DATE OF ISSUE: 1/93

PLUSSING: Backstamp: A special backstamp incorporates the WDCC Society Logo and Charter designation.

PRODUCTION CHANGES: Head Position: Original — Head *straight*. Corrected — Head *tilted* to one side to look more animated.

PARTICULARS: Certificate of Authenticity. Incised Annual Production Mark. GREENBOOK lists amount of membership dues as SRP. Membership was priced at $52 in the U.S. and $54 in Canada. Disney valued the piece at $75. Sold on Secondary as sculpture only (^{S}) or entire kit (^{K}).

STATUS: 1993 Charter Member Gift Sculpture. EDITION CLOSED 12/31/93.

YEAR	MARK	SRP	GBTru	
☐ 1992	✲	$52	$220^S/240^K	Straight
☐ 1992	✲	52	330^S/350^K	Tilted
☐ 1993	§	52	185^S/200^K	Tilted

Charter Membership Gift Sculpture

"'Twas Brillig"

TITLE: "'Twas Brillig"
FIGURINE: Cheshire Cat
ITEM NUMBER: 41057
FILM: *Alice In Wonderland*, 1951
SIZE: 4.75"
DATE OF ISSUE: 1/94

PLUSSING: Backstamp: Special WDCS 1994 Gift Sculpture backstamp.
PRODUCTION CHANGES: Original Version: Smaller and plainer. **Subsequent Version:** More detailed, taller and wider, higher gloss finish.
PARTICULARS: Certificate of Authenticity. Incised Annual Production Mark. GREENBOOK lists amount of membership dues as SRP. Renewing Members dues were $49, new Members paid $55. Canadian rates: $68 and $76, respectively. Disney valued the piece at $75. Sold on Secondary as sculpture only (^{S}) or entire kit (^{K}).
STATUS: 1994 Membership Gift Sculpture. EDITION CLOSED 12/31/94.

YEAR	MARK	SRP	GBTru
❏ 1993		$55	**$120^S/120^K**
❏ 1994		55	100^S/110^K

"Simply Adorable"

TITLE: "Simply Adorable"
FIGURINE: Dumbo
ITEM NUMBER: 41082
FILM: *Dumbo*, 1941
SIZE: 3.5"
DATE OF ISSUE: 1/95

PLUSSING: Backstamp: 1995 WDCS Membership Gift Sculpture backstamp.
PRODUCTION CHANGES: None.
PARTICULARS: Certificate of Authenticity. Incised Annual Production Mark. GREENBOOK lists amount of membership dues as SRP. Renewing Members dues were $49, new Members paid $55. Canadian rates: $68 and $76, respectively. Disney valued the piece at $75. Sold on Secondary as sculpture only (^{S}) or entire kit (^{K}).
STATUS: 1995 Membership Gift Sculpture. EDITION CLOSED 12/31/95.

YEAR	MARK	SRP	GBTru
❏ 1995		$55	**$90^S/100^K**

Membership & Renewal Gift Sculptures

"Time For Something Sweet"

TITLE: "Time For Something Sweet"
FIGURINE: Winnie The Pooh
ITEM NUMBER: 41091
FILM: *Winnie The Pooh And The Honey Tree*, 1966
SIZE: 3.5"
DATE OF ISSUE: 1/96

PLUSSING: Honey: Glistening honey, made of resin, drips from Pooh's honey pot and paws. *Variation:* No honey dripping from paws.
Backstamp: Special WDCS Membership Gift Sculpture backstamp.
PRODUCTION CHANGES: None.
PARTICULARS: Certificate of Authenticity. No Annual Production Mark – beginning in 1996 the Annual Production Mark was replaced with a simple year mark indicating the membership year for which the sculpture is intended. GREENBOOK lists amount of membership dues as SRP. Dues were $49; Canadian $76. Disney valued the piece at $75. Sold on Secondary as sculpture only (^{S}) or entire kit (^{K}).
STATUS: 1996 Membership Gift Sculpture. EDITION CLOSED 12/31/96.

YEAR	MARK	SRP	GBTru
☐ 1996	No Mark	$49	$85^S/95^K

"On With The Show!"

TITLE: "On With The Show!"
FIGURINE: Mickey Mouse
ITEM NUMBER: 41134
FILM: *Magician Mickey*, 1937
Donald is Mickey's ubiquitous heckler in this short. Mickey does something very foolish with his magic tricks, and creates even more Donald Ducks. Fortunately, the spell wears off quickly. Mickey calls the shots and in due course Donald gets his come-uppance.
SIZE: 4.75"
DATE OF ISSUE: 1/97

PLUSSING: Wand: Edge is brushed with gold metallic paint. **Paint Finishes:** Range from glossy to matte.
Backstamp: 1997 Walt Disney Collector's Society Membership Sculpture backstamp.
PRODUCTION CHANGES: None.
PARTICULARS: Certificate of Authenticity. No Annual Production Mark. GREENBOOK lists amount of membership dues as SRP. Dues were $49; Canadian $68. Disney valued the piece at $75. Sold on secondary as sculpture only (^{S}) or entire kit (^{K}).
STATUS: 1997 Membership Gift Sculpture. EDITION CLOSED 12/31/97.

YEAR	MARK	SRP	GBTru
☐ 1997	No Mark	$49	$75^S/75^K

Membership & Renewal Gift Sculptures

"Luau!"

TITLE: "Luau!"
FIGURINE: Timon
ITEM NUMBER: 41197
FILM: *The Lion King*, 1994
SIZE: 4.5"
DATE OF ISSUE: 1/98

PLUSSING: Backstamp: 1998 Walt Disney Collector's Society Membership Sculpture backstamp.
PRODUCTION CHANGES: None.
PARTICULARS: Certificate of Authenticity. No Annual Production Mark. GREENBOOK lists amount of membership dues as SRP. Dues were $49; Canadian $76. Disney valued the piece at $80. Sold on Secondary as sculpture only (S) or entire kit (K).
STATUS: 1998 Membership Gift Sculpture. EDITION CLOSED 12/31/98.

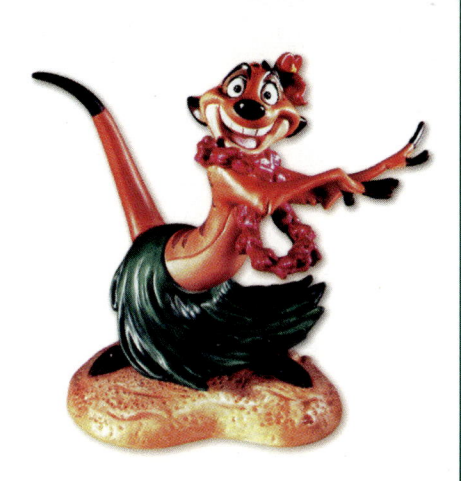

YEAR	MARK	SRP	GBTru
❑ 1998	No Mark	$49	$80^S/$80^K

"A Perfectly Beautiful Little Lady"

TITLE: "A Perfectly Beautiful Little Lady"
FIGURINE: Lady
ITEM NUMBER: 41327
FILM: *Lady And The Tramp*, 1955
SIZE: 3.5"
DATE OF ISSUE: 1/99

PLUSSING: Hatbox: Porcelain with opalescent ribbons. **Backstamp:** 1999 Walt Disney Collector's Society Membership Figurine backstamp.
PRODUCTION CHANGES: None.
PARTICULARS: Certificate of Authenticity. No Annual Production Mark. GREENBOOK lists amount of membership dues as SRP. Dues are $50; Canadian $76. Disney values the piece at $80. (Entire membership kit is Item #43415.) Sold on Secondary as sculpture only (S) or entire kit (K).
STATUS: 1999 Membership Gift Sculpture. EDITION CLOSES 12/31/99.

YEAR	MARK	SRP	GBTru
❑ 1998	No Mark	$50	$80^S/$80^K

Membership & Renewal Gift Sculptures

"I Let 'Em Have It!"

TITLE: "I Let 'Em Have It!"
FIGURINE: Mickey Mouse
ITEM NUMBER: 41048
SERIES: Animators' Choice, 1993 Selection: 1st Issue
FILM: *Brave Little Tailor*, 1938 This short was based on one of Grimm's fairy-tales. It starts with Mickey working away in his tailor-shop. But the buzzing flies won't leave him alone, and he bats at them with a swat, killing seven of them with a single blow. Outside, the townspeople are discussing the giant that is terrorizing the village. They hear his proud boasts and assume him to be a doughty giant-killer. Mickey is offered six million gold pazoozas and the hand of the King's beautiful daughter if he will kill the giant. Off he goes to do battle and win both riches and the fair Princess Minnie.
SIZE: 7.25"
DATE OF ISSUE: 7/93

PLUSSING: Scissors: Matte platinum finish used to resemble well-worn pewter. **Story Book:** A miniature story book, *Mickey Mouse Tales*, was given to Charter Members as a special Thank You.
Backstamp: Animators' Choice Backstamp incorporates the Society Logo.
PRODUCTION CHANGES: Scissors: Original art showed scissors with high shine. Animators felt scissors should not look new.
PARTICULARS: Certificate of Authenticity. Incised Annual Production Mark. (*Found with 1995's ∾ and 1996's ∽ due to replacements for breakage.) Companion piece to 1996's Animator's Choice, *Princess Minnie*.

STATUS: Available to Society Members by Special Order with Redemption Certificate from 7/93 until EDITION CLOSED 3/31/94.

YEAR	MARK	SRP	GBTru
☐ 1993	ʂ	$160	**$250**
☐ 1995	∾	160	**240**
☐ 1996	∽	160	**240**

Animators' Choice Sculptures

Admiral Duck

TITLE: Admiral Duck
FIGURINE: Donald Duck
ITEM NUMBER: 41055
SERIES: Animators' Choice, 1994
Selection: 2nd Issue
FILM: *Sea Scouts*, 1939
Mischievous mayhem ensues as Huey, Dewey and Louie are taught the finer points of seamanship by their uncle, Commodore Donald.
SIZE: 6.25"
DATE OF ISSUE: 7/94

PLUSSING: Gold Plating: On epaulettes and buttons of uniform jacket. **Life Preserver:** A Special Gift of hand-painted resin. It fits neatly over Donald's tail. It reads: "S. S. Rear Admiral." **Backstamp:** Animators' Choice Backstamp incorporates the Society Logo.
PRODUCTION CHANGES: None.

PARTICULARS: Certificate of Authenticity. Incised Annual Production Mark.
STATUS: Available to Society Members by Special Order with Redemption Certificate from 7/94 until EDITION CLOSED 3/31/95.

YEAR	MARK	SRP	GBTru
❏ 1994	♀	$165	**$165**

"Anita Daahling!"

TITLE: "Anita Daahling!"
FIGURINE: Cruella De Vil
ITEM NUMBER: 41088
SERIES: Animators' Choice, 1995
Selection: 3rd Issue
FILM: *One Hundred And One Dalmatians*, 1961
SIZE: 10"
DATE OF ISSUE: 3/95

PLUSSING: Legs & Arms: Made of bronze with feet firmly anchored in a pewter base painted to resemble carpeting. **Handbag:** On left arm, has gold braided cord strap. **Cigarette & Holder:** Are bronze. **Backstamp:** Animators' Choice Backstamp incorporates the Society Logo.
PRODUCTION CHANGES: None.
PARTICULARS: Certificate of Authenticity. Incised Annual Production Mark.

STATUS: Available to Society Members by Special Order with Redemption Certificate from 3/95 until EDITION CLOSED 3/31/96.

YEAR	MARK	SRP	GBTru
❏ 1995	◡	$250	**$390**
❏ 1996	◠	250	**375**

Animators' Choice Sculptures

Princess Minnie

TITLE: Princess Minnie
FIGURINE: Minnie Mouse
ITEM NUMBER: 41095
SERIES: Animators' Choice, 1996 Selection: 4th Issue
FILM: *Brave Little Tailor*, 1938
SIZE: 6.5"
DATE OF ISSUE: 3/96

PLUSSING: Veil: Painted with an opalescent paint. **Shoe Buckles:** Painted in gold. **Backstamp:** Minnie is the first to feature the new design Animators' Choice Backstamp incorporating the Society Logo.
PRODUCTION CHANGES: None.
PARTICULARS: Certificate of Authenticity. Incised Annual Production Mark. Companion piece to 1993's Animator's Choice, *Mickey Mouse as the Brave Little Tailor*.
STATUS: Available to Society

Members by Special Order with Redemption Certificate from 3/96 until EDITION CLOSED 3/31/97.

YEAR	MARK	SRP	GBTru
☐ 1996		$165	**$225**

"Oh, The World Owes Me A Livin'"

TITLE: "Oh, The World Owes Me A Livin'"
FIGURINE: Goofy
ITEM NUMBER: 41138
SERIES: Animators' Choice, 1997 Selection: 5th Issue
FILM: *Moving Day*, 1936

Donald and Mickey are being evicted by the bullying Sheriff Pete who plans to sell off all their furniture because they are seriously behind with the rent. Fortunately Pete leaves and the two begin to rapidly move house. The friendly neighborhood ice-man, Goofy, lends them his truck and his dippy but good-natured services. With classic incompetence, the three of them try to clear out before Pete gets back.

SIZE: 8.5"
DATE OF ISSUE: 1/97

PLUSSING: Hair: Sprigs of real horsehair on his head. **Shoe:** Hole in the sole of the shoe. **Tire treads:** Goofy's truck tire treads on base. **Paint:** Combination from glossy to matte finishes. **Backstamp:** Animators' Choice incorporates the Society Logo.
PRODUCTION CHANGES: None.
PARTICULARS: Certificate of Authenticity. No Annual Production Mark.
STATUS: Available to Society Members by Special Order with Redemption Certificate from 1/97 until EDITION CLOSED 3/31/98.

YEAR	MARK	SRP	GBTru
☐ 1997	No Mark	$185	**$185**

Animators' Choice Sculptures

Sticky Situation

TITLE: Sticky Situation
FIGURINE: Pluto
ITEM NUMBER: 41199
SERIES: Animators' Choice, 1998
Selection: 6th Issue
FILM: *Beach Picnic*, 1939
Mickey and his loyal pup Pluto are busy setting things up to enjoy a beautiful day at the beach, but then Pluto's battle with pesky flypaper changes everything.
SIZE: 3.25"
DATE OF ISSUE: 1/98

PLUSSING: Backstamp: Animators' Choice incorporates the Society Logo.
PRODUCTION CHANGES: None.
PARTICULARS: Certificate of Authenticity. No Annual Production Mark.
STATUS: Available to Society Members by Special Order with Redemption Certificate from 1/98 until EDITION CLOSED 3/31/99.

YEAR	MARK	SRP	GBTru
❐ 1998	No Mark	$150	**$150**

"Tinker Bell Pauses To Reflect"

TITLE: "Tinker Bell Pauses To Reflect"
FIGURINE: Tinker Bell
ITEM NUMBER: 41366
SERIES: Animators' Choice, 1999
Selection: 7th Issue
FILM: *Peter Pan*, 1953
SIZE: Tinker Bell 6.75", Mirror 10" long
DATE OF ISSUE: 1/99

PLUSSING: Mirror: Real mirror with a pewter rim. **Tinker Bell's Feet:** Made of bronze. **Wings:** Opalescent paint is used to create a shimmery look. NOTE: Tinker Bell is created as a completely separate piece from the mirror she stands upon.
PRODUCTION CHANGES: None.
PARTICULARS: Figurine ships in two pieces to reduce breakage. This is the first in a new grouping from the favorite film moments of Walt Disney's original team of animators, "The Nine Old Men." This sculpture honors Marc Davis. A lithograph featuring model sheet sketches comes with the piece. Certificate of Authenticity. Incised Annual Production Mark.
STATUS: Available to Society Members by Special Order with Redemption Certificate from 1/99 until EDITION CLOSES 3/31/00.

YEAR	MARK	SRP	GBTru
❐ 1998	⊤	$240	**$240**
❐ 1999	≜	240	**240**

Animators' Choice Sculptures

Pecos Bill

TITLE: Pecos Bill
FIGURINE: Pecos Bill and Widowmaker
ITEM NUMBER: 41059
SERIES: American Folk Heroes, 1994 Selection: 1st Issue
FILM: *Melody Time*, 1948
In the Old West, a little baby boy tumbles out of a covered wagon. He finds succor in a litter of coyotes and Pecos Bill grows up to be the toughest "coyote" of them all. One day, out in the desert, he saves the life of Widowmaker the horse and a beautiful friendship ensues.
SIZE: 9.5"
DATE OF ISSUE: 7/4/94
PLUSSING: Reins: Made of suede. **Platinum Accents:** Platinum on the studs on Bill's chaps, Widowmaker's bridle and stirrups. **Maximum Com-plexity:** More than 40 separate segments make up each sculpture. **Backstamp:** Backstamp incorporates the Society Logo and American Folk Heroes designation.
PRODUCTION CHANGES: None.
PARTICULARS: Certificate of Authenticity. Incised Annual Production Mark.
STATUS: EDITION CLOSED. Available 7/4/94 to 8/31/94 by commission only, for existing Society Members. New 8/94 Members given courtesy extension to 9/30/94. Announced Edition Size of 10,462 pieces.

YEAR	MARK	SRP	GBTru
☐ 1994	♀	$650	$650

Slue Foot Sue

TITLE: Slue Foot Sue
FIGURINE: Slue Foot Sue
ITEM NUMBER: 41075
SERIES: American Folk Heroes, 1995 Selection: 2nd Issue
FILM: *Melody Time*, 1948
Pecos Bill meets Slue Foot Sue as she rides down the river on the back of a giant fish. It is love at first sight but Bill is thwarted in love when she is thrown from the back of a jealous Widowmaker and bounces right up to the moon.
SIZE: 10.5"
DATE OF ISSUE: 7/4/95
PLUSSING: Special Lasso: Crafted of fine metal. **Backstamp:** Backstamp incorporates the Society Logo and American Folk Heroes designation.
PRODUCTION CHANGES: None.
PARTICULARS: Certificate of Authenticity. Incised Annual Production Mark.
STATUS: EDITION CLOSED. Available 7/4/95 to 8/31/95 by commission only, for existing Society Members. Announced Edition Size of 6,574 pieces.

YEAR	MARK	SRP	GBTru
☐ 1995	∞	$695	$695

Casey At The Bat

TITLE: Casey At The Bat
FIGURINE: Casey
ITEM NUMBER: 41107
SERIES: American Folk Heroes, 1996 Selection: 3rd Issue
FILM: *Make Mine Music*, 1946
The situation is perilous for the Mudville Nine and Casey is ready to show how he can save the day. He needs to do well but contemptuously ignores the first pitch and sits on his bat for the second. Now he steps up to the plate and waits his moment to shine, or alternatively, not.
SEGMENT: *Casey At The Bat*
SIZE: 8.5"
DATE OF ISSUE: 7/4/96

PLUSSING: Bat: Real wood. **Legs & Feet:** Bronze. **Backstamp:** Backstamp incorporates the Society Logo and American Folk Heroes designation.
PRODUCTION CHANGES: None.
PARTICULARS: Certificate of Authenticity. Incised Annual Production Mark.
STATUS: EDITION CLOSED. Available 7/4/96 to 8/31/96 by commission only, for existing Society Members.

YEAR	MARK	SRP	GBTru
☐ 1996		$395	**$395**

Notes:

American Folk Heroes

Display Base for Membership Gift Sculptures

TITLE: Display Base for Membership Gift Sculptures
ACCESSORY BASE: Display Base
ITEM NUMBER: 41052
SIZE: .75" x 3.5" x 4.5"
DATE OF ISSUE: 9/94

PLUSSING: Material: Ivory porcelain. **Legend:** Front of base reads *Walt Disney Collectors Society Membership Gift Sculpture* in teal green.
PRODUCTION CHANGES: Color Variation: 1998 has whiter tone. **Annual Production Mark:** Reissue (1998) is not marked.
PARTICULARS: In September 1994, responding to collector requests, bases that had been intended for dealers to display the Membership Gift Sculptures in stores were made available to collectors. (Note that one does not have to be a Society Member to purchase this piece.) Certificate of Authenticity. Incised Annual Production Mark.
STATUS: SUSPENDED 1996. REISSUED 1998.

YEAR	MARK	SRP	GBTru
☐ 1993	ⓢ	$25	**$35**
	Dealer Version		
☐ 1994	⚘	25	**35**
☐ 1995	∽	25	**25**
☐ 1996	⌒	25	**25**
☐ 1998	No Mark	25	**25**

Display Base for Members-Only Sculptures

TITLE: Display Base for Members-Only Sculptures
ACCESSORY BASE: Display Base
ITEM NUMBER: 41053
SIZE: 1" x 5.75" x 4.25"
DATE OF ISSUE: 9/94

PLUSSING: Material: Ivory porcelain. **Legend:** Front of base reads *Walt Disney Collectors Society Members-Only Sculpture* in teal green.
PRODUCTION CHANGES: Color Variation: 1998 has whiter tone. **Annual Production Mark:** Reissue (1998) is not marked.
PARTICULARS: In September 1994, responding to collector requests, bases that had been intended for dealers to display the Membership Sculptures in stores were made available to collectors. (Note that one does not have to be a Society Member to purchase this piece.) Certificate of Authenticity. Incised Annual Production Mark.
STATUS: SUSPENDED 1996. REISSUED 1998.

YEAR	MARK	SRP	GBTru
☐ 1993	ⓢ	$25	**$60**
☐ 1994	⚘	25	**60**
☐ 1995	∽	25	**25**
☐ 1996	⌒	25	**25**
☐ 1998	No Mark	25	**25**

"Simply Adorable"

TITLE: "Simply Adorable"
ORNAMENT: Dumbo
ITEM NUMBER: 41081
SERIES: Members-Only Ornaments, 1995 Selection: 1st Issue
FILM: *Dumbo*, 1941
SIZE: 4.5"
DATE OF ISSUE: 1/95

PLUSSING: Material & Design: White low-fire flat porcelain plussed with hand-applied gold detailing. A gold hanger cord is attached. Coordinates with 1995 Membership Gift Sculpture. Special gift box.
PRODUCTION CHANGES: None.
PARTICULARS: Certificate of Authenticity. No Annual Production Mark.
STATUS: EDITION CLOSED 3/31/96. 1995 Members-Only Ornament. Was available 1/95 to 3/31/96 with Society Redemption Certificate.

YEAR	MARK	SRP	GBTru
❒ 1995	No Mark	$20	**$48**

"Time For Something Sweet"

TITLE: "Time For Something Sweet"
ORNAMENT: Winnie The Pooh
ITEM NUMBER: 41096
SERIES: Members-Only Ornaments, 1996 Selection: 2nd Issue
FILM: *Winnie The Pooh And The Honey Tree*, 1966
SIZE: 4.5"
DATE OF ISSUE: 1/96

PLUSSING: Material & Design: White low-fire flat porcelain plussed with hand-applied gold detailing. A gold hanger cord is attached. Coordinates with 1996 Membership Gift Sculpture. Special gift box.
PRODUCTION CHANGES: None.
PARTICULARS: Certificate of Authenticity. No Annual Production Mark.
STATUS: EDITION CLOSED 3/31/97. 1996 Members-Only Ornament. Was available 1/96 to 3/31/97 with Society Redemption Certificate.

YEAR	MARK	SRP	GBTru
❒ 1996	No Mark	$25	**$50**

"On With The Show!"

TITLE: "On With The Show!"
ORNAMENT: Mickey Mouse
ITEM NUMBER: 41135
SERIES: Members-Only Ornaments, 1997 Selection: 3rd Issue
FILM: *Magician Mickey*, 1937
SIZE: 4.75"
DATE OF ISSUE: 1/97

PLUSSING: Material & Design: White low-fire flat porcelain plussed with hand-applied gold detailing. A gold hanger is attached. Coordinates with 1997 Membership Gift Sculpture. Special gift box.
PRODUCTION CHANGES: None.
PARTICULARS: Certificate of Authenticity. No Annual Production Mark.
STATUS: 1997 Members-Only Ornament. Was available 1/97 to 3/31/98 with Society Redemption Certificate.

YEAR	MARK	SRP	GBTru
❑ 1997	No Mark	$25	**$25**

Friendship Offering

TITLE: Friendship Offering
ORNAMENT: Timothy Mouse
ITEM NUMBER: 41179
SERIES: Members-Only Figural Ornaments, 1998 Selection: 1st Issue
FILM: *Dumbo*, 1941
SIZE: 3.5"
DATE OF ISSUE: 1/98

PLUSSING: Hat & Jacket: Gold metallic paint highlights on both.
PRODUCTION CHANGES: None.
PARTICULARS: Three-dimensional (Figural) Ornament. Certificate of Authenticity. No Annual Production Mark.
STATUS: Dated 1998 Members-Only Ornament. Available 1/98 to 3/31/99 with Society Redemption Certificate.

YEAR	MARK	SRP	GBTru
❑ 1998	No Mark	$55	**$55**

Members-Only Ornaments

"Luau!"

TITLE: "Luau!"
ORNAMENT: Timon
ITEM NUMBER: 41262
SERIES: Members-Only Ornaments, 1998 Selection: 4th & Final Issue
FILM: *The Lion King*, 1994
SIZE: 4.5"
DATE OF ISSUE: 1/98

PLUSSING: Material & Design: White low-fire flat porcelain plussed with hand-applied gold detailing. A gold hanger is attached. Coordinates with 1998 Membership Gift Sculpture. Special gift box.
PRODUCTION CHANGES: None.
PARTICULARS: Certificate of Authenticity. No Annual Production Mark.
STATUS: 1998 Members-Only Ornament. Was available 1/98 to 3/31/99 with Society Redemption Certificate.

YEAR	MARK	SRP	GBTru
☐ 1998	No Mark	$25	**$55**

"No Time To Say Hello - Goodbye!"

TITLE: "No Time To Say Hello - Goodbye!"
ORNAMENT: White Rabbit
ITEM NUMBER: 41373
SERIES: Members-Only Figural Ornaments, 1999 Selection: 2nd Issue
FILM: *Alice In Wonderland*, 1951
SIZE: 4"
DATE OF ISSUE: 1/99

PLUSSING: Glasses: Wire rim spectacles. **Pocket watch:** Metal trim and chain and metallic gold paint.
PRODUCTION CHANGES: None.
PARTICULARS: Three-dimensional (Figural) Ornament. Certificate of Authenticity. Incised Annual Production Mark.
STATUS: Dated 1999 Members-Only Ornament. Must be ordered by 3/31/2000 with Society Redemption Certificate.

YEAR	MARK	SRP	GBTru
☐ 1998	T	$59	**$59**
☐ 1999	A	59	59

Members-Only Ornaments

"Storybook Sweethearts"

TITLE: "Storybook Sweethearts"
SERICEL: Mickey and Princess Minnie
ITEM NUMBER: 12K-2BLT-010
FILM: *Brave Little Tailor*, 1938
SIZE: 21.5" x 14" framed
DATE OF ISSUE: 2/96

PLUSSING: Frame & Material: Black mica frame, dual aperture with matting.
PRODUCTION CHANGES: None.
PARTICULARS: Animation art companion piece to complement the Animators' Choice sculptures "I Let 'Em Have It" (1993) and "Princess Minnie" (1996), substantiated by a Walt Disney Animation Art Seal and a Certificate of Authenticity. Limited Edition of 1,688.
STATUS: Available by mail order only to Walt Disney Collectors

Society Members who were active between 2/1/96 and 5/15/96. (Orders had to be postmarked by 7/1/96.) EDITION CLOSED 7/1/96.

YEAR	MARK	SRP	GBTru
☐ 1996	No Mark	$225	**$225**

Goofy Delivery

TITLE: Goofy Delivery
SERICEL: Goofy
ITEM NUMBER: 12K-2GOF-050
FILM: *Moving Day*, 1936
SIZE: 15.75" x 18.5" framed
DATE OF ISSUE: 3/97

PLUSSING: Frame & Material: Black mica frame, dual aperture with matting.
PRODUCTION CHANGES: None.
PARTICULARS: Companion piece to the 1997 Animator's Choice sculpture, "Oh, The World Owes Me a Livin'". Each sericel is substantiated by a Walt Disney Studios Animation Art Seal and a Certificate of Authenticity. Offer to Society Members by direct mail with a limit of one per membership.
STATUS: EDITION CLOSED 6/97. Available to Society Members active

between 3/1/97 and 5/31/97 by commission order. Announced Edition Size of 2,622.

YEAR	MARK	SRP	GBTru
☐ 1997	No Mark	$225	**$225**

Members-Only Sericels

Sticky Situation

TITLE: Sticky Situation
SERICEL: Pluto
ITEM NUMBER: 12K-2PLU-020
FILM: *Beach Picnic*, 1939
SIZE: 15.75" x 18.5" framed
DATE OF ISSUE: 3/98

PLUSSING: Frame & Material: Black mica frame, with matting.
PRODUCTION CHANGES: None.
PARTICULARS: Companion piece to the 1998 Animator's Choice sculpture, "Sticky Situation." Each sericel is substantiated by a Walt Disney Studios Animation Art Seal and a Certificate of Authenticity. Offer to Society Members by direct mail with a limit of one per membership.
STATUS: EDITION CLOSED 7/31/98. Available to Society Members active between 3/30/98 and 6/15/98 by commission order.

YEAR	MARK	SRP	GBTru
❒ 1998	No Mark	$195	**$195**

"I'm Late"

TITLE: "I'm Late"
SERICEL: White Rabbit
ITEM NUMBER: 1035092
FILM: *Alice In Wonderland*, 1951
SIZE: 16" x 16" framed
DATE OF ISSUE: 3/99

PLUSSING: Frame & Material: Black mica frame, with matting.
PRODUCTION CHANGES: None.
PARTICULARS: The first 1,500 will be signed by David Pacheco. Each sericel is substantiated by a Walt Disney Studios Animation Art Seal and a Certificate of Authenticity. Offer to Society Members by direct mail with a limit of one per membership. Companion piece to 1999 Members Only Ornament, "No Time To Say Hello-Goodbye!"
STATUS: Available to Society Members active between 3/15/99 and 5/30/99 by commission order.

YEAR	MARK	SRP	GBTru
❒ 1999	No Mark	$225	**$225**

Members-Only Sericels

"The Mistress Of All Evil"

TITLE: "The Mistress Of All Evil"
FIGURINE: Maleficent
ITEM NUMBER: 41177
SERIES: Disney Villains Series – 1st Issue
FILM: *Sleeping Beauty*, 1940
SIZE: 7.5"
DATE OF ISSUE: 6/97

PLUSSING: Staff: Solid bronze. **Orb:** Tops staff and is semiprecious stone Aventurine. **Paint:** Layered, with lighter colors over black, applied by sponge and stipple technique.
PRODUCTION CHANGES: None.
PARTICULARS: The first 3,000 Members to order received a special edition lithograph (11" x 14") of Maleficent, Item Number 11K-20137-0, from the Collectors Society. Hand Numbered Certificate of Authenticity. Incised Annual Production Mark.

Some sculptures are marked "DD" for Dealer Display.
STATUS: Available 6/1/97 to Society Members by special Redemption Certificate until EDITION CLOSED 9/15/97. Final Edition size of 7,047 Hand Numbered Pieces including dealer displays.

YEAR	MARK	SRP	GBTru
☐ 1997	♀	$450	**$465**

"Oh Mighty Evil One"

TITLE: "Oh Mighty Evil One"
FIGURINE: Jafar
ITEM NUMBER: 41280
SERIES: Disney Villains Series – 2nd Issue
FILM: *Aladdin*, 1992
SIZE: 8.75"
DATE OF ISSUE: 4/98

PLUSSING: Hourglass: Hand blown glass with red and gold-painted cobras atop a brick pedestal. **Face & Fingers:** Made out of bronze. **Jafar's Body:** Porcelain. **Turban Jewel:** Genuine red garnet.
PRODUCTION CHANGES: None.
PARTICULARS: Certificate of Authenticity. Incised Annual Production Mark. Some sculptures are marked "DD" for Dealer Display. The Dealer Displays had a different Item Number, 41312; GBTru$ is $400.

STATUS: Available 4/1/98 to Society Members by special Redemption Certificate until EDITION CLOSED 7/98. Final edition size to be announced.

YEAR	MARK	SRP	GBTru
☐ 1998	⊤	$395	**$400**

TITLE: "It's That De Vil Woman!"
FIGURINE: Cruella De Vil
ITEM NUMBER: 41405
SERIES: Disney Villains Series – 3rd Issue
FILM: *One Hundred And One Dalmatians*, 1961
SIZE: 8.75"
DATE OF ISSUE: 5/99

PLUSSING: Headboard & Footboard: Resin. **Arms & Cigarettes:** Bronze. **Nightstand Items:** Pewter.
PRODUCTION CHANGES: None.
PARTICULARS: Certificate of Authenticity. Incised Annual Production Mark. Available for 101 days.
STATUS: Available 5/23/99 to Society Members by special Redemption Certificate until EDITION CLOSES 8/31/99. Final edition size to be announced.

YEAR	MARK	SRP	GBTru
❑ 1999	🎩	$450	**$450**

Notes: _____

Disney Villain Series   281

Mickey's Debut

TITLE: Mickey's Debut
FIGURINE: Mickey Mouse
ITEM NUMBER: 41136
FILM: *Steamboat Willie*, 1928
SIZE: 5.25"
DATE OF ISSUE: 1/97

PLUSSING: Wheel: Steamship wheel turns. **Tail:** Mickey's tail is metal. **Legs:** Mickey's legs are porcelain designed in "rubber hose" look. **Paint:** Monochromatic theme as in original cartoon. **Charter Member Backstamp:** Special backstamp commemorating the Society's 5th Birthday for Charter Members.
PRODUCTION CHANGES: None.
PARTICULARS: First animated film with synchronized sound. Certificate of Authenticity.
STATUS: 5th Anniversary Of Society Charter Membership Edition Sculpture. EDITION CLOSED 3/98.

YEAR	MARK	SRP	GBTru
❏ 1997	No Mark	$175	**$345**

Mickey's Debut

TITLE: Mickey's Debut
FIGURINE: Mickey Mouse
ITEM NUMBER: 41255
FILM: *Steamboat Willie*, 1928
SIZE: 5.25"
DATE OF ISSUE: 1/98

PLUSSING: Wheel: Steamship wheel turns. **Tail:** Mickey's tail is metal. **Legs:** Mickey's legs are porcelain designed in "rubber hose" look. **Paint:** Monochromatic theme as in original cartoon.
PRODUCTION CHANGES: None.
PARTICULARS: First animated film with synchronized sound. Certificate of Authenticity.
STATUS: 5th Anniversary Of Society Non-Charter Membership Edition Sculpture. Available to Society Members upon their 5th Anniversary of Society Membership.

YEAR	MARK	SRP	GBTru
❏ 1998	No Mark	$175	**$175**
❏ 1999	No Mark	175	**175**

Five-Year Anniversary Sculptures

The Touch Of An Autumn Fairy

TITLE: The Touch Of An Autumn Fairy
FIGURINE: Autumn Fairy
ITEM NUMBER: 41281
FILM: *Fantasia,* 1940
SIZE: 8"
DATE OF ISSUE: 7/98

PLUSSING: Fairy: Bronze with opalescent paint highlights. **Wings:** Porcelain with opalescent finish. **Vines & Stems:** Bronze. **Seed Pods:** Porcelain.
PRODUCTION CHANGES: None.
PARTICULARS: Tchaikovsky's *Nutcracker Suite* centers its story on the luminescent fairies grouped by seasons. The Autumn Fairies usher in the harvest season. First Society Limited Edition. Redemption forms included with the May 1998 Member newsletter *NewsFlash*, to be processed on a first-come, first-served basis. Certificate of Authenticity. Incised Annual Production Mark.
STATUS: LIMITED EDITION: 5,000 Hand Numbered Pieces. Collectors Society Members-Only Sculpture. EDITION CLOSED 7/98. (Because of early Redemption Certificate this piece sold out immediately.)

YEAR	MARK	SRP	GBTru
❏ 1998	⊤	$495	**$650**

Members-Only Numbered Limited Edition Sculpture

Double Trouble

TITLE: Double Trouble
FIGURINE: Pumbaa and Timon
ITEM NUMBER: 41416
FILM: *The Lion King*, 1994
SIZE: 5.5"
DATE OF ISSUE: 5/99

PLUSSING: Timon: Cast in pewter. **Backstamp:** Special WDCC Society backstamp. **Anniversary Backstamp:** Special '5th Anniversary' message was added to the WDCC backstamp on 1999 sculptures.
PRODUCTION CHANGES: None.
PARTICULARS: Certificate of Authenticity. No Annual Production Mark. Redemption forms included in the April edition of *Sketches* magazine.
STATUS: Available to Society Members by Special Order with

Redemption Certificate from 5/99 until EDITION CLOSES 3/31/00.

YEAR	MARK	SRP	GBTru
☐ 1999	🎩	$135	**$135**

Notes: _____

Members-Only Scene Completer Sculpture

Announcements As We Go To Press

"Hooray, Hooray, For Pooh Will Soon Be Free!"

TITLE: "Hooray, Hooray, For Pooh Will Soon Be Free!"
FIGURINE: Winnie The Pooh
ITEM NUMBER: 41437
FILM: *Winnie The Pooh And The Honey Tree*, 1966
SIZE: 5.75"
DATE OF ISSUE: 8/99

PLUSSING: None.
PRODUCTION CHANGES: None.
PARTICULARS: Certificate of Authenticity. Incised Annual Production Mark.
STATUS: LIMITED EDITION: 5,000 Numbered Pieces. 1999 Gold Circle Exclusive — 4th Issue.

YEAR	MARK	SRP	GBTru
❏ 1999	⛵	$525	**$525**

New Additions

First Aiders Opening Title

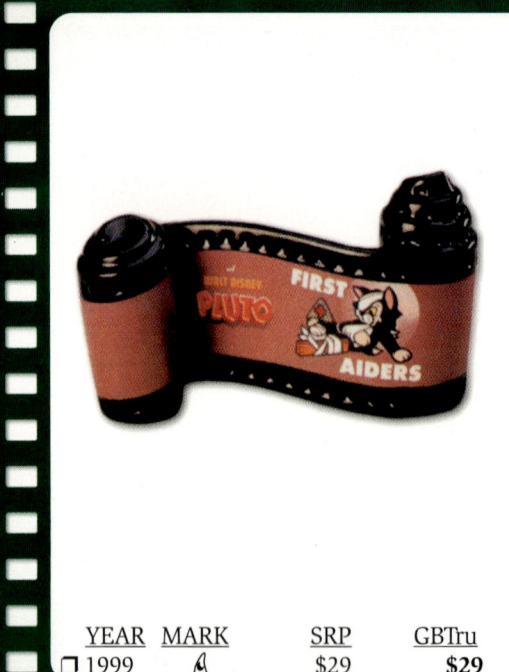

TITLE: *First Aiders* Opening Title
SCROLL: Opening Title
ITEM NUMBER: 41379
FILM: *First Aiders*, 1944.
SIZE: 1.6"
DATE OF ISSUE: 10/99

PLUSSING: None.
PRODUCTION CHANGES: None.
PARTICULARS: Certificate of Authenticity. Decal backstamp with WDCC logo and Annual Production Mark.
STATUS: OPEN EDITION.

YEAR	MARK	SRP	GBTru
❏ 1999	⛵	$29	**$29**

Minnie

TITLE: Minnie
FIGURINE: Minnie
ITEM NUMBER: 41339
FILM: *First Aiders*, 1944. Doing her bit for the war effort in 1944, Minnie Mouse learns first aid — with the help of a couple of energetic, mischievous, volunteer patients.
SIZE: 4.5"
DATE OF ISSUE: 10/99

PLUSSING: None.
PRODUCTION CHANGES: None.
PARTICULARS: Certificate of Authenticity. Incised Annual Production Mark.
STATUS: OPEN EDITION.

YEAR	MARK	SRP	GBTru
❏ 1999	⛵	$110	**$110**

286 New Additions

Pluto

TITLE: Pluto
FIGURINE: Pluto
ITEM NUMBER: 41340
FILM: *First Aiders*, 1944
SIZE: 5.25"
DATE OF ISSUE: 10/99

PLUSSING: Tail: Metal.
PRODUCTION CHANGES: None.
PARTICULARS: Certificate of Authenticity. Incised Annual Production Mark.
STATUS: OPEN EDITION.

YEAR	MARK	SRP	GBTru
❏ 1999	⌂	$95	**$95**

Figaro

TITLE: Figaro
FIGURINE: Figaro
ITEM NUMBER: 41341
FILM: *First Aiders*, 1944
SIZE: 3.75"
DATE OF ISSUE: 10/99

PLUSSING: None.
PRODUCTION CHANGES: None.
PARTICULARS: Certificate of Authenticity. Incised Annual Production Mark.
STATUS: OPEN EDITION.

YEAR	MARK	SRP	GBTru
❏ 1999	⌂	$85	**$85**

New Additions

QUIKREFERENCE

DISNEYANA EXCLUSIVES
			PAGE
9/96	Pongo with Pepper and Penny	41132	143
9/97	Chernabog	41180	76
9/98	Snow White and Prince	41307	199

GOLD CIRCLE DEALER EXCLUSIVES
				PAGE
7/97	Donald Duck	1st Issue	41175	250
1/98	Carp with Harp	2nd Issue	41194	108
1/99	Daisy Duck	3rd Issue	41313	59

THE TRIBUTE SERIES
				PAGE
3/95	Mufasa and Simba	1st Issue	41085	104
3/96	Pocahontas	2nd Issue	41098	171
3/97	Quasimodo and Esmeralda	3rd Issue	41143	88
3/98	Hercules	4th Issue	41253	83
3/99	Mulan	5th Issue	41374	134

Subject Index

A

Alice 21
Alice, Mad Hatter,
   March Hare, Dormouse 23
Alligator 74
Angel Donald 62
Ariel 108, 113
Ariel's Secret Grotto 112
Aurora and Philip 184, 187
Autumn Fairy 283

B

Bagheera 93
Baloo 92
Bambi 29
Bambi and Flower 27
Bashful 195, 204
Belle and Beast 33
Big Bad Wolf 229, 231
Birds with Sash 48
Blackfish 111
Blue Centaurette 78
Blue Fairy 156
Bo Peep 240
Brer Bear 208
Brer Fox 207
Brer Rabbit 208
Briar Rose 187, 189
Broom with Water Pails 77
Bruno 47
Buzz 239

C

Captain Hook 150, 153
Captain Hook's Ship 152
Card Painter 22
Carp with Harp 108
Casey 273
Chernabog 76
Cheshire Cat 265
Chip 'N Dale 167
Chip 'N Dale & Santa Candle 164
Chip 'N Dale with Santa Candle 169
Cinderella 46
Cinderella and Prince 44
Cinderella and Prince Charming 43
Cinderella's Castle 52, 53
Cinderella's Coach 50, 52
Cinderella's Dress 45
Clara Cluck 217
Clarabelle Cow 215
Cogsworth 34
Crocodile 151
Cruella De Vil 269, 281
Cruella's Car 144, 145
Cupid 75
Cupids on a Pillar 79

D

Daisy Duck 59
Devil Donald 63
Display Bases 40, 97, 138, 169, 254, 274
Display Stand 76, 149
Doc 196, 203
Donald and Daisy 129
Donald Duck 62, 138, 218, 225, 250, 269
Dopey 197, 201
Dopey/Sneezy in Coat 199
Dragon 177
Dumbo 68, 265, 275
Dumbo and Mr. Stork 68

E

Eeyore 248
Elliott 258
Evil Queen 198

F

Fairy Godmother 44
Fauna 185
Fiddler Pig 230, 234
Fiddler Pig's Stick House 232
Field Mouse 27
Fifer Pig 230, 234
Fifer Pig's Straw House 232
Fifi 175
Figaro 158
Flora 185
Flounder 112
Flower 30
Fluke 109
Flunky Monkey 93
Friend Owl 28

G

Gazebo 80
Genie 18
Geppetto 158
Geppetto's Toy Hutch 159
Geppetto's Toy Shop 160
Goofy 65, 86, 165, 168, 215, 270, 278
Goofy's Train 256
Grandpa's House 117, 118
Grumpy 202
Grumpy and Pipe Organ 194
Gus 49, 51

H

Hades' Chariot 83
Hamm 240
Happy 194, 203
Hercules 83
Hercules and Pegasus 82
Hippopotamus 74
Hitchhiking Ghosts 259
Horace Horsecollar 216

Subject Index 289

J
Jafar 280
Jane 221
Jaq 50, 51
Jaq & Gus 45
Jiminy Cricket 127, 157, 159, 264
José Carioca 225

K
King Louie 91
King Louie's Temple 94
King of Hearts 22

L
Lady 98, 267
Lady, Tramp, Tony and Joe 97
Large Mushroom 72
Lightning Bug 257
Lucifer 46
Lucky and Ottoman 144
Lucky and Television 142
Lumiere 34

M
Mademoiselle Upanova 75
Maleficent 186, 280
Medium Mushroom 73
Merryweather 186
Mickey and Princess Minnie 278
Mickey Mouse 39, 56, 77, 121, 123, 125, 137, 163, 166, 174, 181, 211, 212, 216, 236, 252, 253, 254, 266, 268, 276, 282
Mickey's Drum 257
Minnie Mouse 56, 121, 126, 137, 165, 167, 174, 270
Minnie Mouse with Cake 115
Mowgli 92
Mr. Smee 148
Mrs. Potts and Chip 35
Mufasa and Simba 104
Mulan 134

N
Nala 102
Nephew Dewey 130
Nephew Huey 131
Nephew Louie 131
Newt 110

O
Open Sewing Book 47
Opening Title 21, 26, 33, 38, 43, 55, 61, 72, 91, 96, 101, 107, 120, 130, 136, 141, 151, 156, 173, 184, 193, 209, 217, 220, 224, 231, 238

P
Pain 84
Panchito 226
Panic 84
Pecos Bill and Widowmaker 272
Perdita with Patch and Puppy 143
Perla 49
Pete 214
Peter 118
Peter Pan 150
Piglet 248
Pink Centaurette 78
Pinocchio 157, 160
Pluto 39, 57, 163, 166, 168, 271, 279
Pocahontas 171
Pongo with Pepper and Penny 143
Pooh Bear's House 246
Practical Pig 229, 233
Practical Pig's Brick House 233
Pumbaa and Timon 284

Q
Quasimodo and Esmeralda 88
Queen of Hearts 23

R
Rafiki with Cub 102
Rex, the Nervous Dinosaur 241
Roger Rabbit and Jessica 243
Rolly the Puppy 142

S
Santa Candle 164
Scrooge McDuck 126, 179
Sebastian 109
Shere Khan 94
Simba 101, 103
Sleeping Beauty's Castle 189, 190
Sleeping Beauty's Dress 188
Sleepy 195, 205
Slue Foot Sue 272
Small Mushroom 73
Snails 111
Sneezy 196, 204
Snow White 193, 201
Snow White and Prince 197, 199
Snow White's Wishing Well 202
Steamboat 212
Suzy 48

T
Table and Rose 36
Tarzan 221
Terk 222
The Beast's Castle 35, 36
The Seven Dwarfs' Cottage 200
The Seven Dwarfs' Jewel Mine 200
The Woodcutter's Cottage 188

Thumper	28
Thumper's Sisters	29
Tigger	247
Timon	267, 277
Timothy Mouse	276
Tinker Bell	148, 149, 271
Tramp	98
Turtle	110, 258
Two Puppies on Newspaper	141

U

Uncle Donald	132
Unicorn	79
Ursula	107

W

White Rabbit	24, 277, 279
White Rabbit's House	24
Winnie The Pooh	246, 247, 266, 275
Witch (The Queen)	198
Woody	239

Z

Zazu	103

Subject Index

Title Index

A

A Castle For Cinderella 52, 53
A Dance In The Clouds 184, 187
"A Dress A Princess Can Be Proud Of" 188
"A Firefly! A Pixie! Amazing!" 149
A Gift From The Gods 82
A Golfer's Best Friend 39
A Kiss Brings Love Anew 199
A Little Bit Of Blue 186
A Little Bit Of Both 185
A Little Bit Of Pink 185
A Little Off The Top 121
"A Lovely Dress For Cinderelly" 45
"A Perfectly Beautiful Little Lady" 267
A Tea Party In Wonderland 23
Admiral Duck 269
"Ah-Choo!" 196
Alice In Wonderland Opening Title 21
Amigo Donald 225
Amigo José 225
Amigo Panchito 226
An Elegant Coach For Cinderella 50, 52
"And A Merry Christmas To You…" 125
" …And The King" 22
"Anita Daahling!" 269
Ariel 113
Ariel's Secret Grotto 112
"Aw Shucks!" 195
"Away We Go!" 138

B

"Bah-Humbug!" 126
Bambi Opening Title 26
Bashful 204
Batter Up 86
Beauty And The Beast Opening Title 33
Beauty In Bloom 78
"Bella Notte" 97
"Bella Notte" Base 97
Ben Ali Gator 74
Beware Of Hitchhiking Ghosts 259
"Bibbidi, Bobbidi, Boo" 44
"Born And Bred In A Briar Patch" 208
Bravo Bravissimo 217
Briar Rose 189
"Bring Back Her Heart…" 198
"Brought You Something." 174
Bucket Brigade 77
Bundle Of Joy 68

C

Calypso Crustacean 109
Canine Caddy Display Base 40
Canine Caddy Opening Title 38
Captain Hook 153
Caroler Minnie 165, 167
Casey At The Bat 273
Cheerful Leader 196
Cinderella Opening Title 43
Cinderella's Sewing Book 47
Clarabelle's Crescendo 215
Classical Carp 108
"Come On, Lucky…" 142
"Cricket's The Name, Jiminy Cricket" 264
Cruella's Car 144, 145

D

Daisy's Debut 59
Dancing Partners 199
"Dear Jessica, How Do I Love Thee?" 243
Deep Sea Diva 111
Display Base for Members-Only Sculptures 274
Display Base for Membership
    Gift Sculptures 274
Doc 203
Donald's Better Self Opening Title 61
Donald's Debut 250
Donald's Decision 62
Donald's Drum Beat 218
Dopey 197, 201
Double Trouble 284
Dribbling Down Court 65
"Duh!" 208
Duke Of Soul 109
Dynamite Dog 57

E

Eeyore 248
"Everyone Runs From Shere Khan" 94
Evil Enchantress 186

F

Fairy Tale Wedding 44
Fantasia Opening Title 72
Fiddler Pig 234
Fiddler Pig's Stick House 232
Fifer Pig 234
Fifer Pig's Straw House 232
Flight Of Fancy 75
Flight Of Fancy Ornament Display Stand 76
Flirtatious Fifi 175
Flounder's Fandango 112
For My Sweetie 115
Friendship Offering 276
From The Top 253
"From Zero To Hero" 83

G

Geppetto's Toy Creations 159
Geppetto's Toy Shop 160
"Go Get Him, Thunder!" 141
"Good Night, Luv" 35
"Good-bye, Father" 157
"Good-bye, Son" 158
Goofy Delivery 278
Goofy's Grace Notes 215
Goofy's Train 256

Grumpy	202
Gus	51

H

Hades' Chariot	83
Happy	203
"Happy Birthday!"	123
"Happy, That's Me!"	194
"He Can Call Me A Flower If He Wants To"	27
"Hee! Hee! Hee!"	28
"Hello, Hello There!"	29
"Hey Diddle, Diddle, I Play On My Fiddle"	230
"Hey Minnie, Wanna Go Steppin'?"	56
"Hey, We Can Do It!"	48
Holiday Series Base	169
Honorable Decision	134
Hop Low	73
Horace's High Notes	216
How To Fly	252
Hula Baloo	92
"Humph!"	194
Hyacinth Hippo	74

I

"I Found My Moving Buddy."	240
"I Got Somethin' For Ya"	130
"I Gotcha, Brer Rabbit!"	207
"I Let 'Em Have It!"	268
"I Toot My Flute, I Don't Give A Hoot"	230
"I'm A Jazz Baby"	56
"I'm A Poor Little Sheep…"	231
"I'm Hungry, Mother!"	142
"I'm Late"	279
"I'm Losing To A Rug"	18
"I'm So Glad You're Not A Dinosaur"	241
"I'm Still Andy's Favorite Toy."	239
"I'm Wishing For The One I Love"	197
"It's Showtime."	240
"It's That De Vil Woman!"	281
"I've Got You This Time!"	150

J

Jaq	51
Jiminy Cricket	159
Jungle Rhythm	222
"Just In Time"	34
"Just Learn To Like Cats"	47

K

King Louie's Temple	94
King Of The Swingers	91

L

Lady And The Tramp Opening Title	96
Lady In Love	98
"Let The Game Begin!"	23
Lightning Bug	257
"Listen With Your Heart"	171
Little April Shower	27
Little Devil	63
Little Mischief Makers	164, 167, 169
Long Live The King	254
Love's Little Helpers	79
"Luau!"	267, 277
Lucky	144

M

"Maestro Michel Mouse"	216
Major Domo	103
Making Dreams Come True	156
Mancub	92
"Meany, Sneaky, Roos-A-Fee"	46
Mickey Cuts Up Opening Title	120
Mickey Mouse	211, 212
Mickey Through The Years Base Set	254
Mickey's Debut	282
Mickey's Drum	257
Minnie's Garden	121
Mischievous Apprentice	77
Miss Jane Porter	221
Money! Money! Money!	179
Monkeying Around	93
Mowgli's Protector	93
Mr. Duck Steps Out Opening Title	130
Mrs. Cratchit	126
Mushroom Dancer	72, 73

N

Nala's Joy	102
Nestled In The Snow…	117, 118
Newt's Nautical Note	110
Night On Bald Mountain	76
"No Time For Dilly-Dally!"	49
"No Time To Say Hello - Goodbye!"	277
"Nobody Calls Pan A Coward!"	150
"Not A Single Monster Line"	88

O

"Oh Boy, What A Jitterbug!"	129
"Oh dear, dear, dear."	148
"Oh, It's Swell!"	174
"Oh Mighty Evil One"	280
"Oh, The World Owes Me A Livin'"	270
"Oh…Gosh!"	30
On Ice Base	138
On Ice Opening Title	136
"On With The Show!"	266, 276
"Once Upon A Dream"	187
One Hundred And One Dalmatians Opening Title	141

P

Pain	84
Pals Forever	104
Panic	84
Pastoral Setting	80
Patient Perdita	143
Pecos Bill	272
Peter	118
Peter Pan Opening Title	151

Title Index 293

Pete's Dragon	258
Piglet	248
Pinocchio	160
Pinocchio Opening Title	156
Playing Card	22
Pluto Helps Decorate	163, 166, 168
Pooh Bear's House	246
Practical Pig	233
Practical Pig's Brick House	233
"Presents For My Pals"	163, 166
Prima Ballerina	75
Princess Minnie	270
Proud Pongo	143
Puppy Love Opening Title	173
"Purty Flower"	29

R

"Rah, Rah, Mickey!"	236
Romantic Reflections	78

S

Santa Candle	164
"Say Hello To Figaro"	158
Seahorse Surprise	108
Simba	103
Simba's Pride	101
"Simply Adorable"	265, 275
Sing-Along Snails	111
Sleeping Beauty Opening Title	184
Sleeping Beauty's Castle	189, 190
Sleepy	205
Slue Foot Sue	272
Sneezy	204
Snow White	201
Snow White And The Seven Dwarfs Opening Title	193
Snow White's Wishing Well	202
"So This Is Love"	43
Somethin' Fishy	181
Song Of The South Opening Title	209
Steamboat	212
Sticky Situation	271, 279
"Storybook Sweethearts"	278
Summoning The Stars	253
Sylvester Macaroni	214
Symphony Hour Opening Title	217

T

Tag-Along Trouble	131
"Take The Apple, Dearie"	198
"Tale As Old As Time"	33
Tarzan Of The Jungle	221
Tarzan Opening Title	220
Tea For Two	45
The Beast's Castle	35, 36
The Circle Continues	102
The Delivery Boy Opening Title	55
The Enchanted Rose	36
"The Fairest One Of All"	193
The Ghost Of Christmas Past	127
The Jolly Roger	152, 153
The Jungle Book Opening Title	91
The Lion King Opening Title	101
The Little Mermaid Opening Title	107
"The Mistress Of All Evil"	280
"The More The Merrier"	177
The Seven Dwarfs' Cottage	200
The Seven Dwarfs' Jewel Mine	200
The Three Caballeros Opening Title	224
The Touch Of An Autumn Fairy	283
The Woodcutter's Cottage	188
"They Can't Stop Me From Dreaming"	46
Three Little Pigs Opening Title	231
"Tick-Tock, Tick-Tock"	151
Tigger	247
"Time For Something Sweet"	266, 275
Tinker Bell	148
Tinker Bell Ornament Display Stand	149
"Tinker Bell Pauses To Reflect"	271
"'Tis The Season To Be Jolly"	165, 168
"To Infinity And Beyond!"	239
Toy Story Opening Title	238
Tramp In Love	98
"'Twas Brillig"	265
Twinkling Turtle	258
Twistin' Turtle	110

U

Unicorn	79
"Up To The Honey Tree"	246

V

Vive L'Amour!	34

W

"Wait For Me, Pinoke!"	157
"Watch Me!"	137
"We Made A Deal"	107
"We'll Tie A Sash Around It"	48
"What A Swell Day For A Game Of Golf!"	39
What An Angel	62
"What's Going On Around Here?"	28
"Whee!"	137
"When I See An Elephant Fly"	68
White Rabbit	24
White Rabbit's House	24
"Who's Afraid Of The Big Bad Wolf?"	229
Winnie The Pooh	247
"With Love From Daisy"	132
"Work And Play Don't Mix"	229

Y

"Yes, Your Majesty."	21
"You Go Get Some Trimmin'"	49, 50

Z

"ZZZzzz"	195

Number Index

Number	Page
11K-20137-0	280
11K-42666-0	107
12K-2BLT-010	278
12K-2GOF-050	278
12K-2PLU-020	279
11098	171
31072	177
31106	214
41000	46
41001	46
41002	47
41003	47
41004	48
41005	48
41006	49
41007	49
41008	50
41009	43
41010	27
41011	28
41012	27
41013	28
41014	29
41015	26
41016	77
41017	77
41018	72
41019	55
41020	56
41021	56
41022	57
41024	129
41025	130
41026	215
41027	215
41028	216
41029	216
41030	45
41031	217
41032	130
41033	29
41034	30
41035	264
41036	229
41037	230
41038	230
41039	229
41040	78
41041	78
41042	79
41043	150
41044	150
41045	149
41046	231
41047	151
41048	268
41049	131
41050	131
41051	75
41052	274
41053	274
41054	151
41055	269
41056	76
41057	265
41058	72
41059	272
41060	132
41061	217
41062	148
41063	193
41064	194
41065	194
41066	195
41067	73
41068	73
41069	195
41070	224
41071	196
41072	177
41073	196
41074	197
41075	272
41076	225
41077	225
41078	226
41079	43
41080	144
41081	275
41082	265
41083	193
41084	198
41085	104
41086	163
41087	166
41088	269
41089	98
41090	98
41091	266
41093	187
41094	231
41095	270
41096	275
41098	171
41099	96
41101	207
41102	208
41103	208
41104	209
41105	218
41106	214
41107	273
41108	44
41109	157
41110	157
41111	158
41112	163
41113	166
41114	158
41116	156
41117	74
41118	74
41119	148
41127	149
41129	141
41130	142
41131	142
41132	143
41133	143
41134	266
41135	276
41136	282
41138	270
41139	156
41140	169
41141	169
41142	168
41143	88
41144	125
41145	126
41146	126
41149	39
41151	137
41152	179
41153	68
41156	33
41157	187
41158	91
41159	93
41160	92
41161	92
41162	93
41163	164
41165	198
41167	82
41169	141
41170	123
41171	91
41172	164
41175	250
41176	246
41177	280
41178	75
41179	276
41180	76
41181	34
41182	34
41183	35
41184	108
41187	109
41188	107
41189	33
41190	167
41191	109
41192	110
41193	110
41194	108
41195	111
41196	111
41197	267
41198	112
41199	271
41200	200
41201	188
41202	24
41203	200
41204	232
41205	232
41206	233
41207	160
41208	50
41209	152
41210	53
41211	117
41212	201
41213	24
41214	189
41215	201
41216	233
41217	160
41218	51
41219	153
41221	118
41222	118
41223	234
41224	234
41225	35
41230	144
41231	246
41232	80
41235	112
41237	79
41238	247
41239	202
41240	113
41241	94
41242	51
41243	152
41244	52
41245	145
41246	83
41247	84
41248	202
41250	84
41251	127
41252	236
41253	83
41254	94
41255	282
41256	103
41257	184
41258	185

Number	Page	Number	Page
41259	185	41345	186
41260	186	41356	101
41261	136	41357	101
41262	277	41358	102
41263	189	41359	102
41264	212	41360	103
41265	212	41363	181
41266	86	41366	271
41267	44	41367	165
41268	252	41368	168
41269	18	41372	199
41270	137	41373	277
41271	203	41374	134
41272	203	41375	21
41273	204	41378	21
41274	247	41384	258
41275	184	41385	258
41277	253	41391	190
41278	253	41396	138
41279	254	41397	121
41280	280	41402	115
41281	283	41403	97
41283	68	41404	65
41284	97	41405	281
41285	107	41410	45
41289	256	41411	205
41290	257	41412	197
41291	257	41413	23
41293	52	41414	22
41294	36	41416	284
41295	23	41417	38
41296	62	41418	259
41297	62	41419	22
41298	61	41423	40
41301	254	41424	211
41304	239	41426	220
41305	239	41427	221
41306	238	41428	221
41307	199	41429	222
41308	165	41433	138
41309	63	41441	21
41311	167	41442	22
41312	280	41443	23
41313	59	41454	22
41314	39	43415	267
41315	159	1023578	121
41318	204	1035092	279
41319	248	1204894	45
41320	240		
41321	240		
41322	243		
41324	174		
41325	174		
41326	173		
41327	267		
41334	241		
41335	159		
41336	175		
41337	248		
41343	36		
41344	188		